Listen, We Need to Talk

LISTEN, WE NEED TO TALK
HOW TO CHANGE ATTITUDES ABOUT LGBT RIGHTS

Brian F. Harrison
and
Melissa R. Michelson

OXFORD
UNIVERSITY PRESS

Oxford University Press is a department of the University of Oxford. It furthers
the University's objective of excellence in research, scholarship, and education
by publishing worldwide. Oxford is a registered trade mark of Oxford University
Press in the UK and certain other countries.

Published in the United States of America by Oxford University Press
198 Madison Avenue, New York, NY 10016, United States of America.

Library of Congress Cataloging-in-Publication Data
Names: Harrison, Brian F., author. | Michelson, Melissa R., 1969– author.
Title: Listen, we need to talk : how to change attitudes about LGBT rights /
Brian F. Harrison, Melissa R. Michelson.
Description: New York : Oxford University Press, 2017.
Identifiers: LCCN 2016030884 (print) | LCCN 2016055362 (ebook) |
ISBN 9780190654740 (hardback) | ISBN 9780190654757 (paperback) |
ISBN 9780190654764 (Updf) | ISBN 9780190654771 (Epub)
Subjects: LCSH: Gay liberation movement—United States. |
Sexual minorities—United States. | Human rights—United States. |
Public opinion—United States. | BISAC: POLITICAL SCIENCE / Public Policy / Social Policy.
Classification: LCC HQ76.8.U5 H38 2017 (print) | LCC HQ76.8.U5 (ebook) |
DDC 306.76—dc23
LC record available at https://lccn.loc.gov/2016030884

9 8 7 6 5 4 3 2 1

Paperback printed by Webcom Inc., Canada
Hardback printed by Bridgeport National Bindery, Inc., United States of America

Contents

List of Figures

List of Tables

Acknowledgments

We would like to thank our colleagues for useful comments and helpful suggestions as our thinking developed over the course of this project. First and foremost, we want to acknowledge the amazing support from Ken Sherrill, the godfather of LGBT political science. We are eternally grateful for his friendship and feedback on earlier chapters and drafts. We also want to thank Gary Segura, Stephen Engel, Dara Strolovitch, Patrick Egan, Don Green, Jessica Lavariega Monforti, Matt Barreto, Tyson King-Meadows, Andra Gillespie, Kathy Melvin, David Broockman, Brian Calfano, Stephen Farnsworth, Mark Hugo Lopez, Lisa Bryant, Chris Mann, Brian Ellner, Thomas Henderson, Sam Marchiano, Andrew Flores, and probably a bunch of other folks that we're forgetting. Brian wants to particularly thank Stephen Engel for his willingness to serve as a sounding board for many aspects of the project and for his willingness to contribute his considerable knowledge about LGBT scholarship for the good of this project. While all errors herein remain our own, the project is significantly improved by the many people who helped us develop it along the way. We also thank discussants, panelists, and audience members at the various conferences through the years who have helped us sharpen our thoughts as the project was underway.

We received valuable financial support from Melissa's home institution Menlo College, a small research grant from the Williams Institute of the UCLA School of Law, and a graduate student grant from SocialSci.com for the religion experiment. We could not have finished the last batch of experiments without the support of a large group of optimistic Kickstarter donors, including a few with deep pockets: Mark and Cheryl Falb (Brian's parents), Trisha London and Laura Chandlee (Brian's sisters), Linda Bernstein and Mei and Arthur Michelson (Melissa's parents), David and Taipai Michelson (Melissa's brother and sister-in-law), Nirmala Patni, and Ron and Lois London. Thank you all for your very generous support of this project. Brian would also like to thank Patrick Egan and New York University for allowing him to serve as an affiliated scholar in the Department of Politics as we worked on the book.

We benefited from feedback presented at various conferences, including the 2013 Marriage Equality Symposium at Stanford University, the 2013 American

Political Science Association annual meeting, the 2012 and 2014 annual meetings of the Midwest Political Science Association, the 2012 and 2014 annual meetings of the Western Political Science Association, and the 2012 meeting of the NYU-CESS Experimental Political Science Conference.

We are especially grateful to the LGBT activists and their affiliated equality organizations for partnering with us to conduct some of our experiments, including Carolyn Jenison at One Iowa, Camilla Taylor and Jim Bennett at Lambda Legal, Bernard Cherkasov and Caroline Staerk at Equality Illinois, Melinda Sheldon and Em Elliott at Georgia Equality, Matthew Patterson and Carrie Wooten at the Capital City Alliance in Louisiana, Carrie Evans and Alex McNeill at Equality Maryland, and Walter Olson in Maryland as well. We are also enormously thankful for the hard work of our research assistants, Liz Lebrón for doing the groundwork for the Louisiana Equality experiment and Seren Mohn for her work on collecting and organizing information from scholarly literature and the popular media. We are thankful for our team of Menlo College research assistants for their work conducting the sports experiments: Nick Acosta, Vanessa D'Amico, Kathryn Dickson, Laurel Donnenwirth, Sean Grey, Haley Mackevich, Karen Perez-Torres, Eric Peterson, Marlana Pierson, and Andrew Vargas. The Menlo College librarians, including Dean of Library Services Linda Smith and librarians Cheryl Collins, Anne Linvill, Rachel Magnusson, Melissa Pincus, and Tricia Soto, provided invaluable research assistance. We also thank our team of student assistants from Lawrence University: Emma Huston, Logan Beskoon, Anastasia Skliarova, Ariela Rosa, Amalya Lewin-Larin, Yuchen Wang, and Manuel Leyva, as well as Lawrence University Vice President for Alumni, Development and Communications Cal Husmann, who graciously helped coordinate the Green Bay Packers experiment.

We are also very grateful to our editor, Angela Chnapko, for her enthusiastic support of the project. We could not ask for a kinder, more supportive editor to work with and we hope she is happy with the result. Our thanks as well to the many folks at Oxford University Press who worked to polish and complete our draft manuscript, including Princess Ikatekit, Rachel Perkins, and Anne Rusinak. Our thanks to Al Brandtner for his patience in helping us work through cover ideas and for his gorgeous final effort that now invites readers into our book.

Finally, thank you to our families, for your love and support. Thanks to our children, Joshua Michelson, Zachary Michelson, Joshua Harrison, and Vivian Harrison, for putting up with so many days and nights of mommy/daddy working on their book, instead of reading one to you. We dedicate this book to our husbands, Christopher Gardner and Shawn Harrison, for their unwavering love and support through years of highs and lows and for helping us focus on the former rather than the latter. In addition, we hope that this book helps pave the way to a future where everyone is treated equally regardless of their sexual orientation or gender identity.

Permissions

Some details of the One Iowa fundraising experiment described in chapter 2 were published in Brian F. Harrison and Melissa R. Michelson, "Not That There's Anything Wrong with That: The Effect of Personalized Appeals on Marriage Equality Campaigns," *Political Behavior* 34, 2 (2012): 325–344.

Some details of the football experiments described in chapter 3 were published in Brian F. Harrison and Melissa R. Michelson, "More Than a Game: Football Fans and Marriage Equality," *PS: Political Science & Politics* 49, 4 (2016): 782–787.

Some details of the SocialSci experiment described in chapter 4 were published in Brian F. Harrison and Melissa R. Michelson, "God and Marriage: The Impact of Religious Identity Priming on Attitudes toward Same-Sex Marriage," *Social Science Quarterly* 96, 5 (2015): 1411–1423.

Photos of David Hasselhoff and Matt Cain in figure 3.5 are reprinted with permission from the NOH8 Campaign.

Listen, We Need to Talk

1 The Theory of Dissonant Identity Priming

How Identity, Source Similarity, and Message Characteristics Influence Attitudes

In 1988, only 11% of the US public supported legalizing same-sex marriage; support increased to 27% in 1996 and 35% in 2006. Subsequent shifts have been even more rapid and by 2013, a variety of polls showed that a majority of Americans supported same-sex marriage, also known as marriage equality. The latest polls, from May 2016, found national support at more than 60%. Support for marriage equality has seen unprecedented increases over the last two decades in nearly every demographic group and a significant number of survey respondents openly admit to having changed their minds. For example, in a March 2013 Pew Research Center poll, 49% of respondents said that they supported the right of same-sex couples to marry, of whom 14% (28% of marriage equality supporters) said that they had changed their mind on the issue (Pew Research Center 2013a).

This rate of attitudinal change is simply stunning and defies typical patterns of public opinion. Usually, public opinion is stable; once formed, attitudes at both the individual and aggregate levels are relatively persistent over time (Erikson, McKuen, and Stimson 2002; Page and Shapiro 1992). For example, according to Gallup Polls, support for the death penalty was 59% in 1936, 68% in 1953, and 61% in October 2015. Support for legal abortion in all circumstances was 21% in 1975 (and opposition in all circumstances at 22%); in May 2015, support for legal abortion in all circumstances was at 29% and opposition was at 19%. In 1957, 55% of Americans said that their federal income taxes were too high; in April 2016, 57% of Americans felt that way.[1] While the news cycle and current events sometimes create peaks and valleys in public support or opposition for certain public policies (e.g., for stricter gun control laws in the wake of a well-publicized mass shooting), opinions generally settle back to their previous levels and trend lines often remain relatively unchanged for decades.

Like any rule in social science, however, there are exceptions; on occasion, attitudes toward a political or social issue shift far more quickly. In 1969, when Gallup first asked the question, only 12% of Americans favored legalizing marijuana; by 2004 that number had risen to 34% and polls since 2011 have shown that a majority of Americans favor decriminalization. Change in opinion on the issue of same-sex marriage has been even more dramatic (figure 1.1).

If public opinion is generally stable, why have we seen such dramatic changes on the issue of marriage equality? Inspired by our desire to answer this question, we developed a theory that integrates identity, source cues, and message effectiveness, particularly in regard to contentious political issues. We posit that the rapid change in opinion on marriage equality occurred because over time, individuals were nudged by members and leaders of their social groups to reconsider their existing opinions. We believe existing explanations of the rapid movement in public opinion toward support of marriage equality are missing a key element: the effects of identity priming from a variety of social identity groups. This book looks at how individual-level identity and identity cues from in-group members affect attitudes toward the prominent and contentious issue of marriage equality. It also expands existing research on identity priming and attitude change in new and interesting ways.

Later in this chapter, we delve into the relevant literature that helped us develop our theory and the details of how it works. That theory-building project began with a relatively small observation: as professional political scientists, we were simply stunned at the rapid rate at which Americans were shifting their opinions on marriage equality. As noted above, this just isn't typical of trends in public opinion.

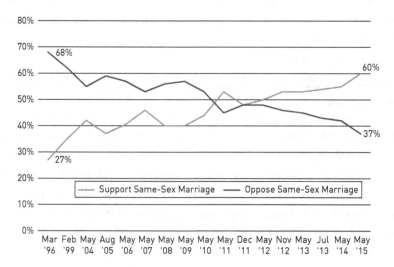

FIGURE 1.1 National Support for Same-Sex Marriage, 1996–2015. *Source:* Gallup Polls. See appendix table A1.1 for question wording and additional details.

When real life doesn't fit with our expectations as scholars, it signals an opportunity to re-evaluate our understanding of how things work. In this instance, it led us to reconsider when and how individuals change their opinions about controversial political issues. The rate of change was too rapid for cohort replacement—in other words, these changes were not simply due to opponents of marriage equality dying and being replaced in the population by younger, more progressive people. Folks were actually changing their minds. Was it just that more people were realizing that they had friends and family members that were members of the gay and lesbian community? Again, the rate of attitudinal shifts seemed too rapid to be due simply to increased contact. The more we delved into our (seemingly) simple observation, the more we were convinced that there were deeper questions to be answered in the intersection of individual-level identity, messaging and source cues, and social issue leadership, questions that deserved further inquiry.

We hypothesized that shifting attitudes were the result of individuals updating their opinions to better align with emerging preferences by people they respected and with whom they identified in some way. In other words, when they heard that someone in a social or political group with which they identified, especially a leader of that group, was a supporter of marriage equality—and particularly if that support was surprising—they reconsidered their own position and even updated their own position in order to better align with that observed opinion.

For example, during most of his first administration, Barack Obama, the first Black President of the United States, was an opponent of marriage equality. In 2012, Obama "evolved" and endorsed marriage equality, an event we discuss further in chapter 3. Black Americans who had previously opposed marriage equality were likely surprised to hear that he had changed his mind and were simultaneously moved to reconsider their own opinions; some then shifted their own opinions to mirror those of the president, becoming marriage equality supporters. We hypothesized that the unexpected nature of such an endorsement, coupled with the strong degree to which many Black Americans identify Obama as an important member of a shared social group (i.e., as Black), enhanced the power of his support to shift attitudes among the Black public. This, we believe, helps explain the rapid shift we have seen on this issue among certain identity groups. We call this the Theory of Dissonant Identity Priming. Our experiments (in chapters 3–6) test that theory; we describe it in greater detail later in this chapter.

While the experimental data we present are focused on lesbian, gay, bisexual, and transgender (LGBT) rights issues and mostly on the issue of marriage equality, the identity-based priming model and theory we describe in this chapter would also be applicable to other contentious social issues. Sinclair (2012) wrote that individuals are "social citizens" embedded in interactive networks and it is well established that references to some social identities can move public opinion. For example, partisanship can generate attitudinal change on non-controversial, non-salient issues (Carsey and Layman 2006; Lenz 2009) or when the partisan cue provides unexpected counter-stereotypical information (Bergan 2012). Building on that scholarship, we argue that individual-level identity plays a significant role in the dramatic change in support for marriage equality observed in the past two decades and has the potential to affect change on other contentious, prominent political and social issues.

OUTLINE OF THE BOOK

Readers may be interested in different aspects of our findings. Our book is meant to offer meaningful information for both academics and those who engage in real-world advocacy and persuasion. For practitioners, non-profit organizations, and those interested in the practical nature of the research we have conducted, we invite you to skip forward to chapter 2. For those more interested in theory and the connections between our contribution and extant work in political psychology, political communication, and political science, we encourage you finish chapter 1; here, we review relevant literature on social identity theory and identity formation as well as the effects identity can have on political attitudes and behavior. The next section discusses theories of attitude change and the limits to which scholars expect attitude change to happen, with a particular focus on the power of priming. Finally, we outline our theory of how seemingly unrelated in-group identity priming can effectively develop feelings of interpersonal closeness and open minds to attitudinal change. We call this the Theory of Dissonant Identity Priming (TDIP). We then preview results from 14 randomized experiments conducted around the United States over a period of five years, often with the cooperation of LGBT advocacy organizations, and in a variety of contexts designed to maximize both internal and external validity. Our full discussion of those experiments and the conclusions we draw from the results comprise the remainder of the book.

Chapter 2 provides an overview of how attitudes and behaviors toward LGBT Americans have changed over time and a brief history of LGBT rights in the United States. We also include a summary of how political science as a discipline has engaged with issues important to LGBT people, noting that it wasn't until somewhat recently that gender and sexuality studies have been viewed as legitimate and included aspects of political science. We then move on to an overview of our methodology and details of a research project that serves as an example of how we have applied theory to real-world contexts, setting the stage for the rest of our findings.

Chapters 3–6 should be of interest to everyone: we present our findings from 14 experiments that investigate four politically relevant and powerful social identities: identity as a sports fan (chapter 3); religious identity (chapter 4); ethnoracial identity (chapter 5); and political partisanship (chapter 6). Chapter 7 provides analysis of our results, their practical implications, and details about how our theory can apply to other issues and future political conflicts and events.

Allport's (1954) contact theory suggests that personal contact with out-group members like LGBT individuals can prompt people to reconsider previously-held prejudices. It is certainly true that more Americans today are aware that they have personal contact with a member of the LGBT community. In 1993, only 22% of Americans said that they had a close friend or family member who was gay or lesbian. In 2014, nearly two-thirds (65%) of Americans reported having such a relationship (Jones, Cox, and Navarro-Rivera 2014). We believe, however, that this is only a partial explanation for observed attitudinal shifts. We argue in this book that support for LGBT rights also increases when an individual realizes that someone who is a member of one of their in-groups shares that they are a supporter of LGBT rights, regardless of that individual's sexual orientation and/or gender identity. In other words, people are likely to be affected by exposure to an attitude shared by a member of their in-group, even if that in-group is based on an unrelated identity, such as partisanship, race, or religion. Individuals who identify as Democrats, for example, should be more likely to become supporters of marriage equality if they see that other Democrats are supporters; Republicans will be more supportive when they see other Republicans are supportive. This effect is even stronger when the support comes from an unexpected source and when it comes from someone with whom the target individual shares a strong in-group identity.

The basic premise of our democratic society is that deliberation and the sharing of opinions generate healthy debate and, eventually, consensus. In *On Liberty*, John Stuart Mill ([1859] 1989, 24) argued that the free marketplace of ideas causes "wrong opinions and practices" to "gradually yield to fact and argument." Democracy presupposes that common ground can be found, even if the public is deeply divided. As anyone who has watched a Sunday news forum or read the comments on a controversial online article can attest, however, the sharing of opinion often causes those who disagree to dig in their heels rather than to reconsider their existing opinions. In a classic series of studies on resistance to change, McGuire (1964) showed that people could be inoculated to counteract messages with which they disagree. If an initial attack on their existing attitudes was perceived as threatening but easily countered, individuals would refute that attack with a counterargument. If later presented with an even stronger attack on the same pre-existing attitude they had successfully defended, they were better able to counterargue the latter attack.

In short, people tend to resist changing their mind. Instead, they use perceptual screens to block out information that might lead them to doubt their own opinions or resolve inconsistencies in their idiosyncratic belief systems (Taber and Lodge 2006). In the end, however, to believe in democracy is to believe that even those on an opposing side of a controversial issue may eventually be persuaded to reconsider and to change their mind. Many scholars have investigated how to cultivate those attitudinal shifts. In this book, we argue that it is normatively positive and substantively possible to encourage discussions about contentious political issues with other people by leveraging the power of group membership and by generating cognitive speed bumps that motivate recipients to be attentive to delivered messages.

Political scientists and scholars who engage with identity studies rarely study personality per se but rather look at self-concepts and identities and how they affect political attitudes and behavior. The "self" is a process; we construct a sense of who we are through interaction with others (Rohall, Milkie, and Lucas 2013). Identity refers to our internalized, stable sense of who we are, including role identities, social categories, and personal characteristics. Identity theory examines the ways society shapes how we view ourselves and how those views, or identities, subsequently affect our attitudes and behavior. Tajfel (1981, 255) describes social identity as "that part of an individual's self-concept which derives from [her or] his membership in a social group (or groups) together with the value and emotional significance attached to that membership." In other words, our social identity is the part of our identity derived from the social groups to which we belong and to which we do not. The latter part of this formula is often the most important (Rohall, Milkie, and Lucas 2013). Social psychologists suggest that we derive self-esteem by positively differentiating our in-group from out-groups ("us" and "them") and therefore tend to categorize our social environment into groups, privileging our in-groups over our out-groups.

To test the effects of group membership, Tajfel (1970) conducted what has become known as his minimal groups experiments. In these studies, test subjects were randomly divided into two groups based on an inconsequential and almost completely irrelevant basis. Participants did not know the other members of their group and had no reason to expect that they would interact with them in the future. Still, members of both groups began to identify themselves with their respective group, preferring other members of their own group and favoring them with rewards that maximized their own group's outcomes. Subsequently, Tajfel and Turner (1981) developed what they called Social Identity Theory. They proposed that people have an in-built tendency to categorize themselves into one or more in-groups, building a part of their identity on the basis of membership in that group and enforcing boundaries with other groups.

Tajfel and Turner (1981) suggested this phenomenon comes about because we all try to give ourselves positive self-identity to increase our self-esteem. The theory posits that first, people derive their identity from the group to which they perceive they belong. Then, to gain a meaningful and positive identity, people categorize both their own group and other groups, perceiving their own to be superior to other groups. Tajfel and Turner proposed four stages of social identity group formation: categorization, identification, comparison, and distinctiveness.

First, *categorization* involves putting others and ourselves into categories. This is not inherently placing a value judgment on those categories; it is simply the process of creating the categories and filing certain people or identities into those categories. Examples include labeling someone as Catholic, female, Black, etc. Again, there is no stereotype or value judgment placed on the categories; it is merely the process of creating discrete groups of people. Second is the stage of *identification,* where we take the extra step of establishing which of the groups or categories are "ours." In other words, after creating the categories, we decide which are our in-groups and which are our out-groups. This is largely to bolster our self-esteem and self-concept (Tajfel 1981). The next two stages are where biases and stereotypes can potentially enter into social identity formation. The third stage of *comparison* is where we make a contrast and assessment of our in-groups in regard to other groups, again tending to find a favorable association toward the groups to which we belong. The final stage, the creation of *psychological distinctiveness,* is our attempt to create clear, concrete differences between our in-groups and out-groups so our in-groups are distinct from and positively compared with other groups.

In sum, in creating our self-identity, we create and form opinions about groups we perceive to be "ours" compared to "theirs," privileging our own groups and their perceived attributes. Existing research shows that people who identify with a social group (e.g., ethnoracial groups) tend to feel close and similar to in-group members (Doosje, Ellemers, and Spears 1995). This self-categorization is extended when group membership is made more salient in social situations (Turner et al. 1987). When a social identity is salient, individuals tend to think and act like group members (Brewer 1991) and to rely on the in-group as a guide for their own thoughts and behaviors (Terry and Hogg 1996). Tropp and Wright (2001) demonstrated the degree to which in-group members feel close to each other and how that closeness drives attitudes and behaviors. This connection induces individuals to be more likely to engage with perceived in-group messengers and the issues they raise; it also confers a sense of legitimacy and source credibility onto the content of their solicitations because of a common social identity (Druckman and Lupia 2000).

Social identity and attitudes are inextricably linked. Lazarsfeld, Berelson, and Gaudet (1948, 27) concluded that "a person thinks, politically, as he is socially. Social characteristics determine political preferences." We define attitudes as "general and enduring positive or negative feelings about some person, object, or issue" (Petty and Cacioppo 1981, 7). People's attitudes create stimulus categories, organize their perceptions of the world, and ultimately affect their behavior (Cacioppo et al. 1991). Further, extant research demonstrates that group identities affect attitude formation toward a variety of public policies, ranging from immigration (Citrin and Wright 2009) to voting behavior (Jackson 2011) and even orientation toward social and fiscal redistribution policies (Scheve and Stasavage 2006). In sum, the social categories in which we do and do not place ourselves drive how we make sense of the social and political world around us.

Before turning to the details of our new Theory of Dissonant Identity Priming, we turn now to the extant literature on attitude change; identity priming and interpersonal closeness; and issue relevance and expectancy violation.

PERSUASION AND ATTITUDE CHANGE

Previous research has generated significant insights about how attitudes can be deliberately changed; in particular, three models or theories document the conditions under which individuals may undergo preference or attitude changes: Zaller's (1992) receive-accept-sample (RAS) model; Sherif, Sherif, and Nebergall's (1965) Social Judgment Theory (SJT); and Petty and Cacioppo's (1986) Elaboration Likelihood Model (ELM). We briefly review them here.

Zaller (1992) suggests that rather than having true attitudes, people make "opinion statements." They are derivative of genuine feelings but are temporary and based on quick, shallow reflection. To explain how people make these reflections, he outlines his RAS model of how individuals come to make sense of their attitudes and opinions. According to the RAS model, people respond to questions based on immediately accessible considerations. The flow of information from members of relevant social groups and peers, media sources and personalities, and political elites determines which considerations are most salient; which information will be received and accepted by an individual is determined by the degree of one's political awareness and their predispositions. The key deduction of the RAS model is called the Ambivalence Deduction: most people are ambivalent, meaning they hold opposing considerations on most issues. These ambivalent citizens are unlikely to resist views that are inconsistent with their predispositions. This deduction can help explain response variation. The most ambivalent people are the most likely to be affected by response effects (such as question order), the race of the interviewer, survey references to groups that might affect opinions (such as religion), and the priming effects of TV news.

Levels of individual political awareness have critical effects on mass attitudes but these effects will differ depending on the nature of the information flows coming from the elite. The *mainstream effect* means that if there is an elite consensus, the public will also display a consensus of opinion and people with high levels of political awareness will be most likely to internalize the elite view (as long as it isn't inconsistent with their values). The *polarization effect* means that if elites are evenly divided, more people will display ideologically consistent views and hence the public will be more polarized. This polarization will be most pronounced among the most politically aware citizens.

According to Zaller (1992), changes in the dominant and countervailing messages affect changes in long-term response probabilities. This implies that attitude changes depend on the reception of new ideas and the acceptance of them as considerations. Resistance to change increases with awareness because more-aware people have stored a wider variety of considerations. Patterns of attitude change are also affected by the intensity and familiarity of messages. People with less information are *less* likely to change their attitudes in response to low-intensity messages (i.e., an environment with a slower flow or density of information) but *more* likely to change their attitudes in response to messages about more familiar issues. Further, less-aware people are most susceptible in very intense communication environments (i.e., presidential elections) because they "receive" a lot of information and "accept" almost everything.

Zaller's model of attitude change predicts that, for example, an increase in liberal messages will be more likely to lead to an attitude change among more aware liberals than less aware liberals (indicating a positive relationship). But for conservative voters, an increase in liberal messages will be more likely to lead to an attitude change among *moderately* aware conservatives than among conservatives with high or low levels of awareness (indicating a non-monotonic relationship). In other words, there is a direct relationship between attitude change and the perceived similarity and credibility of the source that is providing new information for consideration.

Relatedly, Gigerenzer and Todd (1999) determined that people rank available cues and use the best for attitude formation. They coined the phrase "fast and frugal heuristics," which offers a plausible account of how people attend to political issues when faced with multiple cues. One such heuristic is the take the best (TTB) heuristic, where people rank available cues according to how informative and accurate they perceive the cues to be. They then take the best cues and ignore the rest. An important aspect of TTB is that people rank cues according to predictive accuracy, what Gigerenzer and Todd call cue validity. Because a cue enables people to make inferences about an attitude object without knowing all there is to know about it, it stands to reason that people will follow the most informative cues. It is also plausible to assume that cues can build on each other (Eagly and Chaiken 1995; Lau and Redlawsk 2001).

Social Judgment Theory (SJT) offers another key insight into persuasion and attitude change. According to Sherif, Sherif, and Nebergall (1965), messages need to fall into a person's latitude of acceptance, defined as a range of attitudes that a person will engage with or tolerate, if there is to be any likelihood of motivation to process the information. In other words, every individual has a window of acceptable arguments to which they will attend. Any persuasion attempts that lie outside this theoretical window will be immediately rejected; arguments within the window will be at least minimally attended to during the persuasive process. A central assumption of SJT is that attitude change in response to communication is mediated by the individuals' judgments about the position advocated in the message. Again, the key is to create a message that resonates within the realm of persuasion.

Other work also supports the notion that individuals monitor the plausibility of the message and the cue. For example, Sarup, Suchner, and Gaylord (1991) showed that the reduction of contrast or perceived level of difference between the position advocated and individual-level attitudes increases the likelihood of persuasion (i.e., by constricting the latitude of rejection). If the attempted persuasion effort is perceived to be similar to individuals' existing beliefs and within their acceptable limits of issue orientation, they are more likely to change their attitude toward the issue of interest. There have been a number of studies that investigate the impact of cognitive (ego) involvement in persuasive communication, including religion and dogma (Letchworth 1968), the value of congressional politicians (Miller 1965), and the institution of comprehensive exams for college seniors (Petty and Cacioppo 1981, 1984). In each instance, the level of intensity and the level of personal involvement about an issue determined the likelihood of an attitude shift depending on the type of persuasive strategy employed.

Finally, the Elaboration Likelihood Model (ELM) investigates ego involvement and persuasion in political communication (Petty and Cacioppo 1986). According to this model, the first step after the presentation of persuasive messages is the motivation to process the information. People take different considerations into account when deciding whether to process information they have received: personal relevance, the cognitive energy needed to process the information, the amount of personal responsibility, etc. If they are motivated to process the information, they enter the central route of persuasion. If they are not motivated, they enter the peripheral route of persuasion. This is also considered the process of *elaboration*.

If a respondent is motivated to consider the persuasive communication or the issue at hand, the persuader is allowed to elaborate on his or her argument. This shift is crucial to crafting a message strategy. If the motivation to process the thought is not induced, the likelihood of short-term attitudinal change is small and the likelihood of long-lasting attitude change is even smaller. In addition, the attitude of an unmotivated person is not predictive of future behavior. As a result, triggering motivation to process persuasive messages is vitally important to enacting any meaningful attitudinal or behavior changes. Overall, individuals move through either the central or peripheral route of persuasion, depending upon their personal interest as well as their motivation and ability to process new information. Attitude change resulting from the peripheral route tends to be more ephemeral and unstable; the central route results in more durable attitude change.

When trying to persuade someone of something, Zaller's RAS model (1992), Social Judgment Theory (Sherif, Sherif and Nebergall 1965; Sherif et al. 1973), and the Elaboration Likelihood Model (Petty and Cacioppo 1981, 1986) all tell us that the first step down the road to successful attitude change is willingness to receive, listen to, and process new information. Consistent with existing work, the core of our new theory emphasizes the importance of priming a common identity; when a sender of communication establishes themself as a member of one of the receiver's salient in-groups, openness to listening and the likelihood of information processing should be increased. Further, a member of a perceived in-group may be able to change attitudes among other members of the in-group toward an out-group if that desired attitude related to the out-group is interpreted as a credible in-group position. The key to generating the possibility of attitudinal change, then, is increasing the likelihood of information processing. Messages that are sent by in-group members are more likely to be persuasive because they are more likely to be processed in the first place.

In a field experiment, McClendon (2014, 287) found that the promise of social esteem from in-group members increases the likelihood of pro-social behavior and political participation: "Subjects responded positively and dramatically to the promise that their participation would be observed and admired by others" in their in-group. In sum, making connections with targeted individuals through important social identities is crucial to breaking down perceptual screens and opening up minds to the possibility of attitudinal and behavioral change on contentious issues. Individuals will be more likely to reconsider a contentious issue and an unexpected policy preference when presented by a member of their in-group. What is often less clear, and what we describe in this book, is how to do so.

MOTIVATING OPENNESS TO PERSUASION

As Taber and Lodge (2006, 757) wrote, "Once attitudes have become crystallized, persuasion is difficult." Without clearing the initial hurdle of engaging a person's motivation to process an appeal, the likelihood of strong, long-lasting attitudinal change (and therefore the ability to affect behavior) is very small. If this motivation is achieved, the likelihood of attitude shifts that are predictive of behavior is higher. Bringing all of this literature together, we identify three keys to increasing information processing and, more importantly, opening minds to persuasive messages: interpersonal closeness and personal relevance; source similarity and shared identity; and message effects like identity priming and expectancy violation.

Interpersonal Closeness and Personal Relevance

Petty and Cacioppo (1986) suggested that personal relevance is the *most* important variable in determining the likelihood of attitude change. This is a key element of an expansive area of research in social psychology, including studies of ego involvement (Rhine and Severance 1970; Sherif, Sherif, and Nebergall 1965); issue involvement (Kiesler, Collins, and Miller 1969); and personal involvement (Apsler and Sears 1968; Sherif et al. 1973). Apsler and Sears focused on the decreased likelihood of persuasion on issues with which individuals are personally involved, noting, "People are likely to become personally involved with an issue when they expect it to have significant consequences for their own lives" (1968, 162).

A similar method of increasing personal relevance or involvement is linking targets to persuaders by increasing their perceived closeness. In other words, the more closeness felt between the persuader and the target, the more likely the issue will be perceived as personally relevant and the more likely the conversation will lead to attitude and behavioral change. There are a variety of ways to increase personal relevance, including interpersonal contact. Allport's (1954) contact hypothesis suggests that interpersonal contact can reduce antagonism by the majority toward members of unpopular subgroups, possibly leading to reduced prejudice and bias. While originally and most frequently understood as a means of reducing ethnoracial stereotypes, contact theory has also been used to predict attitudes toward other groups, including gay and lesbian individuals, physically disabled individuals, the mentally ill, and the elderly.

Pettigrew and Tropp (2006) also strongly endorsed the power of contact in changing socially charged attitudes. Their meta-analysis of 515 studies of contact theory concluded that intergroup contact can, in fact, reduce intergroup prejudice, even beyond attitudes toward the ethnoracial groups traditionally used in the contact theory literature. While the contact effect varies between studies of various targets and settings, they found that "the largest effects emerge for samples involving contact between heterosexuals and gay men and lesbians" (2006, 763). A number of scholars have found that attitudes toward gay and lesbian individuals are positively impacted by reported contact (see Barth, Overby, and Huffmon 2009; Herek and Capitano 1996; Herek and Glunt 1993). Other laboratory experiments suggest interpersonal contact with gay men and lesbians leads to more positive attitudes toward those groups (Grack and Richman 1996; Scarberry et al. 1997).

Allport (1954) specified several necessary conditions for contact to successfully reduce intergroup antagonism including equal status, common goals, intergroup coordination, and the support of authorities, law, or customs. Pettigrew and Tropp's meta-analysis suggested, however, that although meeting these optimal contact conditions leads to even greater reduction in prejudice, contact is still effective under less-than-optimal conditions. They provide clear evidence that "mere" contact is enough to reduce bias, even if Allport's original conditions are not met. Similar debates surround the issue of mode of contact (e.g., face-to-face, mediated interaction, etc.). Amichai-Hamburger and McKenna (2006, 754) argued for the use of the Internet, positing that it is more practical and less likely to generate anxiety and rejecting Pettigrew and Tropp's condition that contact must involve "actual face-to-face interaction." While Amichai-Hamburger and McKenna's contribution is purely theoretical, the ability of computer-based communications to generate meaningful social interactions is supported by communications scholars (Spears et al. 2002). Hopper (1998) investigated the differences between face-to-face and telephone conversations, finding they are essentially similar. Face-to-face speech and sound-alone speech are almost indistinguishable despite the absence in the latter of visual cues. Contact via mediated communication (i.e., telephone, video, and/or Internet) is a particularly attractive possibility for testing contact theory as it surmounts the practicality obstacle and allows for increased physical distance and lower levels of anxiety. Garretson (2015) found that mere exposure to gay and lesbian characters on television improves evaluations of gays and lesbians among younger viewers, which generates increased support for LGBT rights.

Hewstone and Brown (1986) and Brown, Vivian, and Hewstone (1999) noted that the ability to generalize depends on contact being perceived as an intergroup encounter rather than as an interpersonal encounter. Contact perceived as interpersonal may result in warmer feelings toward the contacted individual but will not also produce warmer feelings for the group that individual is purported to represent. Miller, Brewer, and Edwards (1985) raised a note of caution, noting that to maximize generalization, the psychological linkage between subjects and their respective groups cannot be too salient during the interaction. Scarberry et al. (1997) asked participants to interact with and then evaluate research assistants posing as gay participants trained to use either personal (e.g., "Like when I squeeze every bit of toothpaste out of the tube") or impersonal (e.g., "Like when someone squeezes every bit of toothpaste out of the tube") analogies during the contact session. While participants reported liking each confederate equally, those who interacted with the one who used personal analogies were less likely to generalize those feelings to gay people. Generalization also depends on the degree to which an out-group representative is seen as typical according to an individual's prior attitudes (Skipworth, Garner, and Dettrey 2010).

Personalized messages focusing on individual attributes may trigger a liking heuristic and may add to the credibility of a persuader during an outreach campaign. Conversely, personalized messages may undermine the credibility of the persuader and of the organization that they represent by calling into question the degree to which the persuader and target share a common interest and the degree to which the persuader can be trusted. More importantly, a personalized message may shift the focus away from the larger issue onto the personal attributes of the persuader, thus limiting the ability to generalize. This might be particularly true for very personal messages that are typically made to established friends or family. For example, the sharing of one's sexual orientation during a first-time conversation might be seen as too personal and thus may fail to trigger the desired liking heuristic (Harrison and Michelson 2012).

Prior research suggests that personalized messaging can have both positive and negative effects on political behavior. For example, Han (2009) found that personalization had a positive effect on political fundraising. Her experiment randomly changed an appeal to buy a one-dollar bracelet to support Clean Water Action (a national environmental group) by adding two sentences of personal information about the requester: where the person grew up and how they learned to swim and canoe in a nearby lake. Individuals who were asked to donate and who received the appeal with the added personal information were twice as likely to donate. Reviewing the social psychological literature, Han (2009, 107) noted:

Political appeals which disclose some information about the person making the appeal should be more effective because they trigger a liking heuristic that makes strangers treat each other more like friends or acquaintances. Because people are more likely to comply with requests from people they like, appeals with self-disclosure should be more likely to generate acquiescence with a request for political action.

Han's findings, along with similar fundraising field experiments that test message effects and issue framing, lend support to the view that a personalized appeal will be more effective.[2] As noted above, Scarberry et al. (1997) found that personalizing the analogies used by a gay confederate led to decreases in the contact effect because of the suppression of generalization. Previous work finds that in the absence of personal knowledge about a speaker, individuals will use the heuristic of the group or institute with which they are affiliated to help them determine whether or not the speaker can be trusted.

In chapter 2, we provide details of an experiment where we investigated the theory that a campaign seeking support for and donations to an organization advocating one side of a controversial issue such as same-sex marriage should include messages that include personal information (Harrison and Michelson 2012). On the one hand, when persuaders offer personal information, the liking heuristic may induce potential supporters and donors to respond positively to the request being made. Personalization may also increase the credibility of the persuader. When making requests on behalf of an LGBT organization, for example, gay or lesbian individuals may be seen as more credible because they are personally affected by the work of the organization (Druckman and Lupia 2000; Lupia and McCubbins 1998). On the other hand, however, personalization may decrease the credibility of a persuader and the organization in that the appeal may now be perceived as one motivated by personal self-interest. In addition, personalized messaging may frame the conversation in terms of the individual canvasser or trigger uncomfortable thoughts about gay and lesbian intimacy, taking the focus away from the larger issue (e.g., LGBT rights). Casey (2016) found that for some individuals, thinking about LGBT people or policies triggers feelings of disgust, and this disgust leads to significantly less support for LGBT-friendly policies.

Shared Identity Priming and Expectancy Violation

While dual-processing models have provided significant insight into persuasion and similarity, there is more to uncover. For example, Wilson and Sherrell (1993) found that perceived identity similarity has a relatively small effect on attitudes when compared to the influence of source expertise. Similarly, literature on political party labels that also rely on dual-processing models finds that party labels are not universally successful. These labels affect attitudes when it comes to more novel issues (Kam 2005) but not more familiar social issues (Cizmar and Layman 2009). One potential explanation for these results is that there is an interaction between source characteristics and message content and delivery that is thus far unaccounted for in the dual-process models discussed above (Bergan 2012). Source characteristics may have a more complicated effect on attitudes because of the inferences that recipients draw from these sources and their characteristics. In sum, there is an important interaction between recipients' perceptions of information sources and the content of their messages.

Classic work in rational choice and political decision-making generally focuses on how political actors make poor use of information in political contexts. This can be for a variety of reasons: bias, defensive avoidance, and selective exposure draw these actors further away from the rational ideal (see Janis and Mann 1977, 205; Jervis 1976; and Wicklund and Brehm 1976). However, as Calvert (1985) demonstrated, these phenomena can lead to a decision-maker achieving higher expected utility than a purely unbiased or "objective" source of information. He wrote, "Just because the real world does not meet the conditions of simple rational decision models, the analyst cannot abandon the rigorous study of how goals determine choices" (554). In one model, Calvert showed that if a predisposition is strong enough, so-called unbiased or objective information offers little to the decision-maker while information that leans toward the already-preferred option leads to higher expected utility. Even when a decision-maker has imperfect or incomplete information, having a source that provides information leaning in a predisposed direction leads to better-quality decision-making and optimal behavioral outcomes. In short, relying on source cues, even with so-called biased information, can be helpful in making important attitudinal decisions about public policy.

Relatedly, priming theory captures potential source identity effects by suggesting that communicators can change the basis for evaluation (i.e., different criteria) that individuals use when forming an opinion (Druckman 2003; Druckman and Holmes 2004; Iyengar and Kinder 1987). Issues or attributes that receive the most relative attention are more likely to serve as an overall basis of evaluation (Krosnick and Brannon 1993). Priming is also an increasingly common theoretical framework used to investigate communication effects, identity, and attitudinal change, with existing research suggesting that both issues and image identities can be primed by context and cues (Druckman and Holmes 2004; McLeish and Oxoby 2008). In short, priming theory suggests that when an identity is emphasized or cued, that emphasis increases an identity's salience and subsequently an individual's concern for identity-based interests. Klar (2013) reviewed the literature on priming, identifying three strategies or types of primes: (1) basic (simply mentioning the identity); (2) efficacy (appealing to an identity group's efficacy); and (3) threat (imposing a perceived threat against an identity group). The introduction of identity in these three ways has the potential to affect attitudes and behavior.

One hypothesis about the effectiveness of identity primes and source cues has to do with the degree to which the messages are unexpected from that particular source. For example, if the content in a persuasive message is explained in terms of the character of a source (i.e., self-interest), then the messages are no more successful than if there is no such explanation (Eagly and Chaiken 1975). Sources do tend to be persuasive, however, when supporting messages that are inconsistent or incongruous with their own interests (Walster, Aronson, and Abrahams 1966). In other words, messages can be most effective when they are sent from a trusted source and yet are surprising or unexpected from those particular sources, free from potential biases like self-interest. This is often referred to as expectancy violation.

The literature on expectancy violations, derived from attribution theory (Kelley 1973), suggests that message recipients' explanations of why a source delivers a persuasive message can influence the degree to which recipients' attitudes change. Expectancy violation theory "predicts that extremity in target evaluations is influenced by the interaction between preexisting stereotyped expectations about a target's group and personal information about the target" (Bettencourt et al. 2016, 52). Because stereotype violations are surprising, they garner more attention from the evaluator.

Message recipients are persuaded more by sources that violate expectations than by those that do not. When people are surprised by message content, they engage in greater systematic message processing. This is particularly likely when message recipients initially are not highly motivated to process information or are low in what's known as need for cognition, or when the message is personally irrelevant (Maheswaran and Chaiken 1991). Eagly et al. (1978) found that a source described as pro-business is more persuasive in advocating a pro-environment position than a source described as pro-environment. Unexpected information receives more cognitive processing than expected information (e.g., Bargh and Thein 1985; Hastie 1984; Stern et al. 1984; see also Hamilton and Sherman 1996). Behavior that is inconsistent with personal impressions (i.e., target-based expectancies) or stereotypes is recalled better than is consistent behavior (Jones 1990; Stangor and McMillan 1992). Further, expectancy-violating behavior triggered more effortful causal explanations than expectancy-consistent behavior (e.g., Hamilton 1988; Hastie 1984; Jackson et al. 1993; Pyszczynski and Greenberg 1981).

Consistent with existing research on stereotypes (Ashmore and Del Boca 1981) and party cue violation (Bergan 2012), messages consistent with traits perceived to be typical of the source's group are termed *stereotypical* (see Judd and Park 1993) and messages that conflict with traits typical of the source's group as *counter-stereotypical*. Bergan (2012) also used the term *non-stereotypical* to refer to situations in which sources are attached to messages for which there is no widely held expectation about the source's group. He gave the example of a message supporting a pro-choice view of abortion from a Democrat as being stereotypical, a pro-choice message from a Republican as being counter-stereotypical, and a message in which a new, unfamiliar message from either partisan with no clear ideological or partisan cleavage as being non-stereotypical. Consistent with literature on expectancy violation (Walster, Aronson, and Abrahams 1966), counter-stereotypical messages and endorsements are hypothesized to be more effective and persuasive in terms of support for the advocated object than stereotypical messages or non-stereotypical messages, which typically have little to no effect. Counter-stereotypical messages are cognitive speed bumps, nudging recipients to stop their usual train of thought and pay attention to the information being presented.

OUR THEORY: DISSONANT IDENTITY PRIMING

In this book, we build upon and extend the previously mentioned scholarship on attitude change and identity with our Theory of Dissonant Identity Priming (TDIP). Social group identity, attitude change, and priming have long garnered the attention of scholars in a variety of fields, including political science, political communication, and political psychology. Bergan (2012) claimed that most existing theory ignores the interaction between source characteristics and message characteristics in determining attitude change. We rely on the literature on source credibility and expectancy violation (Eagly, Wood, and Chaiken 1978) to predict that communication sources (senders) will be more likely to increase support for policies among recipients when (a) they share a salient social or political identity with the receiver and (b) the message they deliver is unexpected.

While there is much we know from extant scholarship, we identify three gaps in the literature that TDIP helps to fill. First, most existing studies using identity priming do not identify the conditions under which identity priming can be effective in opening minds on issues that may be counter to existing beliefs. Second, most priming studies investigate the effect of priming identity on an attitude or issue directly related to that identity (i.e., priming Black identity when speaking to a Black target and asking about issues directly relevant to the Black community). Less well understood is how identity priming might affect attitudes and behaviors toward an issue that is not central to or directly related to the identity itself. Third, little work has looked at how identity priming might affect particularly contentious issues or the relative strength of different identities in encouraging attitude change on such issues.

Our Theory of Dissonant Identity Priming draws from the concepts of interpersonal closeness, group identity, and source credibility from social psychology, communication, and political science. Increasing the likelihood of attitude change involves activating cognitive interest and finding the optimal way to focus on the similarities between senders of communication and their targets. On controversial issues like same-sex marriage, abortion rights, or stem-cell research, people often have strong attitudes that they are reluctant to reconsider, putting up perceptual screens to information that might contradict their existing beliefs and generally leaving themselves unwilling or unable to engage in deliberation. Advocacy organizations often struggle to find the recipe for success in reaching out to opponents and generating attitudinal change. TDIP suggests that attitude change will be more likely when messaging activates a salient in-group identity. In other words, if you can induce a person to believe they are speaking with or hearing from a member of a mutually identifying group (e.g., someone from their shared ethnoracial group or political party), they should be more likely to engage in a conversation and to be more open to attitude change, even on contentious political and social issues. Counter-stereotypical or dissonant messages, because they are unexpected, should garner more attention and thus be more effective.

Druckman and Lupia (2000) and Lupia and McCubbins (1998) noted that when individuals do not know each other well, persuasion depends on perceived knowledge and common interest. A heuristic such as association with a known organization or shared membership in another group can generate that credibility. Scholars have shown that such credibility varies based on the level of sophistication of the target individual (Boudreau 2009; Lupia and McCubbins 1998). We add here an additional twist to that model: that source credibility also varies according to activated shared identity and further, that unexpected messages will be even more effective. For example, a messenger seeking to persuade a targeted individual to make a donation in support of an LGBT rights organization or to voice support for same-sex marriage will seem more credible if they are induced to think of the messenger as sharing a group identity; for example, that they are members of the same religion or fans of the same sport.

These cues can come in a variety of forms and we test several different scenarios in chapters 3–6. The overall point is that shared identities among individuals should matter in altering public opinion. Those shared identities are best understood in a framework of values: identity cues—whether from regular people, from celebrities, or from other social group leaders and elites—communicate a set of values associated with that identity. When a signal is sent from a prominent, well-known representative of the Black community, for example, what that representative is communicating is what it means to have Black values. Using elite cues in experiments works because the elites exemplify the identity group and the values it holds; they are unquestionable representatives of that identity.

Different messages and cues have different strengths, of course, depending on the connection between the person and the identity group; knowledge of the cue; and the degree to which the message cues a salient identity. Messages must highlight relevant and easily accessible identities and successfully bring those identities to the attitudinal calculus of the respondent. Each of the examples of identity priming in this book, whether from a regular person, a famous person, or someone who is viewed as a leader of an identity community, was carefully constructed to balance competing interests of believability, context, elites, too much dissonance, not enough dissonance, etc. Ultimately, the success or failure of a prime was dependent upon factors unique to each experiment.

In addition to these factors, we hypothesized that there are message effects; specifically, the hypothesized effect will be more powerful when the message is unrelated to that in-group identity and/or is surprising or unexpected. To summarize, TDIP has four main components:

1. Priming a shared in-group identity can create the perception of reduced social distance between the source of a persuasive message and the receiver, thus motivating willingness to process the information and openness to attitude change.
2. The shared in-group identity that is primed need not be related to the message but must be strong enough to generate interpersonal closeness or source credibility.
3. Messaging and priming effects will be stronger when the primed in-group identity is strongly held.
4. Messaging and priming effects will be stronger when the delivered message is unexpected and yet plausibly held by other members of the primed in-group.

The TDIP process model is illustrated in figure 1.2.

TDIP differs from previous theories about attitude change in that it posits that triggering a shared in-group identity leads individuals receiving a persuasive message to be more likely to be motivated to process the information and be open to attitudinal change, even if the issue at hand does not necessarily have direct, tangible consequences for their own lives. Returning to our focus on same-sex marriage, our hypothesis is that individuals will be more willing to support marriage equality if they are primed to consider themselves as sharing an in-group identity with the individual delivering the appeal. Marriage equality is not personally relevant to most individuals with straight sexual orientations but triggering a sense of shared identity not related to sexual orientation will nevertheless lead targets to consider changing their attitudes on the issue. Note that while our focus in this book is on marriage equality, we expect TDIP would be equally relevant and effective for encouraging straight individuals to be supportive of other LGBT rights such as employment and housing non-discrimination rights, parenting rights, and the rights of transgender and gender non-conforming individuals, as well as to efforts aimed at shifting public opinion on other contentious issues.

BIG-PICTURE IMPLICATIONS

Existing models of persuasion tell us that the first step down the road to successful attitude change is the motivation to process information—in other words, the willingness to listen. We posit that this first step has not, to date, sufficiently considered the influence of individual-level identities. By priming identity, a sender of communication is establishing themselves as a member of the receiver's in-group and therefore the willingness to listen is increased. If the sender then delivers a message that signals a particular attitude that the receiver does not share, the receiver may shift their attitude on that issue in order to be consistent with others in that in-group.

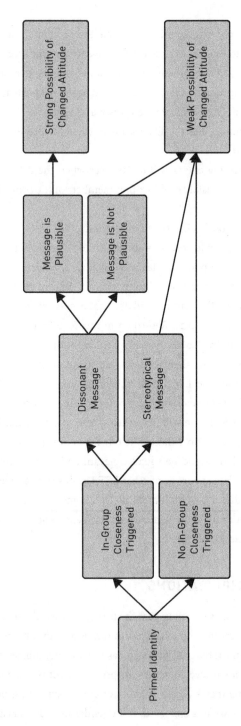

FIGURE 1.2 The Theory of Dissonant Identity Priming Attitude Change Process Model.

This serves to cement their membership in the primed in-group. For example, to foreshadow an experiment described in chapter 3, when individuals who consider themselves to be fans of professional football receive a message in support of same-sex marriage from another dedicated fan of professional football or from a professional football player, they are more willing to consider supporting marriage equality. Doing so reinforces the person's identity as a football fan. This is more likely to occur when the identity that is primed is strongly held (e.g., when the recipient is a dedicated football fan) and when the delivered message is plausibly one held by other members of the primed in-group (e.g., when some other football fans are known to be supporters of marriage equality).

We expect that TDIP will not work if (*a*) the activated identity is weakly held; (*b*) the persuasive cue or message attributed to the activated identity does not capture the attention of the respondent or is not sufficiently surprising; and/or (*c*) there are overwhelming cues in the negative direction such that one identity prime would be unlikely to have a significant effect. For example, scholarship on ethnoracial identity has found that individuals vary in the strength of their identity as Black or Latino (Cross 1991; Rumbaut 1994; Valenzuela and Michelson 2016). Thus, priming a shared ethnoracial in-group identity will work best on those with a strong sense of Black or Latino identity and less well among those with weaker ethnoracial identities. Further, contextual factors may weaken the power of the shared primed in-group identity.

For example, to preview an experiment we describe in chapter 4, a religious prime is likely to work when the sender and recipient share an identity as religious individuals, but not in a context—for example, the Bible Belt—where religious individuals are almost always strongly opposed to the desired attitude. The key to generating the possibility of attitudinal change on a contentious issue is increasing the likelihood of information processing, achieved by identifying and priming a shared identity between the sender and the target. Some core identities such as ethnoracial group or religion are more easily activated and thus have the potential to be effective at reducing perceived social distance and inducing attitudinal shifts. Other identities, those more tangential or less deeply felt, are less easily activated and less effective.

We rely on the prominent social psychological theory of priming to induce or to highlight the salience of individuals' identities (see McGraw and Ling 2003; Valentino 1999; Valentino, Hutchings, and White 2002). A perceived common identity, we argue, is one of the strongest cues possible and the idea of common identity priming forms the core of the experiments we present in this book. We apply our theory to one of the most prominent, contentious issues in US politics: same-sex marriage and rights for lesbian, gay, bisexual, and transgender (LGBT) individuals. We chose these issues because of their prominence in contemporary political debates and the opportunity thus created to test our theory in the real-world arena of advocacy groups fighting for public support. Over the past several years, gay and lesbian people have become the focus of increased attention in political science, building on decades of existing scholarship in the social sciences on the LGBT community (see Vallely

2012 for an extensive review of political science work on LGBT individuals). To illustrate the power of TDIP, we test different methods of increasing the connectedness between sender and receiver and decreasing the perceived social distance between LGBT and non-LGBT individuals and their advocates.

As noted at the beginning of this chapter and as we detail in the next, there has been a rapid increase in support for LGBT issues such as marriage equality over the past few decades. Other explanations for this increase include (1) cohort replacement, the idea that older, more socially conservative Americans are dying and being replaced in the population by younger, more socially progressive respondents and (2) large-scale advocacy campaigns that are attempting to persuade. Neither is adequate for explaining the observed shifts; is it not simply cohort replacement or advocacy campaigns that are persuading the mass public (see Egan 2010). At the same time, however, we have witnessed increased visibility and exposure to LGBT individuals, both in the media and in everyday life.

People are realizing that LGBT people are part of communities that are important to them and that their lives are intertwined with those of LGBT individuals. This leads them to be more supportive in part because it humanizes them, as predicted by contact theory. Members of the LGBT community are no longer abstract unknowns. They are friends, neighbors, coworkers, and relatives. This aspect of increasing support is well documented and consistent with previous scholarship. Further, people are realizing that supporters of marriage equality and other LGBT rights are also members of their communities. Democrats and even some Republicans are realizing that many other members of their political party, including national leaders, are supportive. Blacks, Latinos, and members of other ethnoracial groups are noting increased support from others in their communities, and from ethnoracial elites. Fans of professional sports like football and basketball are learning that their sports heroes and fellow fans are also supporters of marriage equality.

Across a wide range of communities—a wide range of personal in-groups—Americans are realizing that fellow members of their in-groups are supporters of same-sex marriage and other LGBT rights. These shared in-group identities are opening minds to attitude change. Individuals are adjusting their attitudes on LGBT rights to better correspond with opinions shared by other members of their in-groups and thus cement their sense of belonging to those various groups. This is where the Theory of Dissonant Identity Priming comes into play. The interpersonal connection makes people more motivated to process the information that is provided to them and, in the experiments we describe in this book, to be more supportive of marriage equality, gay and lesbian parenting, employment non-discrimination, and rights for transgender people. The effects are especially powerful when the message comes from an unexpected source.

We extend Bergan's (2012) use of partisan identity to look at source similarity and message effectiveness on contentious social issues, finding that the latter depends on the former only when the message is unexpected for the predominant view of that group. We also explore the effects both of elite cues and of non-elite cues. Our biggest contribution is the intersectionality of source and message. Theoretically, cues in general should increase support. When people hear that others (regardless of who they are and what identity they have) are supportive of something contentious like same-sex marriage, it should increase support; however, sometimes cues have little to no effect and sometimes there is a large effect. Some cues fail to be effective because some identity groups are overwhelmingly against LGBT rights and that overwhelming opposition is not easily overcome. These identities tend to be highly salient to people's self-concept and both the high salience and the pre-treatment effects are just too strong. Other cues are effective; while unexpected or dissonant, they are credible and the recipient is motivated to process the information presented. In these instances, respondents may reconsider their original (stereotypical) positions.

To paraphrase Zaller (1992), people are sampling considerations that are available to them, particularly recent and accessible ones, and an unexpected cue will be comparatively weighty compared to others. The people who move are the members of identity groups who receive unexpected but plausible cues. When there is the perception that a community is against (or in favor), one cue in an expected direction may not matter. Hearing a stereotypical and expected message is generally not effective but unexpected messages from a trusted in-group source *are* effective because they are notable and surprising; they are cognitive speed bumps that lead targets to pause and reconsider, to process the information in a new way and possibly change their minds.

CHAPTER SUMMARY AND NEXT STEPS

The Theory of Dissonant Identity Priming would also apply to efforts to change minds on other contentious political and social issues, such as abortion, stem-cell research, or legalizing marijuana, and to other LGBT issues. For clarity, our focus is largely on one issue: same-sex marriage. In some instances, as appropriate, we also test for support for gay and lesbian parenting, employment non-discrimination legislation, and rights for transgender individuals, areas of LGBT rights that in recent years have emerged as a new frontier, particularly as the fight for marriage equality has come to a (legal) close.

In addition to being topically relevant, LGBT studies allow us to address broader questions in American politics by focusing on an issue with new cleavages and divisions in terms of public opinion. A focus on LGBT individuals broadens the applicability and efficacy of this work and highlights important insights on social and identity politics, gender and sexuality roles, and power dynamics. In other words, as one of the most contentious social issues in contemporary American politics, marriage equality is an ideal issue on which to test our theory. Not only is it of interest in real-world political contexts, the study of LGBT rights and marriage equality encompasses many of the central themes of the discipline of political science and social science more generally. As Wald (2000, 6) noted:

Attempts by gays to alter their status through political means gives us the opportunity to study how small, weak and despised groups can use political means to challenge larger and stronger political forces who enjoy the support of entrenched social values.... The clash of social movements over gay rights thus forces us to ask fundamental questions about the nature and distribution of power in the United States, which *is* a central concern of political science.

One of the key innovations of our theory is that the identities we prime do not directly relate to the issues we test. In most other cases, identity priming is used to investigate how identity salience changes attitudes toward issues within that domain (i.e., priming Black identity to then ask questions relating to Black issues or struggles). Our theory diverges from that academic tradition by priming identities that are otherwise unrelated to the policy issues we then test. Further, we bring the power of randomized experiments to bear on the study of identity and political communication; we expand on this point in chapter 2.

The remainder of this book proceeds as follows. In chapter 2, we look at recent survey data on attitudes toward same-sex marriage, followed by a review of the LGBT literature on public opinion and social movements. We then discuss the value of social science experimentation as a research methodology and outline our systematic, scientific tests of advocacy and communication efforts in partnership with LGBT advocacy organizations from around the country.

Various parts of the project were funded or conducted by movement organizations, under our supervision. In each instance of a collaborative effort with an organization, the authors (and the authors alone) were responsible for data analysis and interpretation; at no time were results changed to better suit the goals and aims of these partners. In some instances, the findings were not what our partners would have preferred to hear. We feel strongly that it is important to report honest findings and analyses, even in the face of opposition, and the book contains some inconvenient or unpleasant truths for LGBT rights advocates. In sum, funders and movement organizations had no editorial control over our work. We are tremendously appreciative to those groups who allowed us to work with their staff and volunteers and who contributed time, money, and effort to our experiments, particularly when the results are not what they had hoped to see.

Chapters 3–6 describe the randomized experiments we conducted to test TDIP with various identities: identity as a sports fan (chapter 3), religious identity (chapter 4), ethnoracial identity (chapter 5), and partisanship (chapter 6). We chose to conduct experiments using these identities for a variety of reasons. Some identities—religion and partisanship—are inextricably interwoven in current debates about marriage equality. As noted in chapter 4, for example, those seeking to explain their position on LGBT rights often invoke religious beliefs. Partisanship is not only one of the most powerful social identities in political science but also one of the most reliable predictors of an individual's position on marriage equality (although to a lesser degree as overall attitudes have shifted). Other identities—sports fan and ethnorace—were chosen in response to current events and the real-world concerns of the advocacy groups with which we partnered. As noted in chapter 5, for example, we conducted experiments on the power of Black identity in order to help groups hoping to increase support in the Black community. The relevance of sports fan identity, as detailed in chapter 3, was inspired by elite athletes' efforts to use their celebrity to shift attitudes on the issue. Complete scripts for all of the experiments are in appendix 2.

We conclude in chapter 7 with a review of our overall findings and a discussion of their implications for practitioners and political scientists. Chapter 7 also includes a discussion of experiments conducted in a state that already had marriage equality (Maryland) and one in which attitudes remained firmly opposed to marriage equality (Louisiana). Table 1.1 provides a roadmap to the randomized experiments conducted for this book, including relevant community partners.

In the next chapter, we turn our focus to the politically relevant and contentious topic that will serve as the application of our theory: LGBT rights. We review

Table 1.1 Roadmap of 17 Randomized Experiments in This Book

Chapter	Primed Identity	Target Population	Location	Partner Organization
2	n/a	Supporters of LGBT rights	Iowa	One Iowa
3	NFL fan	Adults	National	n/a
	NFL fan	Adults	National	n/a
	Green Bay Packers fan	Adults	Appleton, WI	n/a
	NHL fan	Adults	National	n/a
	San Francisco Giants fan	Adults	San Francisco, CA	n/a
4	Religion	Adults	National	SocialSci.com
	Religion	Adults	Louisiana	Equality Louisiana
5	Black	Black adults	Cook County, IL	Equality Illinois
	Black	Black adults	Atlanta, GA	Georgia Equality
	Latino	Latino adults	National	Latino Decisions
	Latino	Latino adults	Edinburg, TX	University of Texas, Pan American
6	Partisanship	Registered voters	Virginia	n/a
	Partisanship	Voters	New Jersey	n/a
	Partisanship	Adults	National	n/a
7	Progressive	Supporters of LGBT rights	Louisiana	Capital City Alliance
	Previous supporter or progressive	Supporters of LGBT rights	Maryland	Equality Maryland

the history of same-sex marriage in the United States, including laws and public opinion, noting the rapid shift in attitudes on the issue in the past two decades and evidence that this change is the result not just of cohort replacement but also of individuals actively changing their minds. We also review previous political science scholarship on LGBT issues and clarify how this book takes a unique approach and makes a unique contribution to the literature. This includes a discussion of the science of randomized field experiments and the philosophy of pracademics.

2 Marriage Equality and Other LGBT Issues in the United States

This chapter introduces how LGBT rights in American politics and specifically within the discipline of political science have been addressed over the last several decades. While certainly not an exhaustive history of the fight for LGBT equality, it provides the context and backdrop for our empirical work in chapters 3–6. We start with a broad look at major events in the 20th century before we turn to treatment of those events by social and political scientists. Next, we describe how randomized experiments work and the new insights they can provide for the study of political communication and identity politics, illustrated with details and results from an experiment we conducted with One Iowa in 2009. One of the central tenets of our work is the idea of pracademics, the notion that social science can (and should) engage with real-world practitioners to blend best practices in social science with practical, on-the-ground knowledge from advocates and organizations. Overall, the purpose of this chapter is to familiarize readers with recent events in the LGBT movement; how this movement has been addressed by political scientists; and how we break new ground by applying our Theory of Dissonant Identity Priming to attitudes toward LGBT people and rights in the United States.

THE FIGHT FOR LGBT RIGHTS

American history is fraught with examples of laws and policies that contradict the basic tenets of the American creed. The Declaration of Independence proclaimed that "all men are created equal" despite a system of chattel slavery and the subjugation of women, among other ongoing examples of injustice. Ending slavery led the

United States into a bloody civil war and inequality still persisted, even after the advances that resulted from the Civil Rights Movement. Miscegenation laws banned interracial marriages in many states until 1967, when the US Supreme Court ruled such bans unconstitutional in *Loving v. Virginia*. Women were denied the vote until 1920 and although more than half of American voters today are women, until the historic nomination of Hillary Clinton in 2016, no major political party had chosen a woman as their nominee for President of the United States. In 2016, working women in the United States still make only 77 cents on the dollar compared to men. These persistent inequalities are, in many ways, the consequence of feelings of social group membership and the tendency by dominant groups to prefer their own in-groups at the expense of perceived out-groups. As discussed in chapter 1, social group membership can sometimes create barriers between one's perceived in-groups and perceived out-groups, resulting in disagreement about the rights and freedoms that should be extended to subgroups in American culture.

One of the most prominent, contentious issues in American politics of the past few decades concerns the rights of LGBT individuals, particularly around the ability to marry someone of the same sex. Gay and lesbian individuals have seen recent advances in some of their rights, particularly since the unofficial launch of the modern Gay Rights Movement in 1969 at the Stonewall Inn in New York City's Greenwich Village. In the 1960s, raids on gay bars were routine; police would arrest patrons and publish their names in the newspaper, often with significant negative consequences for the individuals involved. But on June 28, 1969, the patrons of the Stonewall Inn fought back, chanting "gay power" and launching what would become six nights of riots. Stonewall marks the symbolic moment that the LGBT community decided to not accept treatment as second-class citizens but rather to demand that they be treated equally. President Obama marked the significance of that uprising in May 2016 when he declared the Stonewall Inn a national monument, the first national monument in the United States recognizing the struggle for LGBT rights.

Since 1969, the LGBT community has made significant progress in its fight for liberty and equality. Initial efforts focused on freedom from retaliation for being openly gay and the decriminalization of homosexual behavior (Sherrill 1999). The latter goal was attained when the US Supreme Court ruled in *Lawrence v. Texas* (2003) that laws criminalizing consensual sodomy violated the 14th Amendment's due process clause (Egan and Sherrill 2005). In 1977, Harvey Milk became the first openly gay man elected to public office when he won a race to serve on the San Francisco Board of Supervisors. In 1982, Wisconsin became the first state to outlaw discrimination on the basis of sexual orientation and in 2000, Vermont became the first state to legalize same-sex civil unions and domestic partnerships. In 2003, Massachusetts became the first state to legalize same-sex marriage. Gay men and lesbians gained the right to serve openly in the US military in 2011 and the nationwide right to same-sex marriage in June 2015.

Participation in the Stonewall Riots included not just gay men and lesbians but also transgender individuals, many of whom were the leaders of the riots. Rights for transgender people have also advanced significantly since the 1960s. In 1976, the New Jersey Supreme Court ruled that transsexual persons may marry on the basis of their gender identity, regardless of their assigned gender. In 1977, transgender woman Renée Richards won the right to compete as a woman when the New York Supreme Court ruled in her favor in a case filed against the US Tennis Association. In 2010, the federal government extended non-discrimination laws to include transgender civilians who are federal employees. In 2016, the US military changed its policy on transgender service members, allowing those individuals to serve openly without the threat of discharge for their gender identity.

These victories and successes notwithstanding, the fight for equality for the LGBT community is far from over. Federal law provides no protection from discrimination based on sexual orientation or gender identity for non-federal employees. Most states do not provide protection from workplace discrimination based on sexual orientation or gender identity, nor do they have in place anti-bullying policies that protect LGBT children in public schools. In many states, same-sex couples cannot adopt children; in others, they face considerable obstacles to doing so.

Marriage laws have been the predominant conversation around LGBT rights over the past decade. Marriage equality launched into the national consciousness in 1993, when a Hawaii court temporarily ruled that denying same-sex couples the right to marry was discriminatory, and again in 2003 when the Massachusetts Supreme Judicial Court ruled that same-sex couples were legally entitled to wed under the state's constitution. Tanya McCloskey and Marcia Kadish became the first to take advantage of the ruling, marrying on May 17, 2004. After a decade of amendments to state constitutions, lawsuits on the state and federal levels, and ballot initiatives, the fight for the freedom to marry reached the Supreme Court of the United States. Two rulings in 2013 (*Windsor* and *Perry*) led to smaller victories—one invalidating the federal Defense of Marriage Act (DOMA), the other bringing marriage to the state of California. The final word from the Court came on June 26, 2015, when the *Obergefell* decision extended marriage rights to same-sex couples throughout the United States. Further details of these cases are discussed below.

While progress has been made over time in extending equal rights to women, people of color, and the LGBT community, in many ways our laws continue to fail to live up to the grand words of the Declaration of Independence. All men may be created equal but they are not yet treated equally under the law. Progress is slow, with battles won one day at a time, on one issue at a time. These issues are often complex and highly contentious, both among our elected officials and the public at large; different segments of the population have strong attitudes toward these kinds of issues, on each end of the spectrum. In other words, attitudes are divided along demographic, religious, and sociocultural identities.

These divisions are due in part to divisions among partisan elites. There are a variety of studies that come to the same conclusion: the level of elite partisan polarization has been increasing in the United States over time (Aldrich 1995; Coleman 1997; Collie and Mason 2000; Jacobson 2000; Rohde 1991; Stonecash et al. 2003; Theriault 2006). McCarty, Poole, and Rosenthal (2011) showed the trend of increasing partisanship in Congress from 1879 to 2011 for both the House and the Senate, controlling for region among Democrats. It is clear that political parties are becoming more ideologically distinct, with little or no overlap between the two parties among elected officials in Congress. This elite polarization makes partisanship more salient and more determinative of mass attitudes and behavior, generating stronger and more distinct partisan identities among the mass public (see Hetherington 2001; Levendusky 2009).

In addition to the increasing salience of partisanship, an important byproduct of elite polarization is *issue* polarization. That is, as the parties get further apart at the elite level, partisan reasoning increases and the extreme separation of policy attitudes increases as well. Historically, polarization on issues has tended to be around just one policy issue. Contemporarily, however, the two major parties are becoming further and further apart on many (if not most) policies, particularly on social issues (Layman, Carsey, and Horowitz 2006). There is widespread consensus that the major parties have become more sharply divided, both in terms of ideology and in terms of policy stances (Abramowitz and Saunders 1998; Bond and Fleisher 2001; Brewer 2005; Carmines and Layman 1997; DiMaggio, Evans and Bryson 1996; Jacobson 2000, 2005; Layman and Carsey 2002a, 2002b; Levine, Carmines, and Huckfeldt 1997; Pomper and Weiner 2002; Stonecash et al. 2003; Weisberg 2002). While these issues themselves are not necessarily demonstrative of issue polarization, one of the byproducts of this phenomenon is the hardening of attitudes about contentious issues like abortion, stem cell research, marriage equality for same-sex couples, and most recently, transgender rights.

MARRIAGE EQUALITY

Of all of the divisive political and sociocultural issues facing the United States in the last 20 years, marriage equality is one of the most prominent and contentious (Fiorina, Abrams, and Pope 2005). The cleavages across partisan and demographic lines point to a more nuanced understanding of attitudinal shifts beyond mere polarization; recent polling results suggest that in terms of support for marriage equality, there are sharp, clear cleavages along gender, age, ethnorace, party identification, and ideological lines. A June 2015 poll by the Pew Research Center (figure 2.1) measured overall support at 57% of the public, including 76% of younger adults (age 18–29) and 41% of older adults (age 65 and older). There are also significant differences by religious affiliation: only 27% of white evangelical Protestants favor same-sex marriage, compared to 43% of Black Protestants, 62% of white mainline

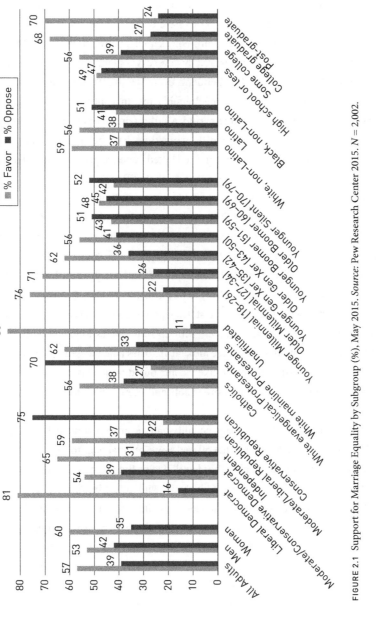

FIGURE 2.1 Support for Marriage Equality by Subgroup (%), May 2015. *Source:* Pew Research Center 2015. *N* = 2,002.

Protestants, and 85% of individuals who are unaffiliated with a formal religion (Pew Research Center 2015).

Support was also relatively high among members of all ideologies except for conservative Republicans: 81% of liberal Democrats, 59% of moderate or liberal Republicans, and 54% of moderate or conservative Democrats reported their support for the freedom to marry compared to only 22% of conservative Republicans. While both Republicans and Democrats have become more supportive over time, important partisan differences remain. For example, between 2001 and 2016, support for marriage equality as measured by Pew surveys increased among Democrats from 43% to 66% and among Independents from 43% to 61%, shifts of 23 and 18 percentage points, respectively. Among Republicans, in contrast, support increased from 21% to 32% during the same period, a shift of only 11 percentage points (Pew Research Center 2015). In other words, while there have been increases in support over time among almost all groups in the United States, support among Democrats and Independents has significantly outpaced that of Republicans.

Despite growing pluralities of support among many subgroups, there have been significant barriers and roadblocks to achieving nationwide marriage equality, with decision-makers in some states continuing to actively work to restrict access to marriage to opposite-sex couples. Victories in the fight for marriage equality have often come in the form of judicial decisions rather than through votes by the public or elected officials (see Pierceson 2013). Massachusetts (2004), Connecticut (2008), and Iowa (2009) were the first three states where judicial decisions established the right to marry for same-sex couples, with 23 other states following suit in 2013, 2014, and 2015. Not only have these judicial victories failed to generate public backlash (Bishin et al. 2016), they also likely contributed to increases in public support by making same-sex marriages more visible and more salient to the general public (Klarman 2013).

Until November 2012, marriage equality had never won at the ballot box, losing 33 times in a row; the few states that offered same-sex marriage to their residents had come to that decision through either legislative or judicial action (Solomon 2014). The November 2012 election proved historic, with voters in Maine, Maryland, and Washington enacting same-sex marriage via ballot initiative. The same day, voters in Minnesota rejected a ballot initiative prohibiting same-sex marriage, only the second time such a ban had lost at the polls; Arizona was the first state to do so in 2006. These advances in marriage equality rights notwithstanding, the overwhelming trend over the last several decades has been one of voters consistently rejecting proposals to allow same-sex couples to marry and to take action to make such marriages illegal or unconstitutional.

In June 2013, the US Supreme Court issued two historic rulings on cases related to marriage equality (see Textbox). *Hollingsworth v. Perry* threw out California's ban on same-sex marriage which had been added to the state constitution in 2008 via ballot initiative (Proposition 8). However, much to the dismay of marriage equality advocates, the ruling was narrowly tailored to address only the issue of standing of the defenders of the ban and did not address the broader constitutional question of the right of same-sex couples to wed. In *United States v. Windsor*, the Court declared section 3 of DOMA to be unconstitutional. DOMA, a bill signed by President Bill Clinton in 1996, defined marriage as between one man and one woman and denied federal benefits to same-sex couples, even if their marriages were recognized by the state in which they lived. Again, however, the ruling was narrow, forcing the federal government to recognize state-sanctioned unions but not ruling that same-sex couples had a constitutionally protected right to marry regardless of their state of residence. In June 2015, the Supreme Court clarified in *Obergefell v. Hodges* that there was a federal right to marry and that the 14th Amendment of the US Constitution requires a state to license a marriage between two people of the same sex.

Box 1 Supreme Court Textbox: *Perry, Windsor, and Obergefell*

In the summer of 2013, the United States Supreme Court issued two rulings on the issue of marriage equality: *Perry* and *Windsor*. While neither case found that the US Constitution guaranteed the right to marry for same-sex couples, the decisions marked major victories for the marriage equality movement. A more definitive statement in favor of marriage equality came in June 2015 with the *Obergefell* decision. Here, we briefly review those three landmark cases.

Hollingsworth v. Perry (2013)

In 2000, California voters approved Proposition 22 which defined marriage as only between one man and one woman. Eight years later, Proposition 22 was declared unconstitutional by the state Supreme Court and in response, proponents put a constitutional amendment (Proposition 8) on the November 2008 ballot. Proposition 8 was approved by California voters with 52.3 percent of the vote, amending the state constitution to provide that "only marriage between a man and a woman is valid or recognized by California." Two same-sex couples in California (Kristin Perry and Sandra Stier, and Paul Katami and Jeffrey Zarrillo) were denied marriage licenses by the state and then filed suit, asking for a preliminary order blocking Proposition 8. The original case was known as *Perry et al. v. Schwarzenegger* because then-Governor Arnold Schwarzenegger was the named defendant in the lawsuit. However, Schwarzenegger and other state officials, including then-Attorney General Jerry Brown, refused to defend Proposition 8. Brown claimed that it was a violation of equal protection rights as protected under the US Constitution. (Under US law, state constitutional provisions can be declared invalid if they are in violation of the US Constitution.) In their place, proponents of Proposition 8 asserted in July 2009 the ability to defend its constitutionality, including Dennis Hollingsworth, a Republican member of the California State Senate. Thus, the case became known as *Hollingsworth v. Perry*.

The plantiffs (Perry et al.) claimed that Proposition 8 was a violation of the federal constitution—namely, the 14th Amendment's right to equal protection under the law. In May 2009, a California District Court ruled that Proposition 8 was unconstitutional and in February 2012, the US Court of Appeals for the Ninth Circuit affirmed that decision. Later that year, the US Supreme Court agreed to hear the case. The Court declined to rule on the merits of the case, however, instead finding by a vote of 5-4 that the defenders of Proposition 8 did not have the legal right to do so. Because Proposition 8 proponents had not suffered any injury due to it being declared unconstitutional, they were found to not have the standing to pursue the case. The case was sent back to the lower court with instructions for it to dismiss the case and on June 28, 2013, same-sex marriage was declared (once again) legal in California.

United States v. Windsor (2013)

In 1996, President Bill Clinton signed into law the Defense of Marriage Act (DOMA) which defined marriage as legal unions between one man and one woman for the purpose of federal law. In 2007, Edith Windsor and Thea Clara Spyer were legally married in Canada; their marriage was recognized by New York state law, the state in which the two women lived. When Spyer died in 2009, she left her estate to Windsor. If they had been a heterosexual couple, Windsor would have been given a marital exemption but because federal law did not recognize their marriage, she was taxed $363,053. Windsor filed suit, declaring DOMA to be unconstitutional.

As in the California case, the government tried to avoid defending the law when it came before the Supreme Court in 2011. President Barack Obama and US Attorney General Eric Holder announced that they would not intervene to defend DOMA, but the Supreme Court ruled in June 2013 that the federal government could not avoid doing so given the federal tax money at stake. In other words, because the government stood to suffer a real economic injury if DOMA were overturned, the Obama administration was required to defend the law in court.

In a 5-4 decision, the Court ruled that DOMA was unconstitutional because it denied same-sex couples the rights that come from federal recognition of marriage and available to other couples with legal marriages under state law. Windsor's tax payment was refunded, with interest. The decision was a victory for supporters of marriage equality, although it stopped short of finding a constitutional right to same-sex marriage. Instead, the Court left the matter to the states, ruling only that the federal government must treat married same-sex and opposite-sex couples the same way under federal law.

Obergefell v. Hodges (2015)

James Obergefell and John Arthur met in the early 1990s and soon moved in together. They had been in a committed relationship for two decades when Arthur was diagnosed with amyotrophic lateral sclerosis (ALS), a fatal disease. When the Supreme

Court issued its decision in the *Windsor* case and with Arthur on his deathbed, Obergefell and Arthur decided to get married. The couple lived in Ohio which did not have marriage equality; they flew to Maryland, the closest state that did, to exchange their vows. Three months later, when Arthur died, Obergefell sought to be listed as the surviving spouse on Arthur's death certificate but Ohio would not allow it. He turned to the courts and ended up being the lead plaintiff in the historic case that eventually extended marriage equality to the entire country.

In 2014, the Supreme Court agreed to hear a case, *Obergefell v. Hodges*, that consolidated challenges to marriage equality bans in Michigan, Kentucky, Ohio, and Tennessee. Each case began in its respective state and US District Court and in each case, the court ruled in favor of marriage equality. Each decision was appealed to the US Court of Appeals for the 6th Circuit which reversed the judgments of the District Courts. The petitioners then appealed to the Supreme Court which agreed to decide two questions: whether the 14th Amendment requires a state to license a marriage between two people of the same sex (presented by the cases from Michigan and Kentucky) and whether the 14th Amendment requires a state to recognize a same-sex marriage licensed and performed in another state (presented by the cases from Ohio, Tennessee, and, again, Kentucky).

On June 26, 2015, the Supreme Court issued its ruling in *Obergefell*. In a 5-4 decision, the Court ruled that states are compelled to issue marriage licenses to same-sex couples under the 14th Amendment's equal protection clause. Writing for the majority, Justice Anthony Kennedy noted four reasons why the Court was ruling in favor of the plaintiffs: (1) that "the right to personal choice regarding marriage is inherent in the concept of individual autonomy"; (2) "the right to marry is fundamental because it supports a two-person union unlike any other in its importance to the committed individuals"; (3) "it safeguards children and families and thus draws meaning from related rights of childrearing, procreation, and education"; and (4) because "marriage is a keystone of our social order." In a stirring final paragraph, Kennedy highlighted how equal marriage rights would grant equal dignity to gay and lesbian individuals:

No union is more profound than marriage, for it embodies the highest ideals of love, fidelity, devotion, sacrifice, and family. In forming a marital union, two people become something greater than once they were. As some of the petitioners in these cases demonstrate, marriage embodies a love that may endure even past death. It would misunderstand these men and women to say they disrespect the idea of marriage. Their plea is that they do respect it, respect it so deeply that they seek to find its fulfillment for themselves. Their hope is not to be condemned to live in loneliness, excluded from one of civilization's oldest institutions. They ask for equal dignity in the eyes of the law. The Constitution grants them that right.

The judgment of the Court of Appeals for the Sixth Circuit is reversed.

In June 2015, just weeks before the Supreme Court's *Obergefell* ruling, lawmakers in North Carolina approved—over the governor's veto—a bill to allow magistrates to refuse to perform marriages if the officials cite a deeply held religious objection, a bill clearly aimed at blocking same-sex marriages. Lawmakers in other states have approved similar measures (Katz 2015). In other states, including Kansas and Missouri, while courts have ruled in favor of marriage equality, implementation of those decisions on the ground has been spotty at best. In Kansas, supporters and opponents disagreed as to whether court decisions required officials in all districts to issue same-sex marriage licenses or if the decisions applied only to certain jurisdictions. Most notably, the Alabama Supreme Court defied a ruling from the 11th Circuit Court of Appeals ordering the state to allow marriage licenses for gay and lesbian couples. Alabama Supreme Court Chief Justice Roy Moore said in an interview, "I can't explain why more than 20 other states have bowed down to unlawful federal authority but Alabama is not one of them. A federal judge has no authority to overturn a state constitutional amendment in the face of a state court's opinion on the same matter" (Faulk 2015).

When the Supreme Court issued the *Obergefell* decision in June 2015, making marriage equality the law of the land, officials in some states continued to resist, particularly in Texas, Mississippi, and Alabama. Two days after *Obergefell*, Texas Attorney General Ken Paxton told county clerks in the state that they could refuse to issue marriage licenses to same-sex couples if they had religious objections to doing so. Mississippi Attorney General Jim Hood continued to block same-sex marriage, claiming the federal courts in his region needed to act first. Alabama Chief Justice Roy Moore issued an order to the state's probate judges (who issue marriage licenses) to ignore the *Obergefell* ruling until the state Supreme Court told them to do otherwise. The order led in May 2016 to ethics charges against him by Alabama's Judicial Inquiry Commission. In September 2016, the state's Court of the Judiciary suspended Moore for the remainder of his term.

This sort of judicial resistance to marriage equality, however, is unusual; most judges have tended to side with same-sex couples in the fight for marriage equality. Before the *Obergefell* decision in 2015, the issue of marriage equality was advanced through judicial decisions rather than through votes by the public or elected officials in 26 states.

Other LGBT rights such as non-discrimination laws also vary in terms of who is covered and in which parts of the country. As of June 2016, 20 states and the District of Columbia prohibit employment and housing discrimination based on sexual orientation and gender identity while an additional two states prohibit discrimination based only on sexual orientation. There are currently only five states with laws banning so-called "conversion therapy," the harmful practice of attempting to change sexual orientation through coercive psychological treatment; there is no ban in the other 45 states. Only seven states have laws officially allowing LGBT couples to be foster parents and one state (Nebraska) specifically prohibits LGBT foster parents;

the other 41 states have no laws in place, in either direction. Finally, only four states have laws recognizing de facto parents, a parent raising a child who is not the legal parent; 25 states and DC allow for limited visitation and custody while status is uncertain in 14 more states and banned in seven more. These de facto parent laws disproportionately affect LGBT parents, who are more likely to have their parenting status called into question (Movement Advancement Project 2016).

In addition to waging battles through legislative and judicial avenues, advocacy organizations on both sides of the marriage equality issue have spent considerable amounts of time and money attempting to alter public opinion and political behavior on the issue of marriage equality. During the 2008 California Proposition 8 campaign to ban same-sex marriage via ballot initiative, spending topped $85 million, shattering social policy initiative spending records (Ewers 2008; Minkoff et al. n.d.; Wildermuth 2010). More recently, during the successful 2011 campaign to lobby state legislators to pass a marriage bill in New York, one organization (New Yorkers United for Marriage) spent $1.8 million over just two months' time (Kaplan 2011).

Despite the time and money being spent, however, little is known about how effective advocacy efforts are in terms of changing individual-level opinion and behavior. Some, in fact, argue that these campaigns have little to no effect. Egan (2010, 10) wrote, "Despite the tremendous attention paid to these initiatives [ballot initiatives on same-sex marriage] and the level of resources devoted to them by both sides, expressed voter sentiment changed little over the course of the typical campaign." At the same time, public opinion on the issue is shifting in a remarkably rapid fashion: as noted above, only 27% of Americans favored gay marriage in 1996, compared to 60% in 2015.

State surveys also show shifts over time in public support for marriage equality. Gelman, Lax, and Phillips (2010) documented the change over time in all 50 states. For polling between 1994 and 1996, support for marriage equality was about 25% and in no state was same-sex marriage supported by a majority of the public. In 2007, national support approached 36% and marriage equality was supported by a majority of residents in Massachusetts, California, and Connecticut. In 2010, nationwide support had increased to approximately 50% and majorities supported marriage equality in 22 states across the country. In addition to marriage equality, some Americans also supported the idea of civil unions, intended to be a similar but different institution than marriage. Many polls asked a three-way question in which respondents were asked which of the following they support: marriage for same-sex couples, civil unions for same-sex couples, or no relationship recognition whatsoever. When civil unions were included in the question, support for same-sex marriage dropped slightly; overall, however, the picture was clear: over time there was a national trend toward approval of legal recognition for same-sex couples.

In terms of attitudes toward LGBT people themselves, thermometer ratings for gay men and lesbians throughout the 1980s, 1990s, and 2000s have been relatively cool (Sherrill 1996; Valelly 2012). Thermometer ratings are survey questions that ask respondents to rate how warmly (or coolly) they feel toward a group or an individual, on a scale of zero to 100. As recently as 2004, respondents in the American National Election Studies (ANES) ranked gay and lesbian individuals lower than Muslims and just above undocumented immigrants, the group at the bottom of the rankings (Bartels 2008, 137). Additional analyses of the 2008 survey suggest that 2008 results do not differ significantly from 2004 responses (Valelly 2012, 315). Four years later, among respondents to the 2012 ANES, warmth toward gay men and lesbians increased dramatically, more than for any other group (Hansen 2014).

Two major factors are often cited in explaining this dramatic rise in support for marriage equality over the last two decades: cohort replacement (the replacement in the population of older individuals by younger generations) and individual-level attitudinal shifts. Lewis and Gossett (2008) concluded from their analysis of California Field Polls from 1985 to 2006 that most of the rise in public support for same-sex marriage in California was due to cohort replacement, not to individuals changing their minds. In other words, they found that most of the increased support for marriage equality over time was due to the entry of younger, more equality-minded individuals to the polity, while older, more opposed individuals were dying. But the rapid pace of attitude shift on the issue across several different identity subgroups means it cannot all be attributed to cohort replacement. In fact, many respondents to surveys openly admit to having changed their minds about marriage equality. By far, the most common explanation for this change given by survey respondents was that they had a gay or lesbian friend or family member (Pew Research Center 2013a).

The visibility of gay and lesbian individuals has increased rapidly over the last few decades, contributing to increases in support for marriage equality and other LGBT rights. A 2015 survey found that 88% of Americans said they know someone who is gay or lesbian, far greater than the 61% of respondents who gave that answer in 1993 (Pew Research Center 2015). Further, nearly three-quarters (73%) of those who know a lot of gay and lesbian individuals support marriage equality, 48% of whom *strongly* support it. Nearly two-thirds (66%) of those who have family members or close friends who are gay or lesbian support marriage equality and 38% of those support it strongly. Unsurprisingly, there is far less support for marriage equality among those who have few or no gay and lesbian acquaintances (32% support, 58% opposition) and those who do not have a family member or close friend who is gay or lesbian (44% support, 46% opposition).

What these and other surveys tell us is that public opinion is shifting rapidly on the issue of marriage equality and that for many individuals this shift is linked to increased personal contact with gay and lesbian individuals. As with cohort replacement, however, a full accounting for the rapid attitudinal shift of the last few decades is still left unexplained. Why do some individuals without known gay or lesbian friends or family members sometimes change their minds? Are other mechanisms besides cohort replacement and contact also at work? Given the tendency of individuals to be biased toward their own opinions, what explains the massive shift in attitudes on same-sex marriage?

The shifting nature of opinion toward LGBT individuals more generally and support for marriage equality more specifically underscores the need for systematic, scientific data with which to draw causal inferences about efforts to change minds. Advocacy groups spend millions of dollars and massive amounts of time and energy to persuade individuals to come to their side of the issue, yet we have limited evidence about the effectiveness of those efforts or the mechanisms through which they might be generating attitudinal change.

Various scholars have used survey experiments to evaluate the effect of framing and question wording on responses to survey questions about marriage equality. Haider-Markel and Joslyn (2008) suggested that framing LGBT individuals as genetically pre-determined to be gay seems to result in warmer feelings and more support for LGBT people. Price, Nir, and Cappella (2005) found differences between liberal and conservative participants when the issue was framed as "granting special marriage rights" as opposed to "extending equal rights." McCabe and Heerwig (2012) found no significant differences in levels of support when the question was worded as allowing "gay and lesbian couples," "same-sex couples," or "homosexual couples" to marry but also found that wording affected the *intensity* of support or opposition. Flores (2015) looked at 136 national polls reporting support for same-sex marriage among registered voters from 1996 to 2014, which includes 36 different question wordings. Overall, he found that "questions that focus on the issue of 'same-sex marriage' garnered less support than questions on legal recognition of marriages for same-sex couples" (Flores 2015, 580).

This book also uses the power of randomized experiments but goes a step further than these simple framing and question wording explorations. We test specific causal claims about the relationships between individual identity, social group membership, and attitudes about a contentious political issue, using marriage equality as the focal example. Before further describing our methods and experiments, we turn now to a discussion of the importance (and relative dearth of) research on LGBT politics.

LGBT RESEARCH IN POLITICAL SCIENCE

In a 1999 book review essay in the *American Political Science Review*, Timothy E. Cook delivered an open call for political scientists to embrace LGBT studies in the discipline. Despite lesbian and gay political movements in the US dating back to the 1950s and tangible political victories dating back to the early 1970s, including the emergence and election of openly gay candidates for office and passage of anti-discrimination laws, few political scientists were studying gay and lesbian politics. Continuing into the 1980s with the AIDS epidemic and the rise of numerous public policy issues, including sodomy laws, gays in the military, marriage equality, and lesbian and gay parenting, political scientists were "notably absent. . . . Until recently, empirical studies on the topic were virtually absent from the pages of major political science journals" (Cook 1999, 679). Among other explanations, Cook suggested that LGBT studies had been neglected because they were particularly difficult from theoretical and methodological standpoints and that we lacked data from which we could derive sociologically and politically rich answers to some of the most pressing LGBT questions.

In the more than 15 years since Cook's assertions, political scientists have made significant inroads in explaining and addressing key aspects of LGBT politics. Richard Valelly posited in a 2012 review article that political scholarship on LGBT politics had become a sophisticated, methodologically rich subfield of political science that has significantly enriched our understanding of key political phenomena. For example, contemporary research addresses key theory and methods in public opinion and political behavior (Brewer 2003, 2008; Egan, Persily, and Wallsten 2008; Harrison and Michelson 2012; Lax and Phillips 2009; Wilcox and Wolpert 2000); legislative and voting behavior (Barth, Overby, and Huffmon 2009; Haider-Markel 2007, 2010; Riggle and Tadlock 1999); social movements and interest groups (Burstein 2003; Chauncey 2004; Eisenbach 2006; Engel 2001; Fetner 2008; Ghaziani 2008; Nownes and Lipinski 2005; Rimmerman 2002, 2007; Seidman and Meeks 2011); and the politics and rhetoric of judicial processes (Engel 2012; Eskridge 1999; Gilreath 2011; Keck 2009; Novkov 2008; Pinello 2003; Rosenberg 2008; Smith 2005; Stoutenborough, Haider-Markel, and Allen 2006).

Despite the substantial and rich scholarship on LGBT rights and issues of the last decade, there are several gaps that remain in our understanding of public opinion and political behavior toward LGBT rights broadly speaking and toward marriage equality in particular. Most of the books investigating the issue in the United States focus on the history or evolution of the fight for same-sex marriage; they tend to provide a chronology of events, highlighting key court cases and demonstrations, public opinion polls and how opinions have changed over time, and how LGBT rights fit into a larger social movements paradigm. There are many attempts to explain shifts in opinion, the elements of advocacy campaigns (without much about their success), and aggregate shifts in opinion. What is lacking, however, is an understanding of individual-level variation in attitudes and the most effective strategies to shift attitudes and key behaviors to be more supportive of marriage equality.

While recounting the history and evolution of LGBT rights is important to understand current events, our book focuses on real-world methods of attitude change on the issue. For example, as documented later in this chapter, we conducted a field experiment in Iowa looking at the behavioral effects of self-disclosure of sexual orientation during a fundraising phone call. In chapter 3, we explore the effect of elite cues from professional athletes on support for LGBT rights among fans of professional baseball, football, and hockey. In chapters 4, 5, and 6, we look at the effect of shared identities of religion, ethnorace, and partisanship (respectively) and of message strategies and tactics in the pursuit of increased support for LGBT rights. As we detail in those four chapters, we find that unrelated in-group identities can be used to open individuals to be supportive of marriage equality. When such an identity (e.g., as a fan of professional football or as African American) is primed, targeted individuals feel interpersonal closeness with the individual making the appeal for support. At the same time, because the message is unrelated to that identity, it is a dissonant form of identity priming, causing a cognitive speed bump that often leads individuals to truly receive the message and thus to be open to reconsidering the issue, the first step toward attitude change.

RANDOMIZED EXPERIMENTS

As described in the subsequent four chapters, we tested our Theory of Dissonant Identity Priming with a series of randomized experiments, many of which were conducted in cooperation with LGBT advocacy organizations, engaging in what is known as pracademics. This cooperation ensured that the questions we were asking were relevant to the ongoing political debate on marriage equality while the experimental methodology maximizes their external validity. Randomized experiments have experienced a renaissance in the last decade and are considered by many scholars to be the gold standard for impact assessment and program evaluation (Gerber and Green 2012; Rossi, Freeman, and Lipsey 2003). What we mean here when we speak of randomized experiments is perhaps best understood as parallel to medical drug trials. In the medical field, controlled trials are often used to test new drugs or procedures. Individuals are recruited for a test and randomly divided into treatment and control groups. Those in the treatment group are administered the new drug or procedure while those in the control group receive a placebo such as sugar pills or sham surgeries. Subsequent differences in health outcomes between individuals in the two groups can be clearly attributed to the treatment.

Similarly, experiments in political science randomly assign individuals to receive a treatment expected to generate a change in attitude or behavior while others are randomly assigned to receive a placebo treatment or to no treatment whatsoever. Subsequent observed differences in attitudes or behavior can then be clearly attributed to the treatment. For example, an experiment seeking to increase voter turnout might expose some individuals to a postcard or telephone blandishment to vote while those in the control group would receive either no message or one encouraging recycling (a message not expected to affect voter turnout). Hundreds of randomized experiments of this sort have been conducted over the last decade, generating valuable insights in a variety of social science disciplines. Political science experiments have most frequently focused on voter mobilization but have also been extended to many different aspects of political science, public policy, and attitude change scholarship (see Druckman et al. 2011). In this book, we extend the science of randomized experiments to the understudied area of individual-level identity and political attitudes, new dependent variables, and prominent contemporary political debates.

While observational studies have produced tremendous advances to our understanding of how people think and act in the political arena, randomized experiments allow for robust hypothesis testing that pinpoints causal mechanisms. In this book, we use a variety of randomized experiments to advance our understanding of how attitudes toward public policy change, with a specific focus on same-sex marriage policy. Over the past five years, we worked with various LGBT advocacy organizations around the country to conduct our experiments. Our Theory of Dissonant Identity Priming, tested in those various experiments, is that in-group priming has the potential to broaden the definition of in-groups to move individuals to be more supportive of marriage equality. When nudged to consider advocates for LGBT rights as "just like me" in some way—because of shared race or ethnicity, shared partisanship, shared religious faith, or shared support for a sport or professional sports team—individuals in our experiments were often moved to be more supportive in their expressed attitudes and observed behaviors. Messengers and messages that were in some way unexpected or dissonant with the stereotype of that identity tended, as expected, to be the most powerful.

On-the-ground organizers have long believed that making identity-based connections helps them in their persuasive efforts. Recounting the 2007 battle to win over legislators in Massachusetts, Marc Solomon, national campaign director for Freedom to Marry, described in his book *Winning Marriage* how he would search for connections with legislators before meeting with them to ask for their support (2014, 109–110):

My own approach to making the case to lawmakers was to figure out ways to connect. I always came to meetings knowing as much as I could about them, and when waiting for a meeting I'd scan the plaques and photos in their reception area to find things we had in common. If they were Republicans, I'd talk about my work as a Republican staffer on Capitol Hill. I could usually chat them up about Boston sports, and always about local politics. My goal was to build a relationship with them that allowed me to stay engaged.

Solomon told other stories of making identity-based connections throughout the book, including bringing a lesbian woman from a rural Polish neighborhood to make her case to a state legislator from another nearby rural Polish neighborhood, or using the author of *Wicked* to reach out to a legislator who was a passionate fan of Broadway musicals. He was priming in-group identities to open minds to attitudinal change.

This book also makes an important methodological and procedural contribution by offering evidence of the validity and causal inference of experiments conducted in cooperation with key organizations in the field. As Gillespie and

Michelson (2011) argued in their *PS* piece on pracademics, conducting experiments in cooperation with real-world political actors and on prominent political issues has multiple benefits, including increased external validity and insights into the political process that academics working independently might otherwise never learn.

Pracademics has the added advantage of helping keep our interest in politics grounded and vibrant: doing this work with real-world actors and with real-world consequences increased our satisfaction with our jobs and our overall quality of life. That the experiments in this book are a form of pracademics means that we formed strategic partnerships with advocacy organizations around the country, reaching out to LGBT groups and asking what questions we might help them answer. Did they want to know how to better raise support among a particular demographic? Were they interested in learning what sort of message was more persuasive? Did they wonder if their current advocacy efforts were having the desired effect? We had questions of our own but we wanted those real-world actors to tell us what questions were relevant to them. As mentioned in chapter 1, however, the authors alone controlled the data and analysis; our results were not swayed or manipulated by any sponsoring group.

Other researchers have done similar work, partnering with elected and appointed officials (e.g., Gerber et al. 2011; Michelson et al. 2012). García Bedolla and Michelson (2012) conducted hundreds of randomized get-out-the-vote field experiments in cooperation with community organizations, with dramatic results. We hope the results shared here will encourage other social and political scientists to consider adding pracademics to their toolbox of methodologies.

TESTING, TESTING: THE ONE IOWA EXPERIMENT

In 2008, as Californians prepared to vote on a proposed constitutional amendment to ban same-sex marriage (Proposition 8), supporters in the field shifted tactics. Believing that the personal touch would increase support, door-to-door canvassers were encouraged to come out as gay or lesbian when speaking to voters. This was expected to personalize the issue and to demonstrate to voters that their vote on Proposition 8 would affect a real person. The theory stemmed from Allport's (1954) contact hypothesis—the idea that contact with an actual gay or lesbian person would reduce discrimination. Canvassers working a few years earlier to build support for marriage equality in Massachusetts had used personal stories when reaching out to legislators to ask for their support, and organizers there believed that strategy contributed to their success (Solomon 2014). While a compelling theory, however, the idea that personal narratives would enhance support was just that: a theory. Without a randomized experiment, it was impossible to say with certainty whether the new strategy was more or less effective than the one that preceded it. Without systematic, scientific experimental data, we cannot know whether it would have been more or less effective if the canvassers had chosen to not share their sexual orientation with contacted voters.

Our initial experiment in the area of political behavior and identity priming was a fundraising experiment in 2011, partnering with One Iowa (see Harrison and Michelson 2012 for more details). One Iowa, formed in 2005, is the state's largest LGBT advocacy organization. The group advocates for full equality for LGBT individuals, including protection from employment and housing discrimination and the freedom to marry. In 2009, One Iowa conducted a phone bank to identify supporters in the state, generating a list of supporters and potential supporters for future outreach efforts. In preparation for their planned fundraising effort in April 2010, this list was supplemented with the names of individuals who had previously donated to the organization, even if they had not been surveyed in 2009.

Prior to the launch of the 2010 outreach effort, we randomly divided One Iowa's pool of 1,561 potential supporters into two equal groups. During the month of April 2010, volunteers for One Iowa made calls to individuals on the list, asking for phone bank volunteers and also for financial donations. Those in the treatment group received a mobilization message identical to those in the control group but with one additional sentence:

As a (**gay man, lesbian, bisexual individual, transgendered individual**) I remember being incredibly proud to be an Iowan when our Supreme Court ruled in favor of equal rights and I'm concerned about the effect rolling back equality in Iowa will have on me and our community.

The script manipulation was based Allport's contact hypothesis as well as on anecdotal accounts from California, where supporters of marriage equality had gradually shifted to a similar script during the unsuccessful No on 8 Campaign in 2008. The campaign used such a script with the belief that it personalized canvassers' appeal and had a positive effect on those targeted. By subjecting the personal appeal to a randomized experiment, we were able to accurately measure its effect on the desired outcomes: more and larger financial donations to One Iowa and an increased willingness to help the organization in the future.

Overall, 292 individuals were successfully contacted, 35 made financial donations or pledges, and 60 individuals agreed to volunteer. Individuals in the control group were more likely to be successfully contacted; of the 292 contacts, 166 were from the control group while 126 were from the treatment group. This generates contact rates of 21.2% for the control group and 16.1% for the treatment group. The different rates of contact between the two scripts reflected the pool of callers available to One Iowa. Many were straight allies and thus were not able to be assigned to the treatment script; also, not all LGBT individuals were willing to use the coming-out script. Logistic regression analysis with contact as the dependent variable (not shown) found that older individuals, Democrats, and residents of Des Moines were more likely to be successfully contacted; there was no statistically significant relationship found for gender, Republican partisanship, or voter history. Overall, individuals in the control and treatment groups did not differ significantly in terms of partisanship, gender, Des Moines residency, or voter history.

Comparing donation request outcomes reveals significant differences in both willingness to donate and the size of those donations. In the control group, 24 individuals (3.1%) made a pledge or donation, compared to 11 individuals (1.4%) in the treatment group. The difference is statistically significant. The frequency of donation was lower in the treatment group (the coming-out script) versus the control group. This difference is best understood as the intent-to-treat effect, in that not all individuals in the treatment and control groups were successfully contacted. Restricting our analysis to those reached by the One Iowa volunteers, we found that rates of donation were 14.5% (24/166) in the control group and 8.7% (11/126) in the treatment group and the difference is statistically significant. The treatment script decreased donation outcomes.

Similarly, there was a statistically significant difference between the treatment and control groups in terms of the amounts of money donated (table 2.1). Donors gave less money in the treatment condition (the coming-out script) as compared to the control script. Looking only at those contacted, we found that the effect persisted and was again statistically significant.

We also calculated a series of logistic regression models to estimate the exact size of the effect of the coming-out script on willingness to make a financial donation, including models adding control variables. Consistently across those models there was a negative coefficient estimate for the treatment variable, indicating that assignment to the coming out script reduced the likelihood of making a financial donation (see appendix table A2.1).

In sum, we found that individuals identified as previous supporters of marriage equality were less likely to donate to an LGBT equality organization when the caller self-identified as an LGBT individual, casting doubt on the theory adhered to by many marriage equality advocates that such personalization of their campaigns is

Table 2.1 Donation Rates (%), One Iowa Fundraising Experiment

	Control	Treatment	Percentage-Point Difference (SE)	Chi-square
Full Experiment (N = 1,561)	3.08% (24/780)	1.41% (11/781)	−1.67* (0.75)	4.956 Pr = 0.03
Contacted Only (N = 292)	14.46 (24/166)	8.73 (11/126)	−5.73 (3.84)	2.227 Pr = 0.136

Note: Respondents were adults in Iowa who were on One Iowa's internal list of potential supporters. Surveys collected April 1–18, 2011. * = $p \leq .05$, two-tailed.

helpful. While a compelling theory, the idea that personal narratives would enhance support turned out to not be true. One Iowa was better served by fundraising messages that did not include a coming-out statement by the canvasser. While disappointing to One Iowa at the time, the experimental findings meant that they had a better sense of how to conduct a successful future fundraising drive and that we had a better sense of best practices for advocacy campaigns on contentious issues.

Note that the message (abstract coming out) and the messengers (LGBT callers) were not surprising for those being called. That an LGBT person is in favor of a pro-LGBT organization was not surprising to potential donors. While not a direct test of the Theory of Dissonant Identity Priming, this experiment provided significant insight into the relationship between individual-level identity and political attitudes and behavior associated with LGBT people and rights. TDIP would predict greater success using a message that reached out to potential donors as fellow Iowans or as fellow supporters of LGBT rights, thus priming a *shared* in-group identity. In chapter 7, we explore this hypothesis with a similar experiment conducted in cooperation with Equality Maryland.

The findings from our One Iowa experiment were called into question by research published in *Science* magazine in December 2014 (LaCour and Green 2014). The piece purported to show that face-to-face conversations with pro-marriage equality canvassers were more persuasive, with long-lasting effects, when canvassers self-identified as gay. The *Science* article made national news, with coverage in the *New York Times*, on the radio show *This American Life*, and other popular outlets, in part because it contradicted conventional wisdom about persuasion. A few months later, doubts about the piece raised by other political scientists (Brockman, Kalla, and Aronow 2015) led to the revelation that LaCour had fabricated the survey data (although the canvassing had actually occurred), and *Science* retracted the article. The scandal brought research on attitude change back to the scholarship we are building on in this book: that the most effective campaigners are those who share an identity with the target population. The best canvassers on behalf of same-sex marriage, we argue, are not necessarily gay canvassers but rather are canvassers who can trigger a sense of shared in-group identity with their targets.

A vivid real-world example comes from Ireland, where voters on May 22, 2015 voted overwhelmingly in favor of same-sex marriage. Days before the vote, an elderly Irish couple, Brighid and Paddy Whyte, just short of their 50th wedding anniversary, posted a video on YouTube urging a yes vote. They reached out to their fellow Irish citizens as Catholics and as people who wanted to make the world a better place for their grandchildren. The video went viral, reportedly inspiring many conversations—and was a perfect example of the power of using in-group messengers.

There are dozens if not hundreds of statewide and national organizations that advocate on behalf of the LGBT community in the United States, all spending resources, time, and energy aimed at persuading elected officials and the public writ large on key issues of relationship recognition, parenting laws, and non-discrimination legislation. Despite enormous amounts of time and effort expended, little is known about how to make this political advocacy as effective as possible. Even fewer political scientists utilize the extensive expertise these organizations have amassed during the last several decades of advocacy work. This book is the magical middle of the Venn diagram where the expertise from political science scholarship overlaps with knowledge from LGBT community organizations. Many of our experiments were conducted in partnership with LGBT advocacy organizations throughout the country, including state organizations from California to Illinois to Georgia to Maryland. We conducted multiple experiments designed to help them answer crucial questions about messaging and tactics. The results from those experiments and the lessons learned are not only helpful to the cause but are also an excellent example of how to use political science, and randomized experiments more specifically, to answer real-world policy questions.

SUMMARY AND NEXT STEPS

Overall, our experiments scientifically test the effect of (*a*) priming different identities and (*b*) using dissonant messages in support for LGBT rights, most often marriage equality. In chapter 1, we provided a review of relevant theories of attitude change and described our theory of how to maximize interpersonal closeness, source credibility, and dissonant identity messages when communicating with the American public on contentious social issues. The experiments described in chapters 3–6 test that theory. We investigate the effectiveness of advocacy communication and identity priming on highly contested issues, using LGBT rights and marriage equality as a case study, on a variety of key identity groups in US politics.

Our Theory of Dissonant Identity Priming suggests that advocacy organizations should encourage campaigns that increase interpersonal closeness between senders and receivers of communication using a relevant and powerful common identity and also using a message from a source that is inconsistent or dissonant with the identity stereotype. In other words, LGBT outreach should encourage people to think about LGBT individuals and their advocates as members of a mutual in-group—not as members of an out-group—to make them more likely to support LGBT rights. The most powerful messages will be surprising, generating a cognitive speed bump that motivates processing of the message by the recipient, and openness to attitudinal change. Overall, as the results in the next four chapters show, we find that our Theory of Dissonant Identity Priming is a consistent and compelling guide to how and when triggering a shared in-group identity can generate attitudinal change.

3 More Than a Game
Sports Fans and Marriage Equality

Loyalty to a sports team is an intense in-group membership for many Americans, whether that team is their college alma mater, the team from their hometown, or simply a team with which they feel a sense of connection. Fans spend significant amounts of time and money on tickets, travel, and official merchandise to show loyalty and to watch and cheer for their team of choice. These identifications with sports teams are enduring and often very strong (Cottingham 2012; Wann and Branscombe 1993; Wann and Schrader 1996). Sports fans categorize themselves and others as in-groups and out-groups (Voci 2006) and exhibit typical in-group-favoring behaviors, including rating in-group members more favorably than out-group members (Wann and Dolan 1994; Wann and Branscombe 1995). Shared identity as a fan of a team can also lead to increased charitable giving (Platow et al. 1999).

Cottingham (2012) noted in her ethnographic study of fans of the Pittsburgh Steelers football team that fans used the team's symbols and engaged in team-specific rituals in a variety of settings, including tailgating, watching games in sports bars, and even weddings and funerals—events not specific to football or sports, and removed from the "peak ritual emotions" of gathering at the stadium to watch the team play. She found that "Steelers fans as a group share a level of group solidarity that extends beyond the stadium experience" (2012, 181) and noted that this emotional attachment to the team extends even to individuals who have never attended a game. Their identity as a member of the group, as a Steelers fan, is powerful, extending to a wide variety of situations and life events. While the Steelers fans studied by Cottingham may be an extreme case—her ethnographic work was conducted during a particularly successful season with fans of a team that are well known to be very strongly emotionally attached to their team—her data and conclusions never-theless indicate that sports fan identity should be understood as a powerful and at times pervasive in-group identity that members are eager to express and reinforce.

Perhaps taking their cue from this research on the power of shared in-group sports fan identities, marriage equality organizations have conducted campaigns to tap into those identities to shift attitudes about LGBT rights. Most well-known among these is Athlete Ally, founded by Columbia University wrestling coach Hudson Taylor in January 2011. A significant portion of the organization's work involves encourag-ing straight athletes to publicly endorse equality and respect for LGBT athletes. As Taylor noted in a *Huffington Post* piece on January 29, 2013, "Fans take cues from professional athletes." Other organizations also seek to use the power of a sports identity to enact social change. For example, in May 2013, an organization called The Last Closet successfully petitioned the Chicago City Council to pass a resolution encouraging the commissioners of four major men's sports leagues—Major League Baseball, the National Football League, the National Basketball Association, and Major League Soccer—to publicly support their gay players, to invite them to come out, and to ensure their safety.

Another sports-based LGBT rights campaign emerged in the winter of 2014 as athletes from around the world headed to Sochi, Russia for the quadrennial Olympic Winter Games. In June 2013, Russian President Vladimir Putin signed federal legis-lation banning "propaganda on nontraditional sexual relationships," a vague defini-tion that was widely understood to include the threat of fine or arrest for speaking publicly about LGBT issues and which was seen as designed to suppress homosexu-ality (Herszenhorn 2013). Some in the West called for a boycott of the February 2014 games and others pointed out the apparent conflict with Olympic principles. The Olympic Charter includes what is known as Principle 6, which states, "Any form of discrimination with regard to a country or a person on grounds of race, reli-gion, politics, gender or otherwise is incompatible with belonging to the Olympic Movement." In October 2013, during a visit from Thomas Bach, the new president of the International Olympic Committee, Putin insisted that there would be no dis-crimination during the games. Not satisfied with this response, LGBT rights organi-zations fought back, using the Olympics to call attention to the new Russian law and to fight for LGBT equality.

Olympic athletes were warned not to make reference to the law or to LGBT rights during the games—Rule 50 of the Olympic Committee's charter states, "No kind of demonstration or political, religious or racial propaganda is permitted in any Olympic sites, venues, or other areas" (Reid-Smith 2013). While complying with this warning, a coalition of two LGBT rights organizations, All Out and Athlete Ally, took the games as an opportunity to fight for support for LGBT rights with what was called the Principle 6 Campaign (www.principle6.org). The campaign sold cloth-ing emblazoned with Principle 6 language (in English and Russian), thus allowing subtle support to be displayed regarding the issue without violating Russian laws or Olympics rules.[1] Gay and straight athletes from around the world supported the Principle 6 Campaign, including dozens of American professional athletes and Olympians. In sum, the campaign aimed to use the visibility of the Sochi Games and American's love of sports to draw attention to the need to protect the rights of gay men and lesbians in Russia and around the world.

The Principle 6 campaign illustrated how to use a primed identity as a sports fan to influence attitudes on a non-sports issue such as LGBT rights. Consistent with our Theory of Dissonant Identity Priming, the movement primed a shared identity as a fan of the Olympic Games in order to move individuals to support LGBT equality in Russia. In this chapter, we describe and discuss five randomized survey experiments testing similar applications of our theory. We posit that cues from members or elites from sports fan in-groups can motivate attitudinal change on issues unrelated to sports (e.g., LGBT rights). As suggested by the real-world advocacy work of organizations like Athlete Ally and the Principle 6 Campaign, we hypothesized that activating a shared identity as a sports fan would cause more individuals to consider persuasive appeals on same-sex marriage and non-discrimination.

Sports leagues in the United States have long traditions of intolerance for gay and lesbian athletes, especially in the major leagues such as the National Football League (NFL) and the National Basketball Association (NBA). Entanglement of sexual orientation and gender identity led in the early 20th century to homosexuality being associated with softness and femininity; men seeking to "prove" their heterosexuality thus were led to perform hypermasculinity. "Hence, males who were successful competitive sportsmen sought immunity from being labeled as soft, weak, feminine, and thus gay" (Hargreaves and Anderson 2014, 12). In other words, by and large, gay athletes in major sports such as football and hockey have stayed closeted in order to avoid calling their masculinity, and by association their athletic ability, into question. In the sports world, "traditional masculine traits thrive and are preserved" (Gregory 2004, 267). "Challenges to the status quo of heteronormativity in sport are met with resistance and retaliation" (Williams 2007, 255). Messner (2002) argued that homophobia (and misogyny) is used to establish hierarchies within male athletic teams. Overall, professional sports are firmly homophobic (Taylor 2014). Given this dynamic within male sports teams, particularly in the hyper-masculine sports of the top leagues, statements of support for marriage equality or other LGBT rights from professional football players or fans will be received by most individuals as an unexpected cognitive speed bump. Scholarship on attitude change and priming, as noted in chapter 1, suggests this will make those statements particularly powerful.

Consistent with this existing scholarship, we predicted that sources (i.e., senders of communication) would be more likely to increase support for LGBT rights among recipients when (*a*) they share a common identity with the receiver and (*b*) the message they deliver is unexpected. In other words, if you can induce someone to believe they are speaking with or hearing from a member of a mutually identifying group (e.g., someone who shares a passion for football or for a particular football team), the individual should be more likely to be supportive. Because of the dominant anti-LGBT atmosphere of certain sports, supportive statements by those sports' athletes to their fans should be unexpected and particularly effective. Marriage equality is not necessarily relevant to individuals with straight sexual orientations; however, triggering a sense of shared identity with the individual or in-group seeking support for marriage equality will lead them to consider changing their attitudes. Doing so reinforces their identity as fans.

In the remainder of this chapter, we first review the degree to which major league sports in the United States are supportive of openly LGBT players, and the history of (in)tolerance in the major leagues. We then turn to a discussion of the power of sports fan identity and the results of our five experiments, targeting football, baseball, and hockey fans. The chapter concludes with a discussion of our findings about the power of in-group identity to influence sports fans' attitudes on same-sex marriage.

(IN) TOLERANCE IN THE MAJOR LEAGUES

Sports leagues in the United States have long, unfortunate traditions of homophobia, particularly in the hyper-masculine sports of the top leagues. Most gay athletes have chosen to reveal their sexual orientation only after they have retired. The first prominent professional female athlete to come out as a lesbian was tennis player Billie Jean King. King was outed in May 1981 not by choice but through a palimony suit filed by a former partner. The resulting scandal caused her to lose over a million dollars in endorsement and coaching deals (Overman and Sagert 2012). The first male major league athlete to come out as gay was former NFL running back David Kopay, who retired in 1972 and came out in 1977. Kopay has noted that he believes his decision to come out had a negative impact on his ability to secure coaching positions (Adkins 2013).

Since then, four additional former NFL players have come out as gay: Roy Simmons in 1992, Esera Tuaolo in 2002, Wade Davis in 2012, and Kwame Harris in 2013. While it is widely believed that there must be some gay players currently in the league, none have revealed their sexual orientation. In 2014, draft pick Michael Sam came out as gay prior to the NFL draft; while initially drafted by the St. Louis Rams, he was released at the end of training camp, briefly joined the Dallas Cowboys practice squad, and eventually signed with the Montreal Alouettes of the Canadian Football League (CFL). After playing just one CFL game, Sam announced via Twitter on August 14, 2015, that he was "stepping away" from football for personal reasons. Other major leagues have similar histories: former players such as baseball's Glenn Burke and Billy Bean have come out of the closet but until February 2014, when Jason Collins was given a (short-lived) contract with the Brooklyn Nets NBA team, not a single current player in one of the four major professional sports leagues was openly gay.

In part, this reluctance to come out is influenced by the reception faced by athletes who do. In 2007, after retiring from the NBA, John Amaechi came out as gay in his memoir, *Man in the Middle*, and in an interview on ESPN. While many offered their support, others were harsh in their homophobic attacks. Retired NBA point guard Tim Hardaway commented, "You know, I hate gay people, so I let it be known. I don't like gay people and I don't like to be around gay people. I am homophobic. I don't like it. It shouldn't be in the world or in the United States" (ESPN 2007). Hardaway's comments were criticized by NBA Commissioner David Stern and others but Amaechi made clear that they were similar to many others he had received:

Every comment that [Hardaway] made is labeled with hate, Amaechi said. The percentage of e-mails I've received overnight that are going to have to go into a little box somewhere just in case I end up dead are unbelievable. He's been a lightning rod for people to finally open the floodgates and decide that they can say some pretty awful stuff.

Negative attitudes towards gay men and lesbians are also apparent in the gay slurs often uttered by athletes during sporting events, although tolerance for such outbursts is waning, and in their comments in locker rooms and in the media. In 2011, two major NBA stars, Kobe Bryant and Joakim Noah, were fined $100,000 and $50,000, respectively, for using the word "faggot." In 2012, the NBA fined New York Knicks star Amare Stoudemire $50,000 for using an anti-gay slur and a profanity in a tweet to a fan. In 2013, Alan Gordon of Major League Soccer's San Jose Earthquakes was suspended for three games and fined an undisclosed amount for a similar outburst. Also in 2013, the NBA fined Indiana Pacers center Roy Hibbert $75,000 for using an antigay slur and an obscenity in a postgame interview, and a NASCAR driver was fined $10,000 for using an antigay slur in a posting on Instagram. As rumors were flying in 2013 about the possibility of an NFL player coming out as gay, San Francisco 49ers player Chris Culliver said he would not welcome gay players in the NFL or on his team: "I don't do the gay guys, man. I don't do that. No, we don't got no gay people on the team, they gotta get up out of here if they do" (Bennett-Smith 2013). An international survey of nearly 9,500 athletes released in May 2015 found that 84% of gay men and 82% of lesbians had heard homophobic language in locker rooms (Denison and Kitchen 2015).

Glenn Burke played baseball for the Los Angeles Dodgers and the Oakland A's from 1976 to 1979. He was openly gay with his teammates and sportswriters but the latter consistently refused to include that information in their reporting. In 1982, he came out as gay in a magazine article and an appearance on the *Today Show*. Years later, promoting his 1995 autobiography *Out at Home*, Burke commented, "My mission as a gay ballplayer was the breaking of a stereotype. . . . I think it worked. . . . They can't ever say now that a gay man can't play in the majors, because I'm a gay man and I made it" (Barra 2013). At the time, however, the news wasn't made public. The media found Burke's sexuality "an inconvenient truth." He told

People magazine, "I think everyone just pretended not to hear me. It just wasn't a story they were ready to hear."

53

More Than a Game

TDIP AND SPORTS FAN IDENTITY

As the previous section makes clear, homophobia and a fear of being identified as gay within professional sports in the United States are widespread. As a result, few professional athletes in the major leagues have come out as gay after retirement and even fewer have come out while still actively competing. Given the strong in-group identity that many fans share with their favorite teams, this long-standing hostility might be expected to generate hostility toward gay men and lesbians among sports fans and resistance to LGBT rights, including marriage equality. On the other hand, messages of inclusion and equal rights linked to opinion leaders within the major leagues might open minds to the issue by demonstrating that one can be both a sports fan and a supporter of same-sex marriage. We hypothesized that instead of persisting in anti-marriage equality opinions, individuals who are strong fans will be open to attitude change on the issue when primed with information about support for marriage equality that cues their identity as a fan.

Our Theory of Dissonant Identity Priming (TDIP) posits that individuals will be more willing to entertain attitudinal change on contentious issues if they are primed to consider themselves as sharing an in-group identity with the individual delivering the appeal, even if the issue at hand may not necessarily have consequences for their own lives. Thus, while same-sex marriage is not personally relevant to most individuals with straight sexual orientations, triggering a sense of shared identity will lead them to consider changing their attitudes. In the experiments described in this chapter, we test the hypothesis that triggering shared sports fan identities— either as a fan of a sport broadly conceived or as a fan of a particular major league team—will generate increased support for marriage equality, particularly when the cue is unexpected or surprising.

Five randomized experiments provide data for this chapter: three aimed at football fans and one each targeting fans of professional hockey and baseball. Two were face-to-face survey experiments and three were conducted online. In each situation, we targeted both fans (or fans of a particular team) and non-fans, exposing individuals to statements of support for marriage equality or non-discrimination either attributed to individuals from the relevant professional sports league or team, or to an anonymous individual. In the three football experiments, we found that support for marriage equality increased among fans exposed to the messages attributed to members of their football in-group; among non-fans, the different messages generated no measurable differences in attitudes (see also Harrison and Michelson 2016). In contrast and for reasons discussed below, we found minimal effects in the experiments conducted with hockey and baseball fans. We turn now to a description of those five experiments.

EXPERIMENT 1: FOOTBALL FANS AND ATHLETE ALLIES

Tolerance for openly gay players within the NFL is weak to negligible but over the past few years, some NFL players have voiced support for gay rights, including former Minnesota Vikings kicker Chris Kluwe and Baltimore Ravens linebacker Brendon Ayanbadejo. In 2013, the Ravens went to the Super Bowl, matched up against the San Francisco 49ers. Ayanbadejo's outspoken support for same-sex marriage and his increased visibility in the weeks leading up to the Super Bowl provided an opportunity to test our theory that football fans would be more supportive of marriage equality when informed of his support.

The experiment was conducted across multiple locations: a small private college in California, a large public university in Texas, and online with the US Internet population. Students at the two institutions were emailed invitations to participate in a survey in exchange for a chance to win a $100 Amazon gift card. In addition, participants from across the United States were recruited using Mechanical Turk (MTurk), with participants receiving $0.50 for their completed responses. Overall, 426 participants completed the survey, including 115 students from the college in California, 99 students from the university in Texas, and 212 MTurk workers. All surveys were completed between January 28 and February 3, 2013 (the Super Bowl was played on February 3, 2013).

Upon clicking on the invitation and giving informed consent, participants were given a false choice to "assign" them to a public policy issue. This was to limit social desirability bias and to induce participants to believe there was not just one issue being investigated in the research. Participants were then randomly shown one of three paragraphs: a statement about same-sex marriage with supportive quotations either with or without attribution to professional athletes or a placebo paragraph about recycling. For the marriage equality treatment groups, participants first saw an opening paragraph that introduced the topic:

Americans fundamentally disagree on many core political issues. One of the issues where people disagree is whether gay and lesbian Americans should be able to marry. **Many individuals have endorsed gay marriage while many others are opposed.**

The on-line text then varied depending on whether the individual had been randomly assigned to the control group (general supporter) or the treatment group (athlete supporter), as indicated in the bolded sections below. Individuals in the treatment group saw a paragraph with statements of support (accurately) attributed to professional athletes while individuals in the control group were told the statements were from anonymous supporters. The paragraph read:

[Brendon Ayanbadejo, All-Pro Linebacker for the Baltimore Ravens in the National Football League, supports gay marriage. He recently said / One supporter of gay

marriage recently said], "Right now it's the time for gay rights and it's time for them to be treated equally and for everybody be treated fairly, in the name of love." **[Chris Kluwe, punter for the Minnesota Vikings and another supporter / Another supporter]** recently wrote that gay marriage would make gays "full-fledged American citizens just like everyone else, with the freedom to pursue happiness and all that entails." **[Sean Avery, forward for the New York Rangers NHL team / Another supporter]** recently said, "I'm a New Yorker for marriage equality. I treat everyone the way I expect to be treated and that applies to marriage. Committed couples should be able to marry the person they love."

After reading their assigned paragraph, participants in all conditions were asked to answer two questions about their own attitudes, including their position on same-sex marriage and how they would vote on a hypothetical state ballot initiative on same-sex marriage. Participants were also asked about their level of interest in sports and a set of demographic questions including age, gender, and partisanship.

We found the highest overall support for marriage equality and the highest percentage of respondents reporting they would vote in favor of a hypothetical ballot initiative in the Professional Athletes condition (figures 3.1 and 3.2). There was a 4.8 percentage-point increase from the anonymous paragraph to the Athletes paragraph in terms of marriage equality support and an 8.9 percentage-point increase in the proportion of respondents responding they would vote in favor of a marriage equality ballot initiative. We then divided the sample based on three measures of

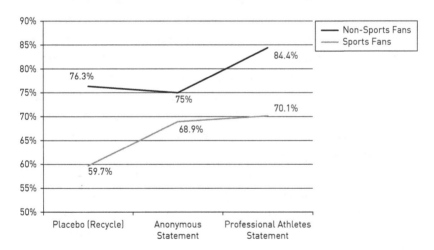

FIGURE 3.1 Support for Marriage Equality, Super Bowl Experiment, by Treatment Assignment and Level of Interest in Sports. *Note: N* = 426 (214 undergraduate students and 212 adult MTurk workers). Surveys completed January 28–February 3, 2013. For Sports Fans, the difference between responses in the Professional Athletes condition and Placebo condition is statistically significant at $p \leq .05$, one-tailed. For Non-Sports Fans, the difference between responses in the Anonymous Statement and Placebo condition is statistically significant at $p \leq .05$, one-tailed. Dependent variable is support for same-sex marriage. Sports Fan index is constructed using three measures of interest in professional sports. See appendix 2 for question wording and additional results.

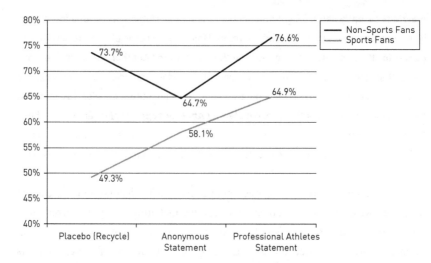

FIGURE 3.2 Support for Hypothetical Ballot Measure, Super Bowl Experiment, by Treatment Assignment and Level of Interest in Sports. *Note: N* = 426 (214 undergraduate students and 212 adult MTurk workers). Surveys completed January 28–February 3, 2013. Dependent variable is support for a hypothetical ballot measure for marriage equality. Sports Fan index is constructed using three measures of interest in professional sports. See appendix 2 for question wording and additional results.

sports identity and behavior: expressed identity as a sports fan, frequency of choosing sports-related coverage (compared to other forms of entertainment), and frequency of watching a sports-related event. We used those responses to generate a Sports Fan index. Respondents exposed to the Professional Athletes paragraph were most supportive of marriage equality compared to the placebo, increasing support by more than 10 percentage points among Sports Fans and by just over eight percentage points among non–Sports Fans. The former is statistically significant, confirming our hypothesis.[2] Support for the hypothetical ballot measure increased even more dramatically among Sports Fans, from 49% in the placebo condition to almost 65% in the Professional Athletes condition, a statistically significant increase of 15.7 percentage points. Support also increased among non–Sports Fans but the differences are not statistically significant.[3]

The elite in-group cue also had a strong effect in terms of intended vote on a hypothetical marriage equality ballot initiative: an 11.2 percentage-point increase in intention to vote in favor of marriage equality between the anonymous and Athletes conditions among strong sports fans. In sum, the elite in-group cue induced respondents who were strong sports fans to be more supportive of marriage equality.

EXPERIMENT 2: AND THEN MICHAEL SAM CAME OUT

In February 2014, Michael Sam, a defensive end from the University of Missouri, came out as gay prior to the NFL draft, inspiring a rash of news analyses about how the news might affect his draft prospects. Reaction from NFL leaders and fans was swift and divided, including a flurry of homophobic tweets and a story in *Sports Illustrated* that provided negative reactions from anonymous NFL coaches and executives. Other observers noted that what mattered was Sam's abilities on the field, not his sexual orientation. The NFL issued an official statement of support, noting that the league had adopted a sexual orientation anti-discrimination and harassment policy in April 2013. The statement read (NFL 2014a):

We admire Michael Sam's honesty and courage. Michael is a football player. Any player with ability and determination can succeed in the NFL. We look forward to welcoming and supporting Michael Sam in 2014.

NFL Commissioner Roger Goodell also spoke out personally in support of Sam, stating (Goodbread 2014):

He's proud of who he is and had the courage to say it. Now he wants to play football. We have a policy prohibiting discrimination based on sexual orientation. We will have further training and make sure that everyone understands our commitment. We truly believe in diversity and this is an opportunity to demonstrate it.

In the midst of these events, we tested the effect of Goodell's statements of inclusion and anti-discrimination on the openness of football fans towards LGBT rights. Our experiment was conducted using Google Consumer Surveys. We used a screening question to select only football fans and individuals not at all interested in professional football: "On a scale of one to five, how interested are you in professional football?" Five possible responses ranged from "not at all interested" to "extremely interested," with the order of the responses randomly reversed. Only individuals responding as "not at all interested" or "extremely interested" were selected to be exposed to the second question; those giving one of the other three answers were not included in the experiment. The second question randomly exposed participants to one of two quotations:

Treatment
NFL's Roger Goodell recently said discrimination based on sexual orientation is inconsistent with NFL values. Do you agree?

Control
A corporate leader recently said discrimination based on sexual orientation is inconsistent with modern values. Do you agree?

Respondents could choose from one of five possible answers, displayed in randomly reversed order: strongly agree, somewhat agree, neither agree nor disagree, somewhat disagree, and strongly disagree. We hypothesized that football fans would

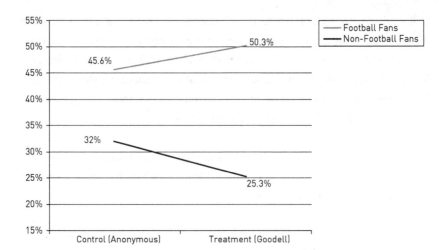

FIGURE 3.3 Support for Non-discrimination Statement, Michael Sam/Roger Goodell Experiment. *Note: N* = 811. Data collected online from a national sample of adults using the Google Consumer Survey product. Surveys completed February 18–20, 2014. Football Fans are those who said they were "extremely interested" in professional football; non-fans are those who said they were "not interested at all" in professional football. See appendix 2 for question wording and additional results.

be more likely to agree when exposed to the treatment quotation compared to non-football fans. We also hypothesized that while football fans would be more likely to agree when exposed to the treatment condition as opposed to the control condition, non-fans would not vary in how they responded to the two quotations. Although the quotations did not reference Michael Sam directly, any serious football fan would have been aware of the ongoing discussion. A photo of Sam was featured on the cover of the issue of *Sports Illustrated* that hit newsstands the day before our experiment began and his decision to come out was the topic of hundreds of news stories.

The survey experiment was in the field February 18–20, 2014. A total of 811 responses were collected, including 409 individuals who said that they were "extremely interested" in professional football and 402 who said that they were "not interested at all." Of the 409 fans, 208 were randomly assigned to the control quotation and 201 to the treatment quotation; of the 402 non-fans, 228 were assigned to the control quotation and 174 to the treatment condition.

As shown in figure 3.3, football fans exposed to the Roger Goodell prompt were twice as likely as non-fans to say that they supported the statement of non-discrimination, a difference of 25 percentage points. Priming fans' identity as football fans led to increased support for non-discrimination.[4]

EXPERIMENT 3: PACKERLAND

For our third football experiment, we focused on a specific team: the Green Bay Packers, a team that enjoys widespread and deeply held loyalty among its fans. We conducted a randomized survey experiment on the sidewalks of Appleton,

Wisconsin in the fall of 2014. In exchange for a Starbucks or Dunkin' Donuts gift card, respondents agreed to complete a paper survey that collected information about their interest in professional sports, their support for the Green Bay Packers, their attitude about same-sex marriage, and various demographic variables. Half of these respondents were exposed to a photo and statement that noted the support for marriage equality of Green Bay Packers Hall of Famer LeRoy Butler; the other half were exposed to parallel information from entertainer Jay-Z.

We hypothesized that the in-group elite cue (Butler) would increase support for marriage equality and LGBT rights among Packers fans but not among non-fans. Survey responses were collected by a team of undergraduate students recruited through the career services office of the local college, Lawrence University. The survey began by asking questions measuring the degree to which respondents were fans of sports in general, the NFL, and the Green Bay Packers.[5] Respondents were then exposed to a picture of either Butler or Jay-Z with the following prompt:

[Green Bay Packers Hall of Famer LeRoy Butler / Rapper and music producer Jay-Z] (seen in the photo on the left) supports same-sex marriage. What do you think? Should gays and lesbian individuals (check one):

- be able to get married
- be able to enter into a legal partnership similar to but not called marriage (such as a domestic partnership or civil union)
- have no legal recognition given to their relationships

Additional survey questions collected demographic information including age, gender, race, homeownership (as a proxy for income), and partisanship. A total of 306 surveys were collected from October 19 to November 12, 2014, including 156 with the Butler prime and 150 with the Jay-Z prime.

Overall, 66% (202/306) respondents said that they supported same-sex marriage, including 69.2% of those shown the Butler prime (108/156) and 62.7% of those shown the Jay-Z prime (94/150). Support for marriage equality was stronger among female respondents than among male respondents (72.2% vs. 57.4%) and stronger among Democrats (82.2%) than among Republicans (42.9%) and those claiming to prefer neither major political party (63.4%). We also found support for same-sex marriage inversely related to the amount of time respondents reported watching professional sports on television. As professional sports viewing increased, support for marriage equality decreased—from 76.7% among those reporting that they never watch sports, to just 33.3% among those who watch sports daily.

We then separated respondents into two groups based on their response to the question "Thinking specifically now about the Green Bay Packers, which of the following best describes how you feel about the team?" Possible responses included "I'm a huge fan," "I'm somewhat of a fan," "I'm not much of a fan," and "I'm not at all a fan." We coded respondents giving one of the first two responses as Packers fans

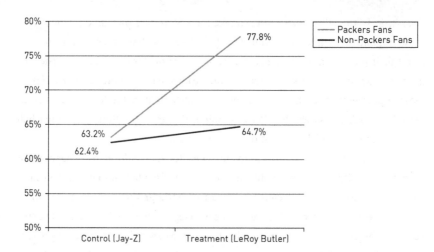

FIGURE 3.4 Support for Marriage Equality, Green Bay Packers Experiment. *Note: N* = 306. Respondents are adults in Appleton, Wisconsin. Surveys completed October 19–November 12, 2014. For Packers Fans, the difference between the control and treatment conditions is statistically significant at $p \leq .05$, one-tailed. See appendix 2 for question wording and additional results.

and respondents giving one of the two latter responses as non-Packers fans. As predicted by TDIP, the difference in levels of support for marriage equality among non-Packers fans was not affected by the treatment (exposure to the Butler photo and prime). Among Packers fans, however, exposure to the treatment increased support by more than 14 percentage points, as shown in figure 3.4, with additional details in appendix table A3.5. This difference is statistically significant. This relationship persists in a multivariate analysis controlling for other variables, as shown in appendix table A3.6.

EXPERIMENT 4: REAL MEN WEAR SKATES

Perhaps to a greater degree than the other three big professional sports leagues in the United States, the National Hockey League has been a consistent supporter of LGBT rights. The You Can Play organization, an organization that supports "equality, respect and safety for all athletes, without regard to sexual orientation," was founded by NHL Director of Player Safety Patrick Burke (the son of Calgary Flames President and Team USA General Manager Brian Burke). Burke founded the organization in honor of his younger brother, Brendan, who came out while a student manager for the Miami, Ohio, RedHawks hockey team and was killed in a car crash shortly afterward. On January 7, 2014, team captain for the Colorado Avalanche Gabe Landeskog added a video to the You Can Play website, the last team in the league to have a player do so. With that entry, every one of the 30 teams in the NHL was represented in a You Can Play video; every team likewise has a current player who has spoken out against homophobia and in favor of inclusion and equality.

According to our Theory of Dissonant Identity Priming, this widespread and fairly well known support for LGBT rights in the NHL raises doubts about the power of a shared identity as a hockey fan to provide a sufficiently powerful speed bump to shift attitudes on marriage equality. An NHL player interviewed in Anderson's book *In the Game* said, "In the NHL we are professionals, and guys really aren't all that homophobic" (2005, 41). On the other hand, the NHL is the only one of the major professional sports leagues to never have had a player come out as gay, either while active or after retiring. While fewer in number compared to other leagues, there are some examples of homophobic behavior in the NHL: in 2016, Chicago Blackhawks Center Andrew Shaw was caught on video using a homophobic slur during a game. He was fined $5,000 and was suspended for one playoff game, which turned out to be pivotal to the series for Chicago.

In sum, it was unclear the degree to which the effects found in our experiments priming football fan identity would also work among hockey fans. We tested this question with another Google Consumer Survey. The screener question mirrored that of Experiment 2, asking respondents on a scale of one to five how big a fan they were of professional hockey. Because far fewer Americans are hockey fans than are football fans, we included in the experiment not just individuals who were "not at all interested" and "extremely interested" (ones and fives), but also those stating that they were "very interested" (fours). The treatment and control conditions then exposed respondents to one of the following prompts:

Treatment

A recent ESPN survey found that a large majority of NHL players support same-sex marriage. How about you?

Control

A recent survey found that a large majority of Americans support same-sex marriage. How about you?

The treatment quotation is based on an anonymous survey of professional athletes published in *ESPN The Magazine's* October 15, 2012 issue (ESPN 2012). Among surveyed NHL players, 92.3% said yes when asked, "Should the U.S. legalize gay marriage?"

Possible responses (displayed in randomized order) included "Yes, I support same-sex marriage," "No, but I support civil unions," and "No, I oppose same-sex marriage." We hypothesized that hockey fans would be more likely than non-hockey fans to say that they supported same-sex marriage when exposed to the treatment quotation as opposed to the control condition while non-fans would not vary in how they responded to the two quotations.

The survey experiment was in the field February 21–26, 2014. A total of 832 responses were collected, including 443 hockey fans and 400 non-fans. While the results were in the hypothesized direction, the differences are not statistically

Table 3.1 Support for Marriage Equality (%), Hockey Experiment

	Control	Treatment	Percentage-Point Difference (SE)	Chi-square
All (N = 832)	50.37% (205/407)	54.12% (230/425)	3.75 (3.47)	1.1713 Pr = 0.279
Hockey Fans (N = 432)	59.42 (123/207)	62.22 (140/225)	2.80 (4.71)	0.3554 Pr = 0.551
Non-hockey Fans (N = 400)	41.00 (82/200)	45.00 (90/200)	4.0 (4.96)	0.6528 Pr = 0.419

Note: Data collected online from a national sample of adults using the Google Consumer Survey product. Surveys completed February 21–26, 2014. See appendix 2 for question wording and additional results.

significant (table 3.1, additional details in appendix table A3.7): hockey fans were more likely to be supportive of marriage equality when exposed to an NHL identity prime (a 2.8 percentage-point difference between treatment and control) and non-hockey fans were more likely to be supportive as well (a 4.0 percentage-point difference between treatment and control), though non-fans were considerably less supportive overall.

EXPERIMENT 5: TAKE ME OUT TO THE BALL GAME

The San Francisco Giants baseball team has in many ways been at the forefront of efforts by professional sports teams to support LGBT rights. Every year, the Giants dedicate one game to LGBT fans, called LGBT Night Out, with a portion of ticket proceeds donated to non-profits in the LGBT community. In 2011, the Giants became the first professional sports team to join the It Gets Better Project, a worldwide movement launched in September 2010 by syndicated columnist and author Dan Savage in response to LGBT youth committing suicide after being bullied in school. The organization urges LGBT youth to not take their own lives and promises, "It gets better." The message is spread through video messages uploaded by groups and individuals; as of June 2015, the It Gets Better website included over 50,000 user-created videos viewed more than 50 million times.

On June 1, 2011, the Giants released a 58-second It Gets Better video featuring pitchers Matt Cain, Barry Zito, and Sergio Romo, as well as centerfielder Andres Torres and batting coach Hensley "Bam Bam" Meulens. In May 2013, the LGBT advocacy group GLAAD awarded the Giants that year's Corporate Leader award for sending a message of inclusiveness, noting the years of support through the LGBT Night Out, the It Gets Better video, and advocacy and fundraising to raise awareness of and fight HIV/AIDS. As a corporation, the team is far ahead of the field in its support for LGBT rights. Individuals on the team, most notably pitcher Matt Cain, have also taken a leadership role, with Matt Cain posing for several "NOH8" photos in opposition to Proposition 8, the constitutional amendment that voters approved in November 2008 to end gay marriage in California.

The Theory of Dissonant Identity Priming predicts that individuals who are supporters of a sports team will be more likely to be influenced to support same-sex marriage if cued to think of it as a shared in-group attitude. The effects are predicted to be strongest when the cued attitude is unexpected, generating a cognitive speed bump. That dissonance was weak to non-existent here; support for marriage equality and other LGBT rights is widespread among residents of San Francisco generally, including among Giants fans, and support for LGBT rights is well known to be an attitude shared by the Giants team and its members, as noted above. Thus, while we were hopeful that the experiment would generate attitudinal shifts, there was reason to believe the effort would, at best, generate only weak effects.

On a day that the Giants were playing a home game, June 23, 2013, we conducted a survey experiment among individuals encountered on the sidewalks of San Francisco in the two blocks surrounding the Giants stadium. A team of 10 undergraduate students invited pedestrians to take a one-page paper survey, for which they were compensated with a $5 Starbucks gift card. In-group identity was cued in two ways. In the treatment group, five randomly selected students were given Giants T-shirts to wear and instructed to distribute surveys that noted Giants pitcher Matt Cain's support for gay marriage. Cain was pitching for the Giants on the day of the experiment. In the control group, the other (randomly selected) five students wore plain T-shirts and distributed surveys that noted support for gay marriage by actor David Hasselhoff. Both surveys included a picture of either Cain or Hasselhoff posing with "NOH8" painted on their cheeks, taken from the NOH8 website (see figure 3.5).

FIGURE 3.5 NOH8 Photos of Actor David Hasselhoff and San Francisco Giants Pitcher Matt Cain, San Francisco Giants Experiment.

The first question on the survey was a manipulation check and also was designed to heighten awareness of the accompanying photo. The question asked:

In the photo on the left, **[San Francisco Giants Pitcher Matt Cain / actor David Hasselhoff]** is showing his opposition to Prop 8, the 2008 initiative that banned same-sex marriage in California and is currently being reviewed by the U.S. Supreme Court. What do you think the photo is supposed to mean? (check one)

• **[Matt Cain / David Hasselhoff]** opposed Prop 8 and supports gay marriage
• **[Matt Cain / David Hasselhoff]** supported Prop 8 and opposes gay marriage

Respondents were then asked three questions about their level of support for LGBT rights: (1) a general attitude about whether LGBT individuals should be able to marry, get a legal partnership like a civil union, or have no recognition; (2) vote choice on a hypothetical ballot initiative on marriage equality; and (3) support for LGBT parenting. Later in the survey, we asked about their level of interest in professional sports generally and support for the San Francisco Giants baseball team, in particular, to construct a Sports Fan Index, as well as a variety of demographic questions. A total of 490 completed surveys were collected.

Reminiscent of the confusion reported by California voters when asked to decide Proposition 8, many respondents were confused by the first question and incorrectly identified Cain or Hasselhoff as opposing gay marriage. Reviewing multiple surveys about same-sex marriage and Proposition 8, Lewis and Gossett concluded (2011, 15): "We find substantial numbers of people telling pollsters they opposed Proposition 8 even though they did not favor same-sex marriage. We could find little explanation for this other than misunderstanding." Similar misunderstandings are evident in results from our survey at the Giants game. While initially designed as a manipulation check, we were struck by the large percentage of respondents (40%) who either declined to answer or incorrectly answered the question; only 301 of 490 respondents accurately interpreted the photo. As shown in table 3.2, individuals who correctly answered the question were much more likely to support same-sex marriage; almost 75% of respondents who correctly interpreted the photo said that they supported marriage equality, compared to only 36% of those either declining to answer the manipulation check question or answering it incorrectly.

In our further analysis of the Giants experiment data, we included answers to the manipulation check question as a predictor, with the expectation that those able to correctly answer the question would be more likely to be affected by the intended treatment (primed identity as a fan of the San Francisco Giants). What we found, however, was that there was no difference in support for marriage equality or LGBT parenting between the two groups, regardless of how individuals answered the manipulation check question. In other words, respondents exposed to the photo of Matt Cain while interacting with a student wearing a Giants T-shirt were no more supportive of marriage equality than were those exposed to the photo of David

Table 3.2 Support for Marriage Equality (%), San Francisco Giants Experiment

	Control	Treatment	Percentage-Point Difference (SE)	Chi-square
All (N = 490)	60.16% (148/246)	59.43% (145/244)	−0.74 (4.44)	0.0276 Pr = 0.868
Sports Fans (N = 229)	69.52 (73/105)	71.77 (89/124)	2.25 (6.06)	0.1391 Pr = 0.709
Non-Sports Fans (N = 261)	53.19 (75/141)	46.67 (56/120)	−6.52 (6.22)	1.1040 Pr = 0.293
Successfully Answered Manipulation Check Survey Item				
All (N = 301)	76.47 (117/153)	72.97 (108/148)	3.57 (7.57)	0.4876 Pr = 0.485
Sports Fans (N = 161)	82.43 (61/74)	85.06 (74/87)	2.63 (5.85)	0.2035 Pr = 0.652
Non-Sports Fans (N = 140)	70.89 (56/79)	55.74 (34/61)	−15.15 (8.12)	3.4404 Pr = 0.064

Note: Respondents are adults in San Francisco, California. Surveys completed on June 23, 2013. Sports Fan is a dichotomized index created using responses to three survey items. See appendix 2 for question wording and additional results.

Hasselhoff while interacting with a student in a plain T-shirt. This is true for those who answered the manipulation check correctly and incorrectly and for those who were strong sports fans and for those who were not.

Simply put, the experiment did not work. Whether due to confusion about the meaning of the photos or the relatively pro-LGBT context of the city of San Francisco and the Giants baseball team, cueing an individual's identity as a supporter of the San Francisco Giants did not lead to increased support for same-sex marriage. It could be that the treatment was not adequately received (i.e., respondents did not take the time to carefully read the paragraph). We believe a more likely explanation is that the overwhelming supportive cues from the community and the team outweighed our single priming treatment and that the support was not surprising enough to have a measurable effect.[6]

SUMMARY AND DISCUSSION

The world of professional sports and of the National Football League in particular is one of predominant heteronormativity and resistance to gay rights. Support for same-sex marriage equality from NFL elites such as Commissioner Roger Goodell or current or former members of well-loved teams thus constitute a speed bump for individuals who strongly identify as fans. Primed with that football fan identity and presented with an unexpected cue of support for marriage equality, fans are motivated to reconsider their attitude on the issue, and even to change their opinions, in order to cement their in-group membership. We found that football fans assigned to a treatment group that primed a football fan identity and provided a cue of support for LGBT rights (same-sex marriage or non-discrimination) were more supportive of those rights compared to fans assigned to a control group. Among non-fans, in contrast, exposure to the same cues produced negligible differences in attitudes. Because non-fans do not consider themselves part of the in-group of football fans, the cueing of football fan identity did not make those treatment conditions more compelling or constitute as notable a cognitive speed bump. As noted above, Athlete Ally's Hudson Taylor recently claimed: "Fans take cues from professional athletes." In the football experiments, we found empirical support for that sentiment.

Not all of our sports fan experiments moved attitudes, however. In situations where support for LGBT rights was less unexpected—when paired with identity either as a fan of professional hockey or as a fan of the San Francisco Giants baseball team in the LGBT-friendly city of San Francisco—the primed identities had negligible effects. Only among football fans, when the prime generated a cognitive speed bump, were attitudes shifted. These results are consistent with our Theory of Dissonant Identity Priming.

In January 2013, *Sports Illustrated* released its annual Super Bowl preview issue. Included on page 48 was a picture of a man-on-man kiss between two 49ers fans, taken at the Hi Tops gay sports bar at the moment the team clinched its spot in the game. Reporting on the photo, NBC Bay Area quoted bartender Logan Chavarria: "A lot of people that come in don't even know that it's a gay sports bar, and that's the best part, you know, and then we find that we have that common bond." Hi Tops owner Jesse Woodward noted, "Sports fans come from all walks of life and we're a great big melting pot here and everyone can get along." These sentiments illustrate exactly the theory tested in our experiments: that thinking of oneself as a sports fan leads individuals to feel that they are members of a distinct group, individuals with a shared identity, regardless of other differences in identities or attitudes. Pulled together in the excitement of watching a football game, patrons at the Hi Tops bar that night—gay and straight, Black and white, young and old—felt more alike than different, members of the same 49ers fan club, united in their goal of rooting for the home team.

Several real-world examples provide further evidence of the power of a sports fan identity to generate support for LGBT rights. After Jason Collins signed his 10-day contract with the Brooklyn Nets in February 2014, his jersey quickly became the top-selling jersey in the league. After joking that the sales were due to gay basketball fans finally having "their guy" on a team, cohost of the *Boomer and Carton in the Morning* radio program Craig Carton told listeners, "I'm getting the jersey and I'm not gay, 'cause I'm supportive" (www.cbssports.com). In Arizona, lawmakers on February 20, 2014 passed a bill that would allow business owners to deny service to LGBT individuals on religious grounds. As Arizona Governor Jan Brewer considered whether to veto the measure (and ultimately she did), the NFL joined the conversation, warning that it would consider moving the Super Bowl, scheduled to be played in Arizona in 2015, were the bill approved. In a statement, the NFL noted, "Our policies emphasize tolerance and inclusiveness, and prohibit discrimination based on age, gender, race, religion, sexual orientation or any other improper standard" (NFL 2014b). Pressure from NFL fans, among others, contributed to the governor's decision to veto. And while the Twitterverse and conservative commentators including talk radio's Rush Limbaugh were critical of Michael Sam potentially joining the NFL, overall the reaction to his coming out was largely positive. Ralph Vacchiano, sportswriter for the *New York Daily News*, commented: "Those who react in horror or with insensitivity are part of a minority that thankfully is diminishing. The majority of the human race hears news of a gay colleague or friend and greets it with a shrug" (Vacchiano 2014).

Sports fans and sports teams are tightly knit communities, with strong in-group identities that encourage shared worldviews and attitudes. As more individuals in these in-groups come out as supporters of gay and lesbian rights or as gay or lesbian themselves, others in those groups are influenced to re-think their attitudes about those rights. When Michael Sam came out as gay in February 2014 and was greeted with open arms at the NFL combine and with supportive statements from the NFL and its commissioner, that signaled to football fans around the country that it was consistent with their identity as football fans to also support an openly gay player.

People are realizing that LGBT people are part of other communities that are important to them, that their lives are intertwined with those of LGBT individuals. This leads them to be more supportive in part because it humanizes LGBT people as predicted by contact theory. Gay men and lesbians are no longer abstract unknowns. They are friends, neighbors, coworkers, and relatives. This aspect of increasing support is well documented and consistent with previous scholarship. In addition, people are realizing that supporters of marriage equality and other LGBT rights are also members of their communities. Fans of professional sports like football are learning that their sports heroes and fellow fans are also supporters of marriage equality and our experiments suggest these shared in-group identities can be particularly powerful in changing minds. Individuals are adjusting their attitudes on LGBT rights to better correspond with opinions shared by other members of their in-groups and thus cement their sense of belonging to those various groups. As evidenced by the results of our survey experiments, support for LGBT rights and same-sex marriage among sports fans will increase as more gay and lesbian players are welcomed by their leagues with open arms and as more players, sports elites, and fellow fans publicly endorse those rights.

4 God and Marriage
Activating Religious Identity to Influence Attitudes on Same-Sex Marriage

Religion is a core aspect of US identity. On a variety of measures including church attendance, the importance of religion, and belief in God, America is by far the most religious advanced country in the world (Putnam and Campbell 2010). In 2012, eight out of 10 surveyed Americans identified with a religion and seven in 10 said that religion was important in their daily life and that they attended religious services frequently (Newport 2012b). Religiosity is one of the most robust in-group identities (Ben-Nun Bloom et al. 2015; Weeks and Vincent 2007). A number of scholars have noted the importance of religiosity in many individuals' self-conceptions (see Ysseldyk, Matheson, and Anisman 2010); individuals with strong religious group identities tend to perceive their religious identity as central to their self-concept (Luhtanen and Crocker 1992).

In short, Americans are extremely religious. Mostly, this generates neighborliness and good citizenship. They are more likely to volunteer for both religious and secular causes, to donate money to charity, to be involved in their communities, to give blood, to return excess change to a clerk, to give money to panhandlers, and to let a stranger cut in front of them in line. They are happier. But religious people are also less tolerant of dissent and of extending civil liberties to atheists, LGBT individuals, or those expressing unpopular views (e.g., defending Osama bin Laden or al-Qaeda), although tolerance has increased in recent years (Putnam and Campbell 2010). A number of studies have documented the effect of religious belief on political attitudes as well as the power of priming religious belief to generate cooperation and tolerance (or intolerance).

That religion is such a widely and strongly held identity also makes it a good candidate for activation to generate openness to attitudinal change. Activating religious identity is also of interest when it comes to debates about LGBT rights in general and marriage equality specifically because the issue of religious freedom is often raised during debates about those issues. Supporters of LGBT rights argue that the US Constitution prohibits individuals or groups from imposing their beliefs on others and that marriage is a matter of civil law, not of religious freedom. Opponents, in contrast, generally argue that their religious rights are being trampled by those who want to move away from the traditional one-man, one-woman understanding of the institution.

Biblical verses are often invoked and references to God and Jesus Christ feature prominently in debates on LGBT rights. Denominations and individuals vary in how they interpret those biblical verses; this variation allows for religious identities to be triggered in advocacy messages about those rights, in line with our Theory of Dissonant Identity Priming. In this chapter, we discuss the results of two randomized experiments conducted to test the effect of triggering religious identity on attitudes about marriage equality. First, we review previous scholarship on the effect of religiosity on desirable (e.g., tolerance and cooperation) and undesirable (e.g., racism) attitudes and behaviors. We next review the role that religion has played in contemporary debates on marriage equality. We then describe our randomized experiments, one conducted with a national online sample and one conducted by telephone in Louisiana, in cooperation with a local advocacy organization. We find significant support for our hypothesis that triggering a shared religious identity can influence individual attitudes on same-sex marriage but also confirm the limits of the power of identity priming, as predicted by our theory.

THE POWER OF RELIGIOSITY

Religiosity has been the focus of extensive investigation by scholars interested in its origin and consequences, including the degree to which priming it can influence various psychological outcomes. Religiosity is credited with increasing altruistic behavior and empathy and other virtuous behaviors (Hood, Hill, and Spilka 2009; Saroglou et al. 2005), increasing compliance with group norms and interpersonal trust (Baumeister, Bauer, and Lloyd 2010), and reducing abuse of drugs and alcohol (Myers 2000). Experimental economic studies have found that religious priming increases prosocial behavior, including increased generosity and cooperation (see Shariff et al. 2016). Other studies have found that religious priming increases honesty and charitable intentions (Pichon, Boccato, and Saroglou 2007; Randolph-Seng and Nielsen 2007).[1]

Scholars have theorized that the power of religiousness to generate prosocial behavior may derive from the perception of being watched by supernatural entities

(McCullough and Willoughby 2009). In other words, when religious identity is primed, individuals are reminded that their actions are being monitored and thus prosocial behavior is encouraged via the "sanctification" of goals (Baumeister et al. 2010; Koole et al. 2010; McCullough and Willoughby 2009). Gervais and Norenzayan (2012) called this the "supernatural monitoring hypothesis."[2]

Priming religion can also generate less desirable attitudes, including enhanced prejudice toward African Americans and gay men (Johnson, Rowatt, and LaBouff 2012). As Johnson et al. pointed out, while some scripture encourages tolerance, "Christians' behaviors and attitudes often reflect other Biblical scriptures that advocate treating out-groups, such as nonbelievers and gay men, with discrimination" (154). In one study, they found that more religious and spiritual participants have more negative attitudes toward Muslims, atheists, and gay men. In a second study, participants exposed to religious words via subliminal primes were more likely to report colder feelings toward Muslims, atheists, and gay men. Overall, research on religiousness and prejudice finds a consistent positive relationship, with rare exceptions, as shown in a recent meta-analysis of 55 studies by Hall, Matz, and Wood (2010).

A meta-analysis of 64 studies by Whitley (2009) found that nearly all measures of religiousness predicted negative attitudes toward gay men and lesbians. Whitley noted that while most religions teach tolerance, they also have historically condemned homosexuality, thus defining prejudice against lesbians and gay men as a permitted prejudice and as contrary to (or even a threat to) their value systems. The link between religion and intergroup bias extends to findings from priming experiments: when exposed to religious primes, individuals are more likely to express racial prejudice and prejudice against members of groups perceived to be value violators, including gay men and lesbians, Muslims, and atheists (Johnson, Rowatt, and LaBouff 2010, 2012; Preston and Ritter 2011). Rutchick (2010) found that people voting in churches are more likely to support conservative candidates and bans on same-sex marriage.

In a recent meta-analysis, Shariff et al. (2016) reviewed 92 religious priming experiments. Overall, the authors found a small but statistically significant difference between religiously primed and control groups. Seventeen of the 92 studies in the meta-analysis report differences between religious and non-religious participants; however, the effect of religious priming on subjects is generally reported as an overall effect on all participants without consideration of the degree to which those participants are religious. Our Theory of Dissonant Identity Priming predicts that identity primes will primarily affect individuals from within the primed identity group. In other words, we would not expect a religious prime to have an effect on non-religious respondents. Looking at the 17 studies, Shariff et al. found that there is indeed a significant difference: religious respondents are affected by religious primes while respondents who are non-religious or described as of low religiosity are not. Even stronger evidence for TDIP comes from the few studies examining the effect of in-group priming on members of a religious community: participants are more tolerant of and more likely to agree with messages attributed to religious in-group members (Djupe and Calfano 2014; Robinson 2010).[3]

RELIGION AND LGBT RIGHTS

Discussions of LGBT rights in general and same-sex marriage more specifically often include references to religious belief and surveys show that individuals who are more religious are also more likely to oppose those rights (Cox, Navarro-Rivera, and Jones 2014). Some Christians believe that "homosexual passions and acts are unnatural, shameful, contrary to sound doctrine and deny entrance to the Kingdom of God" (Edmiston 2002). Many Christians believe that their religious identity requires that they work to oppose same-sex marriage, to speak out against what they believe to be a sin and an abomination, and to save others from damnation. The Family Research Council, a prominent conservative advocacy group, argues that allowing same-sex marriage "pushes out traditional views on the family, leading to the erosion of religious liberty" (www.frc.org). Similarly, the evangelical Christian group Focus On the Family argues that marriage is a religious institution and that same-sex marriages, because they do not conform to the traditional definition of marriage as described in scripture, are an attack on the religious beliefs of evangelicals.

There is a particularly strong sense of conflict between religious beliefs and LGBT rights among white evangelical Protestants, 72% of whom say there is a conflict between homosexuality and their religious beliefs and 64% of whom report "a lot" of conflict (Pew Research Center 2015). Black Protestants also see significant conflict, with 48% reporting "a lot" of conflict and 12% reporting "a little" conflict between their religious beliefs and homosexuality. By comparison, only 38% of white mainline Protestants report "a lot" of conflict and 10% report "a little." Finally, 38% of Catholics report "a lot" and 14% report "a little" conflict. Frequency of attendance at religious services is also correlated with feelings of conflict: 61% of those who attend services weekly report feeling a conflict, 51% of whom perceive "a lot" of conflict. Among less-frequent attendees, only 34% think there is a conflict while 64% do not (Pew Research Center 2015).

Religious opposition to marriage equality is not universal, however. Official positions on the issue are growing increasingly diverse. On December 19, 2013, Pennsylvania Pastor Frank Schaefer was defrocked by the United Methodist Church for officiating at his son's same-sex marriage (in Massachusetts, where it was legal at the time) and for refusing to pledge to comply with church law on the issue. The punishment was meant to deter other pastors from performing similar ceremonies but instead had the opposite effect. Schaefer's trial and defrocking inspired a wave of Methodist ministers to step forward in their support of same-sex marriages, including the posting on the Internet of a list of such ceremonies by Methodist clergy in New York (www.mindny.org). As reported by the *New York Times* (Goodstein 2013):

Members of the United Methodist Church, the nation's third-largest Christian denomination, have been battling bitterly over homosexuality for four decades. The church now faces an increasingly determined uprising by clergy members and laypeople who have refused to cede, even after losing the most recent votes, at the Methodist convention last year, on proposals to change church teaching.

Other denominations have also come forward in recent years to support marriage equality. In July 2012, the Episcopal Church's General Convention voted to approve an official rite for blessing same-sex marriages, building on the momentum started three years earlier when church leaders voted to allow priests to bless same-sex couples if their bishops allowed it. The United Church of Christ voted in 2005 to support marriage for same-sex couples as did the Evangelical Lutheran Church of America in 2009. In 2011, the Presbyterian Church voted to ordain gays and lesbians as pastors and in March 2015, they voted to amend the church constitution to include same-sex marriage. Other religious denominations that allow their clergy to perform same-sex marriages include the Quakers, the Unitarian Universalist Association of Churches, and Reform and Conservative branches of Judaism (Goodstein 2012, 2015).

Leaders of the Catholic Church remain firmly opposed to same-sex marriage but at the same time, there have been recent glimmers of support for gay and lesbian individuals. In July 2013, Pope Francis told reporters: "If someone is gay and he searches for the Lord and has good will, who am I to judge?" (speaking in Italian but using the English word "gay"). As Donadio (2013) reported in the *New York Times*, "Francis's words could not have been more different from those of [former Pope] Benedict XVI, who in 2005 wrote that homosexuality was 'a strong tendency ordered toward an intrinsic moral evil,' and an 'objective disorder.'" In October 2014, an interim report (later revised) from a worldwide meeting of Catholic bishops called for greater acceptance of gay and lesbian individuals. In February 2015, the pope gave VIP treatment to members of a prominent American Catholic gay rights group, the first time the group had been welcomed in that way by the church (Pullella 2015). However, Pope Francis has also made clear his opposition to same-sex marriages, calling them a threat to traditional families (Richinick 2015).

The Church of Jesus Christ of Latter-day Saints has taken a high-profile position against marriage equality, including a pivotal role in funding Proposition 8, the 2008 ballot initiative in California that amended the state constitution to ban same-sex marriage. In 2013, the marriage equality battle heated up in Utah, a state where nearly two-thirds of all residents are Mormons and home to the church's world headquarters. In November 2004, two-thirds of Utah voters had approved a state constitutional amendment defining marriage as between one man and one woman; nine years later, on December 20, 2013, US District Judge Robert J. Shelby ruled the ban unconstitutional, a violation of the guarantees of due process and equal protection under the US Constitution. Over the next 17 days, 1,360 same-sex couples were married, until January 6, 2014, when Shelby's ruling was stayed by the US Supreme Court while the matter was appealed.

The Utah Attorney General and the U.S. Attorney General both supported the legality of the same-sex marriages that had taken place in Utah during those 17 days (Horwitz 2014). The leadership of the Church of Jesus Christ of Latter-day Saints continued to push back against the legal tide but in October 2014, the Supreme Court declined to hear the case, leaving in place a lower-court decision making same-sex marriage legal in the state (Liptak 2014). This legal decision and others notwithstanding, opposition to marriage equality is widespread among Mormons. In a 2012 survey, about two-thirds of Mormons said that homosexuality should be discouraged by society. The official position of the church is that acting on same-sex attraction is a sin and that same-sex marriage is "contrary to the laws of God" (Burke 2015).

Broadly speaking, religious beliefs are a powerful influence on attitudes about same-sex marriage and civil rights for LGBT individuals and have become even more important over the past few decades (Olson, Cadge and Harrison 2006; Sherkat et al. 2011). Conservative religious groups were key proponents for congressional passage of the Defense of Marriage Act in 1996 (see chapter 2) and a host of state-level prohibitions (Camp 2008; Campbell and Monson 2008; Lax and Phillips 2009; McVeigh and Diaz 2009; Soule 2004). This underscores the context in which our experiments that activated religious identity were conducted: religious Americans are more likely to oppose same-sex marriage, especially if they are members of a denomination that has taken an official position in defense of "traditional" marriage and particularly when that identity is primed to be more relevant to their self-concept.

Opponents of LGBT rights often frame their arguments as about preserving religious liberty. In early 2014, Arizona state lawmakers approved HB 1062, legislation that would have broadened protections for the free exercise of religion to include non-governmental entities including individuals, corporations, and businesses. Those entities would have been allowed to deny service to customers on the grounds that doing so would violate their religious beliefs and it was widely understood to mean that businesses would be allowed to deny service to gay men and lesbians. The bill was opposed by major corporations such as Apple, AT&T, and American Airlines, by Major League Baseball and the National Football League, and by prominent Republicans including Arizona's two US senators, John McCain and Jeff Flake, and former presidential candidates Mitt Romney and Newt Gingrich (Kopan 2014). Leading conservative voices such as Glenn Beck and Rush Limbaugh, however, focused on the religious freedom aspect of the legislation, arguing that the bill was about respecting the religious beliefs of all Arizonans. *Forbes* columnist Ilya Shapiro (2014) wrote:

While governments have the duty to treat everyone equally under the law, private individuals should be able to make their own decisions on whom to do business with and how—on religious or any other grounds. Gay photographers and bakers shouldn't be forced to work Southern Baptist celebrations, Jews shouldn't be forced to work Nazi rallies, environmentalists shouldn't be forced to work job fairs in logging communities, and pacifists shouldn't be forced to work NRA conventions.

Discussion of the Arizona law reflected ongoing controversies elsewhere, some of which were working their way through the courts at the time. In one instance, a professional photographer in New Mexico was being sued for declining to take pictures at a lesbian couple's commitment ceremony. Citing her right to freedom of expression (photography is a constitutionally-protected form of freedom of speech, protected by the First Amendment), the photographer said that forcing her to celebrate "something her religion tells her is wrong" was a violation of her rights (Liptak 2013). In Colorado, a baker refused to make a cake for a gay couple's wedding celebration, claiming that doing so would be "displeasing God and acting contrary to the teachings of the Bible" (Fields 2013). And in Washington a florist declined to provide flowers for a gay couple's wedding, claiming she could not do so "because of (her) relationship with Jesus Christ" (Porterfield 2013). In defying the Supreme Court's decision in June 2015 that same-sex couples had a constitutionally protected right to marry, Texas Attorney General Ken Paxton said his office would legally defend any county clerks who chose to refuse to do so based on religious objections.

Over and over again, the courts disagreed. The florist in Washington State, the baker in Oregon, the photographer in New Mexico, and others who had denied services or venues to couples related to their same-sex wedding and commitment ceremonies lost their cases. As the judge in the florist case noted, "For over 135 years, the Supreme Court of the United States has held that laws may prohibit religiously motivated action, as opposed to belief. In trade and commerce, and more particularly when seeking to prevent discrimination in public accommodations, the Courts have confirmed the power of the Legislative Branch to prohibit conduct it deems discriminatory, even when the motivation for that conduct is grounded in religious belief" (Ford 2015).

Crucial to understanding religious opposition to same-sex marriage is that those opponents see marriage equality as an attack on their religious freedom, a core component of the First Amendment of the US Constitution and a value highly cherished by Americans. A majority of Americans believe that the US Constitution established a Christian nation (First Amendment Center 2013). A number of recent polls indicate that religious Americans believe that religious freedom is under attack in this nation and that the group most responsible for those attacks is gays and lesbians (Markoe 2013).

On February 26, 2014, Arizona Republican Governor Jan Brewer vetoed SB 1062 (see chapter 3). Many media outlets reported the breaking news with a tweet similar to this one from the *Washington Post*: "#BREAKING: Arizona governor vetoes controversial anti-gay bill." But some outlets, including the *Wall Street Journal*, focused on the religious-freedom argument put forward by the bill's supporters. The WSJ tweet for the news was "Breaking: Arizona governor vetoes religious freedom bill." Brewer acknowledged the religious arguments in her veto message, noting, "Religious liberty is a core American and Arizona value, so is non-discrimination" (Shoichet and Abdullah 2014). The focus on religious freedom rather than LGBT rights illustrates that contemporary battles over marriage equality are entangled with religious belief and religious identity.

IDENTITY PRIMING AND IN-GROUP IDENTITY

As the previous sections make clear, there is often a clear tie between religious identity and attitudes toward LGBT rights such as marriage equality. What is less clear, however, is how priming religious identity and communicating support from people of faith might affect the opinions and behavior of Americans who identify as religious. Priming religious identity among individuals with a strong religious identity might increase hostility toward LGBT rights because of preexisting religion-based opposition to those rights. On the other hand, priming religious identity with an elite religious cue that is a message of inclusion might increase support for LGBT rights by demonstrating that one can be both a person of faith and a supporter of same-sex marriage.

We believe the latter is more plausible; in the experiments described in this chapter, we hypothesized that religious individuals would be more supportive of marriage equality when primed with information about support for marriage equality from a religious elite, as predicted by our Theory of Dissonant Identity Priming. When the primed identity was deeply held and particularly when the delivered opinion was unexpected, generating a cognitive speed bump, we expected to see increased levels of support. Priming a religious identity with a message in favor of same-sex marriage meets these requirements. Specifically, we theorized that the influence of a primed shared in-group identity through exposure to a statement of support for same-sex marriage from a religious elite would generate increased support for same-sex marriage among religious individuals but would have no effect among those who do not have a religious identity. At the same time, given the strong link between religious belief and attitudes about homosexuality, we also posited that the power of a single prime might be insufficient to move attitudes, particularly in contexts where religion is very salient and overwhelmingly linked to opposition to LGBT rights.

We conducted two experiments to test these hypotheses: one with a national online sample, and one in the state of Louisiana using live telephone conversations and in cooperation with a local advocacy organization. Results from the two experiments support our Theory of Dissonant Identity Priming. In the online experiment, religious respondents whose religious identities were triggered through religious elite cues were more likely to be supportive of marriage equality. In the second experiment, in contrast, religious adults in Louisiana showed consistent levels of openness to LGBT issues regardless of whether the script they were read triggered religious identity. Examined together, the experiments provide intriguing empirical evidence of when and where triggering religious identity can be used to open minds on an issue often closely linked to religious belief. We turn now to our two experiments.

EXPERIMENT 1: THE SOCIALSCI EXPERIMENT

We conducted a randomized survey experiment with a nationwide sample through SocialSci.com; data were collected May 17–28, 2013 (Harrison and Michelson 2015). SocialSci is a private company that works with academics to provide access to a large pool of compensated opt-in study participants. The experiment was conducted online via the SocialSci.com survey platform, using a random national sample of adult participants recruited by SocialSci. In order to limit the experiment to participants who were either religious or secular (non-religious), participants were first asked to indicate their level of religious identity on a seven-point scale ranging from extremely secular to extremely religious. The survey item was embedded within a list of other questions in the screening survey, including items about employment and marital status, income, and smartphone use, in order to camouflage the intent of the screening question. We divided participants into two groups: Secular / Not Religious (responses 1–3) and Religious (responses 5–7). Individuals who indicated that they were neither religious nor secular (response 4) were not included in the experiment. To further camouflage the intent of the experiment, dependent variable items in the main survey experiment were also embedded within a larger set of questions on other issues, such as cigarette taxes and protecting the environment.

Participants were randomly assigned to read one of two paragraphs regarding marriage equality, different only in the attribution of the source of the quotation as either from an anonymous citizen or Reverend Richard T. Lawrence, pastor at St. Vincent de Paul Church in Baltimore, Maryland. The paragraph read:

[In a recent newspaper op-ed, a citizen wrote / Reverend Richard T. Lawrence recently told members of his church], "It seems to me, therefore, that one might easily judge that even if we do not believe that gay marriage ever could or should be allowed in the church, we could live with a provision that allows civil marriage of gay and lesbian couples. Personally, however, I would go farther than that ... we could come to recognize the total, exclusive, permanent, interpersonal commitment of gay and lesbian couples as a part of the sacrament of matrimony."

The quotation from Reverend Lawrence was real, delivered to members of his congregation in Baltimore, Maryland, on Sunday, October 28, 2012 (Ramsey 2012).

Respondents were then asked whether they supported same-sex marriage, civil unions, or neither; how they might vote on a hypothetical ballot initiative in their state legalizing gay marriage; and whether they supported gay and lesbian parenting. A total of 500 surveys were completed, including 250 by religious participants and 250 by secular participants, each randomly divided into groups of 125 each for the treatment and control conditions. Responses were recoded into dichotomous variables indicating whether the respondent was supportive of same-sex marriage or same-sex parenting.

Additional survey questions measured demographic and attitudinal variables that we expected to predict attitudes on same-sex marriage, reflecting previous survey-based research (Baunach 2012): age, gender, education, partisanship, and religious affiliation.[4] Partisanship was measured on a seven-point scale ranging from Strong Democrat (partisanship = 1) to Strong Republican (partisanship = 7); we hypothesized that those who were closer to the Strong Republican end of the spectrum would be less supportive of same-sex marriage. Identity as a Fundamentalist Christian is an indicator variable based on responses to two survey items: whether the respondent self-identified as a Christian and also self-identified as someone who is an evangelical or "born again." We hypothesized that Fundamentalist Christians would be less supportive of same-sex marriage than individuals with different religious identities. We also expected support for same-sex marriage to be weaker among older respondents and men.

The data support our hypotheses: assignment to the treatment or control paragraph had negligible effects among secular (non-religious) respondents but consistently generated significant differences in responses among religious respondents. Religious participants exposed to the quotation attributed to Reverend Lawrence were more likely to say that they supported marriage equality, more likely to say that they would likely vote for a ballot measure in their state establishing marriage equality, and more likely to approve of gay and lesbian parenting.

As shown in figure 4.1, there was a statistically significant increase in support of marriage equality among religious respondents who received the religious elite cue. For secular respondents, there was a negligible difference in support for marriage equality between those exposed to the secular cue (92.0%) and the religious cue (89.6%). Among religious respondents, in contrast, support among those exposed to the secular cue was 51.2%, compared to 62.4% of those exposed to the religious cue, a statistically significant difference of 11.2 percentage points. Support for a hypothetical ballot initiative showed a similar pattern, with no true difference in support among secular respondents but a 14.4 percentage-point difference among religious respondents (figure 4.2). Support for gay and lesbian parenting did not differ among secular respondents while there was a 9.6 percentage-point difference for religious respondents (figure 4.3). Across all three dependent variables, religious respondents exposed to a religious elite cue were much more likely to support LGBT rights than were those exposed to an anonymous cue.[5]

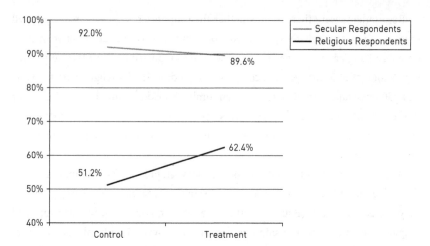

FIGURE 4.1 Support for Marriage Equality, SocialSci Experiment. *Note: N* = 500. Respondents are a national sample of adults. Surveys completed May 17–28, 2013. Difference between treatment and control for religious respondents is statistically significant at $p \leq .05$, two-tailed. See appendix 2 for question wording and additional results.

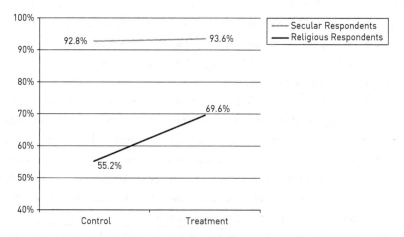

FIGURE 4.2 Support for Hypothetical Ballot Measure, SocialSci Experiment. *Note: N* = 500. Respondents are a national sample of adults. Surveys completed May 17–28, 2013. Difference between treatment and control for religious respondents is statistically significant at $p \leq .05$, two-tailed. See appendix 2 for question wording and additional details.

We were also interested in whether exposure to the treatment paragraph with the religious cue was moderated by inclusion of other variables known to be predictors of attitudes on marriage equality, as noted above. This was explored with multivariate logistic regression models and an interaction term.[6] Results from these models indicate that support for same-sex marriage and parenting dropped as religiousness increases, as expected. More religious respondents primed by the treatment paragraph were more supportive of same-sex marriage, although this effect did not persist for the same-sex parenting item. Individuals who are religious and who were exposed to the treatment paragraph, triggering their religious identity, were more

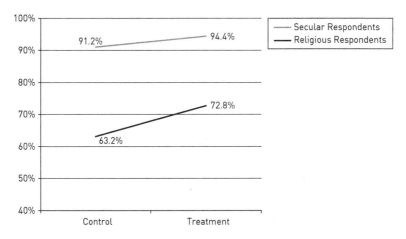

FIGURE 4.3 Support for LGBT Parenting, SocialSci Experiment. *Note:* N = 500. Respondents are a national sample of adults. Surveys completed May 17–28, 2013. Difference between treatment and control for religious respondents is statistically significant at $p \leq .05$, two-tailed. See appendix 2 for question wording and additional details.

likely to say that they would vote in favor of same-sex marriage on a ballot initiative in their state.

Other variables were also good predictors of attitudes about same-sex marriage and parenting. Individuals who were older, more strongly Republican, or who identified as fundamentalist Christians were consistently more likely to oppose marriage equality and same-sex parenting. Support for same-sex parenting increased with education. Controlling for these variables, triggered religious identity performed as expected among secular and religious respondents (see appendix table A4.2). The results are consistent across a variety of models and with a variety of methods of statistical analysis.

EXPERIMENT 2: EQUALITY LOUISIANA

The degree to which religion is an important and pervasive part of people's lives varies considerably by geographic location. In the American South, in particular, religious attitudes are so much a part of daily life that the region is commonly referred to as the Bible Belt; socially conservative evangelical Protestantism is a pervasive part of the culture. Barton (2012) described the religious-based homophobia faced by gay men and lesbians in the Bible Belt, where they are subject to constant oppression, silencing, and discrimination, and where same-sex attraction is considered "bad, sinful, and disgusting." Barton noted (2012, 13):

While there may be great variation in church norms throughout the Bible Belt . . . most Christian denominations in the Bible Belt, from Baptist to Methodist to Holiness to Catholic to Jehovah's Witness to Mormon to nondenominational, are uniform in their construction of homosexuality as sinful. . . . [T]he vast majority of places one might worship in the Bible Belt are homophobic.

This homophobia is not restricted to places of worship but pervades the culture of the entire region.

This particular brand of Christianity permeates the multiple environments in which residents work, socialize, and worship. Christian crosses, messages, paraphernalia, music, news, and attitudes saturate everyday settings. Bible Belt Christianity thus influences a wide range of local secular institutions like schools and workplaces, and Bible Belt Christians exert a powerful influence on city, county, and state political and cultural institutions. (14)

Further, Barton pointed to nonprofit organizations and Christian right political groups as driving the acceptance of anti-LGBT sentiment:

Homophobic messages from organizations like the AFA [American Family Association] and the FRC [Family Research Council] encourage prejudice, confusion, and fear in the parents and relatives of gay people. . . . This conservative Christian antigay platform trickles down into churches and homes across the country. A large percentage of people in the Bible Belt listen to conservative Christian programming and really do believe that homosexuality is destroying the family. (49)

Our second religious identity priming experiment was designed to test the limits of TDIP. Specifically, in an environment with such pervasive opposition to LGBT people and rights, can priming religious identity and exposing religious individuals to a supportive cue still open minds? Or are religious anti-LGBT messages too strong and pervasive in the Bible Belt to be pushed aside by such a subtle manipulation?

This experiment was conducted in Louisiana, a state where support for LGBT rights lags behind most of the country. In September 2004, 78% of voters approved a state constitutional amendment that banned both same-sex marriage and civil unions. In October 2004, State District Judge William Morvant declared the amendment invalid because it violated state law restricting constitutional amendments to a single legal purpose. On appeal, the Louisiana Supreme Court in January 2005 reinstated the constitutional ban on same-sex marriages (CNN 2012); that ban held until June 2015, when the Supreme Court ruled in *Obergefell v. Hodges*. Mirroring the rapid nationwide shifts in opinion on the issue, support for marriage equality in the state has increased considerably in recent years but has also remained a minority position. In February 2013, only 25% of Louisiana voters supported same-sex marriage; by late 2014, support had increased to 42%, still one of the lowest rates in the country, while 48% were opposed (Piacenza 2015; Public Policy Polling 2013). On May 19, 2015, just two hours after the state legislature killed a bill that would have allowed businesses to discriminate against same-sex couples, then-Governor of Louisiana Bobby Jindal issued an executive order to enforce the intent of the bill. In a statement, Jindal noted that the order would "prevent the state from discriminating against persons or entities with deeply held religious beliefs that marriage is between one man and one woman" (Lane 2015; Lerner 2015).

Given the strength and persistence of public opposition to same-sex marriage in Louisiana, advocacy organizations have pursued equality through legal challenges, focusing their persuasive efforts on other LGBT rights such as support for workplace non-discrimination laws. Two major cities in Louisiana, New Orleans and Shreveport, have local non-discrimination ordinances that ban discrimination based on sexual orientation or gender identity in housing, employment, and public accommodation and facilities. The New Orleans ordinance has been in place since June 1999; Shreveport's since December 2013. Efforts to overrule such local protections at the statewide level have died in committee, reflecting public support: a November 2013 survey found that nine out of 10 Louisiana residents are opposed to discrimination in housing and employment against gay or transgender individuals (McGaughy 2013, 2014b; O'Donoghue 2013).

We conducted a telephone-based survey experiment with Equality Louisiana (EQLA), a group that has worked since 2011 to coordinate statewide efforts in favor of LGBT rights. We purchased a list of Louisiana adults from a commercial vendor, TargetSmart, restricting our pool to individuals who were identified as members of a religious household and for whom we had a recently confirmed telephone number. Undergraduate students made the calls from a calling center at Louisiana State University (LSU) on weekends and evenings from February 4 to 27, 2014.

The experiment included several manipulations to test various hypotheses. First, in order to test for desirability bias, we randomly assigned contacted individuals to hear a script that identified the caller as a student from LSU or as calling from Equality Louisiana. We hypothesized that respondents told that the call originated from the LGBT equality organization would be more likely to say that they supported LGBT rights. Second, we randomly assigned contacted individuals to hear a script that either included a religious prompt or that included an anonymous prompt. We used two versions of each script, either noting the relevant paragraph as originating from 40 community groups or from 40 faith groups (Religious Action Center 2013), designated Script A, or as originating from an anonymous citizen or from Pastor Steve Chalke (Chalke 2013), designated Script B. The exact wording was:

Script A (control/treatment)

Forty **[community/faith]** groups recently signed a letter to members of the US Senate that stated the following: "As a nation, we cannot tolerate arbitrary discrimination against millions of Americans just because of who they are. Lesbian, gay, bisexual and transgender (LGBT) people should be able to earn a living, provide for their families and contribute to our society without fear that who they are or who they love could cost them a job."

Script B (control/treatment)

[*Name*], **[a citizen / Pastor Steve Chalke]** recently wrote an article in **[a national/ *Christianity*]** magazine about his belief that same-sex marriage is consistent with Jesus's teaching. He wrote, "When we refuse to make room for gay people to live in loving, stable relationships, we consign them to lives of loneliness, secrecy, and fear.... Christ-like love calls us to go beyond tolerance to want for the other the same respect, freedom, and equality one wants for oneself."

After hearing one of the previous four paragraphs (either Script A or B, treatment or control), respondents were asked a series of four questions about LGBT rights: whether they supported a non-discrimination law, whether they supported gay and lesbian parenting, their position on same-sex marriage, and how they might vote on a state ballot initiative on same-sex marriage. A total of 381 surveys were completed, including 93–98 in each of the four treatment conditions. Because our initial analysis indicated that respondents did not vary in their answers depending on whether the caller identified as calling from LSU or EQLA, we collapsed those categories for the analysis presented here. This allowed us to retain relatively large cell counts for each of the four script conditions.

As shown in table 4.1, assignment to treatment and control scripts failed consistently to predict support for LGBT rights as measured by our four dependent variables.[7] This null finding persisted in multivariate logistic regression models (not shown) controlling for a variety of other demographic variables. Instead, frequency of attendance at religious services and identity as a born again or evangelical Christian were consistent predictors of attitudes toward LGBT rights.

Table 4.1 Support for LGBT Rights (%), Louisiana Experiment

	Control	Treatment	Percentage-Point Difference (SE)	Chi-Square
Support for marriage equality (N = 263)	24.24% (32/132)	23.66% (31/131)	−0.6 (5.3)	0.0121 Pr = 0.913
Support for hypothetical ballot measure (N = 274)	32.61 (45/138)	30.88 (42/136)	−1.7 (5.6)	0.0942 Pr = 0.759
Support for gay and lesbian parenting (N = 271)	48.91 (67/137)	49.25 (66/134)	0.3 (6.1)	0.0033 Pr = 0.954
Support for ENDA (N = 275)	65.22 (90/138)	67.15 (92/137)	1.9 (5.7)	0.1151 Pr = 0.734

Note: Respondents are adults in Louisiana who are members of religious households. Surveys completed February 4–27, 2014.

The results from this experiment were disappointing but not terribly surprising. Taking our fieldwork to the Bible Belt and focusing on triggering religious identities among religious individuals amounted to stacking the deck against the power of in-group identity priming. In an environment where homophobia is widespread and clearly linked to religious belief, reinforced in daily life by local organizations, it is reasonable that our one-time exposure to a religious cue with a pro-LGBT rights message did not substantially move respondents to be open to supporting those rights. In other words, given the frequency and one-directional nature of religious cues against LGBT rights in Louisiana, our single priming treatment could not overcome the situational factors on the ground in the state. Issues that hew too closely to central facets of one's identity or belief system are more resistant to contradictory cues than are more secondary or tertiary ones. Further, in the context of overwhelming social group norms, one statement or prime is unlikely to generate a large effect; in other words, the treatments were not strong enough to overpower the predominant opposition to marriage equality among people of faith in the South. The treatment primes may have failed to trigger a shared in-group identity, or may not have been plausible.

As the rest of the country moved over the past two decades from opposition to majority support of marriage equality, residents of Louisiana remained firmly opposed. As other state attorneys general were backing away from enforcing local bans on same-sex marriage, responding to advice from the US Attorney General that they are not bound to defend laws they consider discriminatory, Louisiana hired backup: in February 2014, Special Attorney General Kyle Duncan left his position at the Becket Fund for Religious Liberty to take a full-time job defending legal challenges against Louisiana's constitutional amendment banning same-sex marriage (McGaughy 2014a). The null findings from this experiment illustrate the limits of TDIP and the likelihood that the fight for marriage equality (and other LGBT rights) will be harder and longer in environments such as the Bible Belt. This is evident in recent real-world events in the region. In advance of the US Supreme Court's June 2015 ruling on the matter, the Southern Baptist Convention vowed to continue to fight same-sex marriage (Brydum 2015). Officials in Louisiana, along with Texas, Alabama, and Mississippi, all took steps in the days after the Court ruling to delay or resist offering marriage licenses to same-sex couples (Worland 2015).

SUMMARY AND DISCUSSION

Individuals who are more religious are also more likely to believe that their religious beliefs are under attack by gay men and lesbians and that same-sex marriage is inconsistent with God's commandments. In our national experiment, however, we found that priming religious identity with an elite cue of support for marriage equality had a powerful effect on attitudes about marriage equality among religious respondents. While our results cannot confirm long-term attitude change, they do show that public opinion toward a divisive issue like LGBT marriage can be changed in a significant way by priming in-group identity and using identity-salient elite cues.

In a context more hostile to LGBT rights and where religious identity is more salient, as is the case in Louisiana, a single religious prime was insufficient to generate attitudinal shifts. After the historic *Obergefell* decision in June 2015, elected officials in Louisiana were the last to comply and to allow the issuing of same-sex marriage licenses. In a poll conducted by Louisiana State University in February 2016, a full eight months after the ruling, only 41% of Louisiana residents said they supported same-sex marriage, the same proportion as a year earlier, before the Court ruling. Simply put, opposition to marriage equality in Louisiana is and remains strong.

That our Theory of Dissonant Identity Priming worked as hypothesized in the national experiment is evidence of the possibility of in-group primes generating openness to attitudinal change. More denominations and religious leaders are becoming supporters of marriage equality. The likelihood of such a shift in some religious faiths is unlikely to come soon: leaders of the Church of Jesus Christ of Latter Day Saints and the Catholic Church, in particular, are firmly opposed to marriage equality, and Pope Francis's openness towards gay men and lesbians is tempered by continued church teaching that homosexual acts are sinful. Other denominations, however, are moving toward equality. Attitudinal shifts among adherents of those religions are thus likely to continue to follow as more individuals in more religious traditions are motivated to revisit their attitudes about marriage equality and cement their ongoing membership in those salient in-groups.

5 It Does Matter If You're Black or White (or Brown)

Ethnoracial Identity Priming

As noted in chapter 2, public support for same-sex marriage has increased dramatically over the last two decades. Support has not increased equally among all segments of the public, however. Our focus in this chapter is on support among Blacks and Latinos; here there are significant differences in public opinion. In a May 2015 Pew survey, 59% of whites and 56% of Latinos said that they favor marriage equality but only 41% of Blacks agreed (Pew Research Center 2015). These ethnoracial differences persist even when taking into account religious affiliation, religiousness, and age. Whites, Latinos, and Blacks have all become more supportive over time, as shown in figure 5.1. In 2001, only about a third of whites and Blacks supported marriage equality; Pew began tracking support among Latinos in 2006. Support among all three ethnoracial groups was still quite low that year: 35% of whites, 25% of Blacks, and 31% of Latinos. In 2012, a majority of Latinos said that they supported marriage equality; whites followed suit a year later. Support among Blacks is still notably lower, just 42% in the latest surveys (in 2016).

A common refrain in popular and scholarly examinations of Latino political attitudes is the apparent disconnect between their preference for the Democratic Party and their relatively conservative attitudes on public policy issues, particularly on social issues such as abortion and LGBT rights. As a number of scholars have pointed out, this apparent paradox is easily solved if we recognize two realities of Latino politics. First, Latinos tend not to vote based on social issues and second, Latinos are actually not as conservative as some observers have assumed, holding more liberal positions than whites on issues of redistributive policies and provision of public services such as public schools and protecting the environment (Bowler

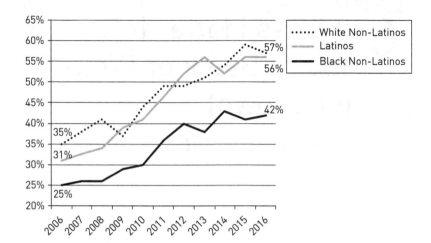

FIGURE 5.1 Support for Marriage Equality, by Race and Ethnicity, 2006–2016. *Source:* Pew Research Center polls, aggregated by year, compiled by the authors. See appendix table A5.1 for additional details.

and Segura 2011; Fraga et al. 2011). Segura (2012, 2) noted: "Latinos are significantly to the left of non-Hispanic whites on virtually every issue of public policy." Despite support for the conservative norm of self-reliance, "Latinos' underlying ideology appears to be solidly progressive" (8).

In this chapter, we examine Black and Latino support for same-sex marriage and the power of in-group identity primes to influence that support as predicted by the Theory of Dissonant Identity Priming. We first turn our attention to Black Americans. We review existing scholarship on the power of in-group priming on Black attitudes and behavior and the history of Black public opinion on marriage equality and various sources of those attitudes. We then describe two randomized experiments we conducted to test the power of identity priming to influence Black support for same-sex marriage. Next, we shift our focus to Latinos, paralleling our discussion of Blacks: we review existing scholarship on the effect of in-group identity priming on Latino Americans and the history of Latino public opinion on marriage equality. We then describe two randomized experiments conducted to test TDIP. Overall, this chapter includes four experiments. Two were conducted with Black populations in 2011 and 2012 in partnership with community organizations in Chicago and Atlanta, and two with Latino populations in 2013 with professional bilingual survey organizations, one with a national sample and one focused on Latinos in the South Texas city of Edinburg.

AFRICAN-AMERICAN ATTITUDE FORMATION AND IDENTITY PRIMING

Placement within the racial social structure of the United States causes most African Americans to identify as part of a broader Black community. The strength of this identity varies and has important individual consequences for political attitude formation and behavior. Dawson (1994) sought to explain why, given the social diversity of the Black population, there is not more diversity in their political attitudes. He found that institutions and networks in the Black community reinforce racial schemas, generating strong feelings of group identity and group political consciousness. Because they live within a racialized environment, they have a racialized view of the world. While African Americans are not monolithic in their political attitudes, they are bunched together on the left of the ideological spectrum and are more united in their political attitudes across class lines than are whites.

Hutchings and Valentino (2004, 392) noted that "racial attitudes, broadly conceived, represent one of the fundamental influences on contemporary mass political attitudes." Scholars have found that racial group identification is more powerful in generating individual Black political attitudes than competing influences such as partisan identification or political ideology (Dawson 1994; Kinder and Sanders 1996; Tate 1993). White (2007) found that explicit racial cues consistently affect Black attitudes on public policy (although implicit racial cues do not, particularly when the policy issue is linked to a marginalized subgroup). Dawson (2001) wrote that African Americans in particular have a strong sense of collective identity that helps explain existing huge racial gulfs in public opinion.

Reflecting existing racial social schemas and the power of Black in-group identity, previous research has found that Blacks are influenced by race-of-interviewer effects. In other words, they give different answers when surveyed by someone who is Black compared to when they are surveyed by someone who is not Black. These effects are most prominent on issues that are race-related or sensitive (but they also exist for more general items such as voting, political knowledge questions, and perceptions of citizens' duties) and they persist even when contact is made via telephone or a video recording (Cotter, Cohen, and Coulter 1982; Davis 1997a, 1997b; Davis and Silver 2003; Davis et al. 2010; Krysan and Couper 2003). Another potential source of Black identity priming is Black elite opinion. Many citizens use elite cues as shortcuts to understanding politics, relying on those they trust and consider more knowledgeable. Kuklinski and Hurley (1994) found that this effect is particularly strong among Blacks.

BLACK SUPPORT FOR MARRIAGE EQUALITY

Black people tend to be much more strongly opposed to same-sex marriage than white people. Various scholars have sought to explain why Blacks are more strongly opposed to marriage equality than are whites, pointing out the apparent inconsistency of a historically oppressed minority group seemingly unwilling to extend equal rights to another oppressed minority group. The lack of Black support for LGBT rights has been attributed to the intensity of their religiosity and religious beliefs (Schulte and Battle 2004; Taylor 1988; Taylor and Chatters 1996), to underlying homophobia (Brandt 1999), and to opposition to the framing of LGBT rights as a civil rights issue (Gates 1999). Even controlling for religion and education, Blacks were still more likely to express negative attitudes toward homosexuality (Egan and Sherrill 2009; Lewis 2003). Craig and Richeson (2014), examining both national surveys and results from a laboratory experiment, found that Blacks and Latinos who perceived discrimination toward their own group were less supportive of gay and lesbian rights. While perceptions of racism increased identification with other racial and ethnic identity groups, it decreased identification with a stigmatized group that is not identified by ethnorace.

In November 2008, Californians voted in favor of both Barack Obama, the Democratic nominee for president, and Proposition 8, an amendment to the state constitution banning same-sex marriage. Obama received 60.9% of the votes cast in the state and 95% of votes cast by African Americans. During an interview on MTV prior to Election Day, Obama stated his opposition to the ballot measure but also reiterated his opposition to marriage equality.

I've stated my opposition to this. I think [Proposition 8 is] unnecessary. I believe marriage is between a man and a woman. I am not in favor of gay marriage. But when you start playing around with constitutions, just to prohibit somebody who cares about another person, it just seems to me that's not what America's about.

On Election Day, Proposition 8 was approved by 52.5% of California voters, and according to National Election Pool estimates was supported by 70% of Black voters. Egan and Sherrill (2009) disputed this figure; their analysis of precinct-level data indicated that 57–59% of Black voters supported Proposition 8. Regardless of which estimate is correct, Black support for Proposition 8 was clearly higher than was white support.

Observers inaccurately blamed increased Black turnout (inspired by Obama's presence on the ballot) for the proposition's success. While such blame was misplaced (see Abrajano 2010), the episode nonetheless reinforced the understanding that African Americans were more opposed to same-sex marriage than other Americans. Not only were Black Californians more likely to support Proposition 8 than were white Californians but Blacks who identified as born-again Christians were twice as likely to oppose marriage equality and to support Proposition 8 as whites with the same religious identity (Abrajano 2010). A post-mortem analysis written for the National Gay and Lesbian Task Force laid the blame for Black support for Proposition 8 on their higher levels of religiosity (Egan and Sherrill 2009). Ghavami and Johnson (2011, 398) noted:

Because the church serves as a guiding principle for many Blacks, its teachings, ideologies, and political positions can carry a significant weight in determining the social and political views of Blacks. Thus, it is reasonable to expect that if the church takes a conservative view on homosexuality and same-sex marriage, so will those who attend such traditional or conservative Black churches.

89

It Does Matter If You're Black or White (or Brown)

Black opposition to marriage equality has also been linked to a backlash effect against the equating of the Gay Rights Movement with the Civil Rights Movement. A 2009 report by the Arcus Foundation suggested that appeals to African Americans using the phrase "equal rights" instead of "civil rights" might be more effective when framing the issue of marriage equality, as using the term "civil rights" might induce Blacks to consider the differences between sexual identity and racial identity rather than the similarities between them (Victoria and Belcher 2009).

The Arcus report also suggested that African Americans do not relate the fight for LGBT rights to the historical fight for racial equality. When asked whether progress on LGBT rights was a logical extension of the Civil Rights Movement, only 23% of respondents agreed, while 53% responded that they did not see such a link. At the same time, 76% of respondents said that they believed that LGBT individuals were discriminated against "a lot" or "somewhat." In sum, while Blacks do not explicitly tie the struggle for racial equality to the fight for LGBT equality, a large majority of Blacks recognize the discrimination suffered by LGBT individuals. In fact, public opinion polls have consistently found that Blacks are more supportive of anti-discrimination laws protecting gay men and lesbians, even as they have been stronger opponents of same-sex marriage (Lewis 2003).

Cohen (1999) argued that individuals in Black communities are pressured to maintain consensus on political issues and to focus on issues related to race; gay sexuality and support for LGBT rights threaten individuals' sense of belonging and identity with the Black community. At the same time, Black members of the LGBT community perceive themselves as facing more disapproval from their families and from other African Americans and feel less supported by LGBT social groups (David and Knight 2008; Jones and Hill 1996; Moore 2010a; Stokes and Peterson 1998). Moore (2010b) noted that the fight for same-sex marriage has often been framed by gay and lesbian activists as "their" civil rights issue, suggesting that the fight is not significant to Black people. In sum, existing literature suggests that Blacks are less likely to support LGBT rights including same-sex marriage as a result of their identity as a member of the Black community and the desire to maintain standing with that identity group. This tendency has been reinforced by messages of exclusion from the predominantly white LGBT community.

On May 9, 2012, President Obama became the first US president to endorse same-sex marriage, stating, "I've just concluded that for me personally it is important for me to go ahead and affirm that I think same-sex couples should be able to get married." The LGBT community hailed the announcement as a victory, and *Newsweek* magazine featured him on the cover with a rainbow halo, dubbing him the first gay president. Observers of Black politics, however, wondered if he would lose support from Black voters in his bid for reelection in 2012 given the community's well-documented opposition. While few believed Black voters would vote for the Republican candidate, Mitt Romney, there was some media speculation that the announcement would dampen their enthusiasm, leading some of them to stay home on Election Day and possibly cause the president to fail to win battleground states such as North Carolina and Virginia (Newport 2012a; Touré 2012).

Rather than reducing their support for Obama, many other Black elite individuals and political institutions followed the president's lead. On May 19, the board of the National Association for the Advancement of Colored People (NAACP) voted 62–2 for a resolution in support of same-sex marriage and Republican Colin Powell, former Chairman of the Joint Chiefs of Staff, endorsed marriage equality on May 23. The chorus of Black voices in support of marriage equality increased daily: African American political leaders, including Jesse Jackson, Al Sharpton, then-Newark Mayor Cory Booker, then-Massachusetts Governor Deval Patrick (at the time, the nation's only Black governor), most of the Congressional Black Caucus, and entertainers 50 Cent, Jay-Z, and Will Smith all publicly announced their support shortly after the president had done so (Thrasher 2012).

Black religious leaders, on the other hand, were more critical. The Coalition of African American Pastors asked President Obama to reconsider, saying Black Christian voters felt betrayed by his endorsement of same-sex marriage. Emmett Burns, a prominent Black minister who said he supported Obama in 2008, held an event at Rising Sun Baptist Church in Baltimore, Maryland, to publicly withdraw support from the president. The Reverend Patrick Wooden, senior pastor of the Upper Room Church of God in Christ, in Raleigh, North Carolina, called the president's announcement "appalling." He commented: "I am going to do all that I can to influence as many people as possible to think for themselves and allow the God of Christianity and the teachings of Christianity to have more influence in their lives than any person who may be holding any political office, even if that office is the presidency of the United States of America" (NPR 2012). One of the dissenters from the NAACP board vote, the Reverend Keith Ratliff, a pastor from Des Moines, Iowa, resigned from the NAACP board in protest (Stanley 2012).

And the Black public? While some Black voters voiced disapproval, the broader effect demonstrated the ability of President Obama to lead African American public opinion. Polls conducted after his announcement found that his overall approval ratings among Blacks did not suffer and that Blacks were increasingly supportive of marriage equality. In Ohio, support for same-sex marriage among Black voters increased from 16% to 42% and opposition decreased from 63% to 35% (Siddiqui 2012). In North Carolina, a poll conducted just before the president's announcement measured Black voter support for same-sex marriage at 44%, while a poll conducted just after the announcement found that number had increased to 55% (Demby 2012). In Maryland, support for same-sex marriage among Blacks shifted from 41% to 59% (Weigel 2012). Rather than punishing the president, Black voters seemed to be changing their minds. And on Election Day, Black turnout surpassed white turnout for the first time in US history, contributing to Obama's 2012 reelection victory. Circumstantial evidence thus strongly suggests that Obama's leadership on the marriage equality issue led to a new openness to same-sex marriage among the Black public. This is consistent with previous research on African American attitude formation and the power of Black group political consciousness and also with our Theory of Dissonant Identity Priming.

THE BLACK IDENTITY PRIMING EXPERIMENTS

In our two randomized experiments focused on Black in-group identity, we investigate how Black opinion on same-sex marriage responds to counter-stereotypical (dissonant) race-of-interviewer cues and elite cues that support same-sex marriage. We primed in-group identity in two ways: through the use of Black callers and through the use of quotations from Black leaders. In 2011, we used a quotation from Coretta Scott King, widow of Martin Luther King, Jr.; in 2012, we used a quotation from President Obama. In 2011, when we were designing the first experiment, few Black leaders were vocal supporters of same-sex marriage. As described below, we used a quotation from Coretta Scott King but it may have been too weak of an elite cue to trigger our desired identity-priming effect. In a January 2011 poll of experts, Coretta Scott King was not rated as an influential Black American leader. Her husband, in contrast, was named the most influential, while President Barack Obama came in second (TheGrio 2011). For the second experiment, we used the stronger cue of President Obama, who by that time had stated his support for marriage equality. As noted above, public opinion polls conducted before and after the president's statement of support strongly suggested that his shift on the issue influenced Black public opinion.

Both experiments tested the power of primed Black identity to influence the willingness of Blacks to voice support for marriage equality. In other words, we expected Blacks to be more likely to voice support for same-sex marriage when primed that other members of their racial in-group were supporters. The experiments asked African Americans whether they supported same-sex marriage, with randomized manipulation of the way in which the question was asked (either with or without a Black elite cue) and of the race of the individuals making the queries (either Black or not Black). In both experiments, we considered both the race-of-interviewer and elite primes to be dissonant, given the widespread opposition to marriage equality among African Americans. As detailed below, the results support our Theory of Dissonant Identity Priming. When respondents were cued that support for marriage equality is consistent with their in-group identity as Black, they were more likely to voice support for marriage equality.

The main dependent measure of interest for each experiment asked respondents, "Can I add you to our list of supporters for marriage equality?" We also asked respondents to donate money and to volunteer for an upcoming event. Both of these higher-cost behaviors resulted in negligible differences between groups, largely because so few individuals agreed to donate either money or time. As a result, we focus solely on the lower-cost behavior of willingness to be added to a list of supporters.

Experiment 1: Equality Illinois

For the first experiment we partnered with Equality Illinois, an LGBT advocacy organization located in Chicago. Equality Illinois has worked since 1991 to secure, protect, and defend equal rights for LGBT people in Illinois. The organization is primarily responsible for building support for a statewide non-discrimination bill (2005), a statewide civil unions bill (2011), and eventually, a marriage equality bill (2013). In April 2011, we purchased a list of contact information for Black adults in Cook County, Illinois (Chicago) from the List Company, a commercial vendor. Calls were made from the Equality Illinois headquarters in Chicago. Interviewers included a mix of longtime Equality Illinois volunteers as well as Black students recruited from local Chicago universities. Calling was conducted on four separate evenings in 2011, April 26, May 26, May 31, and June 20, a schedule chosen to accommodate other commitments by Equality Illinois. A total of 285 conversations were completed.

Blacks on the county list were randomly assigned to either the treatment or control group, clustering at the household level. Contacted individuals heard a nearly identical script with one key difference: the treatment script adds a quotation from Coretta Scott King noting her support for marriage equality, noted in bold below. The script read:

Hi! Is [first name] available? My name is [your name]. I'm a volunteer with Equality Illinois, the statewide organization working to secure and protect rights for individuals of all sexual orientations and identities. On June 1, a new statewide law will allow civil unions. While this is an important step toward equality, civil unions are not the same as marriage. **Coretta Scott King once said that she stood with gay and lesbian people just as they stood with her husband in places like Selma and Montgomery.** We want to keep fighting to ensure marriage equality for all residents of Illinois. We believe that everyone should be allowed to marry, regardless of sexual orientation. [Name], can I add you to our list of supporters for marriage equality?

In the control condition, the script did not include the bolded quotation from Coretta Scott King.

The experimental design randomly assigned respondents *and* randomly assigned interviewers, allowing us to simultaneously test two different approaches to activating a shared in-group identity: through race-of-interviewer effects and elite cue effects.

Interviewers did not at any point during the conversation mention their own racial identity or their own sexual orientation and respondents were never asked if they could identify the race or sexual orientation of the interviewer. Previous research has demonstrated that individuals are able to determine racial identities during telephone conversations with fairly good accuracy (Lass et al. 1979; Lass et al. 1980; Walton and Orlikoff 1994). There is less evidence that individuals can correctly discern the sexual orientation of interviewers by voice cues alone (Gaudio 1994; Smyth, Jacobs, and Roberts 2003). Thus, we expected that respondents would know with relative certainty whether or not they were speaking with a Black interviewer but would not have similar knowledge regarding interviewers' sexual orientation.

Our primary dependent measure of interest asked respondents, "Can I add you to our list of supporters for marriage equality?" Overall, 27.7% of those contacted (79/285) expressed support for same-sex marriage. This percentage was slightly lower than national levels of Black attitudinal support for same-sex marriage at the time, likely reflecting the script request that the respondent "add their name"—a behavior—rather than just report their opinion. There was a difference of 1.5 percentage points when comparing responses to the control script to responses to the King script (28.4% vs. 26.9%), indicating that the addition of a quotation from Coretta Scott King did not alter the willingness of contacted Blacks to express support. Looking only at responses to non-Black interviewers, levels of support garnered were separated by 2.7 percentage points (26.3% vs. 23.5%); for Black interviewers the difference between the two scripts is negligible (0.02 percentage points, 30.67% vs. 30.65%). In sum, we found that the inclusion of the elite cue had no measureable effect.

Race-of-interviewer effects, on the other hand, were larger and more robust (figure 5.2). As expected, we found that Blacks are more likely to indicate that they are supporters of marriage equality when contacted by a Black interviewer than

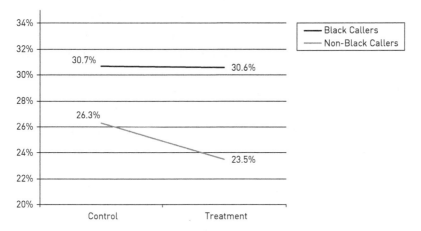

FIGURE 5.2 Black Support for Marriage Equality, Equality Illinois Experiment. *Note:* $N = 285$. Respondents are adult African Americans in Cook County, Illinois. Surveys completed April–June 2011. The dependent variable asked, "[*Name*], can I add you to our list of supporters of marriage equality?" See appendix 2 for question wording and additional results.

when they are contacted by a non-Black interviewer. For the control script there was a 4.4 percentage-point difference when comparing outcomes by race of caller (26.3% vs. 30.7%), with Black interviewers much more likely to obtain verbal statements of support; for the treatment script, the difference was even larger, 7.1 percentage points (23.5% vs. 30.6%). Individuals contacted by Blacks were more likely to agree to add their name to a list of same-sex marriage supporters (see appendix table A5.2 for details).

Caller characteristics varied on dimensions in addition to race including gender, sexual orientation, and age. We were also interested in whether respondents varied in how they responded to this variation, although the results here must be interpreted with caution because these characteristics were not randomly assigned. Of the 13 interviewers, eight were men, five were women; six were straight and seven identified as members of the LGBT community; seven identified as Black and six did not; they ranged in age from 19 to 50. Using multivariate logistic regression, we also tested for effects of these variables. In addition to the strong race-of-interviewer effect, we also found statistically significant coefficient estimates for interviewer gender, age, and sexual orientation. Contacted individuals were more likely to support marriage equality when contacted by a Black caller, a woman, an older caller, or a member of the LGBT community (see appendix table A5.3).

Experiment 2: Georgia Equality

After President Obama's announcement of support for marriage equality on May 9, 2012, we sought an opportunity to again test the Theory of Dissonant Identity Priming with Black respondents. We hypothesized that using the president as an elite cue rather than Coretta Scott King might prove more effective, although we also considered that the widespread attention to the president's endorsement of marriage equality might limit our ability to isolate a control group and to avoid pre-treatment effects. Further, given the publicity around President Obama's statement, we wondered if a presidential cue would be sufficiently dissonant to generate the cognitive speed bump crucial to TDIP. To test the power of race-of-interviewer and elite cues in the wake of Obama's evolved position, we conducted a follow-up experiment in cooperation with Georgia Equality, an LGBT organization headquartered in Atlanta. Georgia Equality has worked for LGBT equality, safety, and opportunity in the state since 1995. This includes work on hate crimes (2000) and anti-bullying legislation (2010), state laws protecting the rights of domestic partners, non-discrimination workplace ordinances, and support of LGBT candidates for elected office.

The design of the experiment was generally identical to that of the Illinois experiment, with one important exception: the quotation from Coretta Scott King was replaced by one from President Obama's May 9 announcement. A list of African American adults in Atlanta was purchased from the same commercial vendor, the

List Company, and randomized, again clustering by household. Calls were made from the organization's headquarters on nine different days and evenings between July 18 and September 13, 2012, using a mix of Black and non-Black interviewers who were regular Georgia Equality volunteers; this fairly lengthy period of data collection was necessary in order to accommodate the organization's schedule.

As in the first experiment, the dependent measure of interest asked respondents, "Can I add you to our list of supporters for marriage equality?" Overall, 32.8% of those contacted (60/183) expressed support for same-sex marriage, a stronger base level of support than in the Equality Illinois experiment and consistent with the pro-marriage equality shifts seen nationally among African Americans after President Obama's endorsement.

Results for the experiment are shown in figure 5.3. Those contacted by Black interviewers were more likely to voice support for same-sex marriage but the difference was small and not statistically significant; the difference for those hearing the control script compared to those hearing the treatment script was much larger, almost 10 percentage points. For non-Black callers, the difference was almost six percentage points (28.1% vs. 34.0%); for Black callers, the difference was over 14 percentage points (27.3% vs. 41.3%) (see appendix table A5.4 for details).

Using multivariate logistic regression, we found statistically significant effects for the Obama script: respondents hearing the Obama cue were more likely to be willing to be added to a list of supporters, as predicted by TDIP. As with the Equality Illinois experiment, we again examined the effect of other interviewer characteristics, although these were not randomly assigned. Of the 18 interviewers, nine were men and nine were women; eight were straight and 10 identified as LGBT; six identified as Black and 12 did not; they ranged in age from 18 to 68. In contrast to the

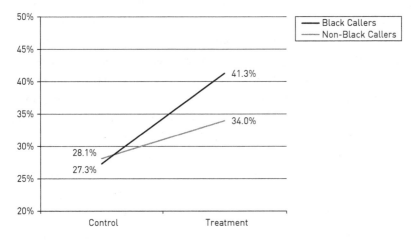

FIGURE 5.3 Black Support for Marriage Equality, Georgia Equality Experiment. *Note:* N = 183. Respondents are adult African Americans in Atlanta, Georgia. Surveys completed July–September 2012. The dependent variable asked, "[*Name*], can I add you to our list of supporters of marriage equality?" See appendix 2 for question wording and additional results.

findings from the Illinois experiment, interviewer age and sexual orientation were not statistically significant but individuals contacted by a male interviewer were more likely to be willing to be added to the list of same-sex marriage supporters (see appendix table A5.5).

African Americans around the country became more supportive of marriage equality after President Obama announced his support. An NAACP Battleground Poll conducted November 1–4, 2012, found that a majority of African American voters in Georgia favored a constitutional right of gay men and lesbians to marry (Jealous, Lee, and Barreto 2012). Exit polls from November 6, 2012 by the Pew Research Center found that 51% of Black voters nationwide supported same-sex marriage while only 41% were opposed, almost double the level of support (26%) from a Pew survey just three years earlier (Connelly 2012). Yet even after these national shifts and considerable media attention to the president's announcement, Blacks in Atlanta were moved by the cue of Obama's support to themselves voice more support for marriage equality.

As noted above, Black support for marriage equality lags behind that of whites and Latinos. These two experiments provide considerable evidence for how to use counter-stereotypical in-group identity priming to increase that support. Another major community of color in the United States, Latinos, is more supportive than is the Black community but close to half of Latinos are still opposed. We turn now to a discussion of Latino attitude formation, Latino attitudes about marriage equality, and our two experiments with Latino populations.

LATINO ATTITUDE FORMATION AND IDENTITY PRIMING

Compared to Blacks, Latinos comprise a much more diverse group in terms of their history, culture, and political attitudes (Beltrán 2010; García Bedolla 2009). While some Latinos have strong in-group attachments to a panethnic Latino identity, others identify more strongly as Americans or as members of their national origin group (e.g., Mexican, Puerto Rican, Salvadoran). The 1990 Latino National Political Survey (LNPS) reported that about one-third of Latinos self-identified using a panethnic term (Latino or Hispanic). In the 2006 Latino National Survey, over 87% of respondents said that they "somewhat" or "strongly" identify with one of those terms (Lavariega Monforti 2014). Feelings of commonality with other Latinos, also known as linked fate, are powerful determinants of Latino attitudes and behaviors, including increased trust in government (Lavariega Monforti and Michelson 2014), increased support for Latino-centric and social welfare policies (Branton, Franco, and Wrinkle 2014), and increased desire for Latino elected representatives (Schildkraut 2013; Wallace 2014). Latinos with strong feelings of Latino identity are more likely to be moved to vote by a message that cues their ethnic identity (Valenzuela and Michelson 2016).

Other scholars have found evidence that Latinos are influenced by in-group elite cues. Wallsten and Nteta (2011) found that Latino attitudes about the degree of commonality between Latinos and African Americans could be influenced by elite cues. Multiple studies have documented the effect of co-ethnic candidates on Latino voter participation and vote choice. Barreto (2007) found that the presence of a Latino candidate on the ballot primes Latino identity, increasing both voter turnout and co-ethnic voting. Jackson (2011), in a set of three laboratory survey experiments priming Latino identity using mock newspaper articles, found some evidence that identity priming can influence reported vote choice. McConnaughy et al. (2010) tested the effect of ethnic priming on support for fictional city council candidates; Latino respondents with strong in-group identities (strong feelings of Latino linked fate) were significantly more likely to prefer a Latino candidate over a white candidate.

LATINO SUPPORT FOR MARRIAGE EQUALITY

Until quite recently, Latino opposition to same-sex marriage was considered rock solid, linked to their overwhelming preference for the Catholic religion. While the Catholic Church still remains firmly opposed to homosexual behavior, however, Latino religious affiliation is becoming more diverse. In 1990, the Latino National Political Survey found that 77.4% of respondents identified as Catholic, and the Latino National Survey of 2006 found that 71.3% of Latinos were Catholic. Reviewing these numbers, Garcia (2012, 21) noted: "The centrality of Catholicism is a major aspect of Latino communities." More recent surveys have found that this centrality is waning: 67% of Latinos identified as Catholic in 2010 but only 55% did so in 2013; these recent surveys have found that Latino Catholics are less likely to be opposed to same-sex marriage than are Latino evangelicals and Mormons (Ellison, Acevedo, and Ramos-Wada 2011; Funk and Martínez 2014).

In 2012, as the Supreme Court prepared to hear arguments in the case of Proposition 8, the constitutional amendment banning same-sex marriage in California, Latino leaders spoke out in support of marriage equality. National Council of La Raza (NCLR) President and CEO Janet Murguía said, "When one group is denied the dignity and the right to marry, it diminishes us all." Similar statements of support came from California Democratic Congressman and Democratic Caucus Chairman Xavier Becerra and then-Los Angeles Mayor Antonio Villaraigosa. During oral argument in *Obergefell v. Hodges* (2015), Justice Sonia Sotomayor, the only Latino on the Supreme Court, asked how barring same-sex couples from marriage could possibly strengthen marriage for opposite-sex couples: "How does withholding marriage from one group—same-sex couples—increase the value [of marriage] to the other group?"

Some activists have suggested that Latino family values underlie increasing support for marriage equality. In August 2014, Lisbeth Melendez-Rivera, director of Latino and Catholic Initiatives for the Human Rights Campaign (an LGBT advocacy organization), noted, "A strong sense of family is the foundation of the Latino community, and marriage provides many LGBT families with the support and security they need to thrive" (HRC 2014). Other studies have also found that Latinos are more supportive of marriage equality when it is tied to the issue of family, for example, stressing that every gay or lesbian individual is a member of someone's family (Nevarez 2015). US Representative Joaquín Castro (D-TX) spoke in March 2015 about support for LGBT rights among Latinos, noting, "They don't give the community enough credit about how accepting and compassionate this community is, with respect to family members. Whatever your sexual orientation is, whatever your station in life is, the Latino community is a very accepting community. Period" (Garcia 2015).

THE LATINO IDENTITY PRIMING EXPERIMENTS

We conducted two randomized field experiments in 2013 to test our Theory of Dissonant Identity Priming on Latino support for marriage equality. The first was a national effort, contracted with Latino Decisions, the country's leading Latino public opinion research firm; the second was conducted in South Texas in cooperation with the University of Texas–Pan American Survey Research Center. Both experiments asked Latinos whether they supported same-sex marriage, with randomized manipulation of the way in which the question was framed (either with or without a Latino elite cue). Respondents could choose to complete the surveys in either English or Spanish. As detailed below, the results provide strong evidence for the power of identity priming when respondents are cued that support for same-sex marriage is an attitude held by elite members of their ethnic community.

Paralleling our experiments with Black respondents, we hypothesized that noting the support of marriage equality by a prominent Latino leader would increase support among Latinos. Given the widespread perception that Latinos are conservative and overwhelmingly Catholic as well as the lack of prominent Latino advocates for LGBT rights, we expected these cues to be perceived as counter-stereotypical and dissonant. In the first experiment we used a quotation from Latina civil rights leader Dolores Huerta; in the second experiment we enhanced the quotation from Huerta to also note support from Supreme Court Justice Sonya Sotomayor and civil rights leader César Chavez. Two main dependent measures of interest were asked, one about support for same-sex marriage (vs. civil unions or no legal recognition for same-sex relationships) and one about how respondents would likely vote on a hypothetical ballot measure to allow same-sex marriage in their state.

Experiment 3: National Latinos and the Dragon Lady

Our first randomized survey experiment was conducted by Latino Decisions, the leading US survey company for Latino public opinion research.[1] The survey was in the field April 10–22, 2013. A total of 800 responses were collected, embedded within a larger Latino Decisions survey that focused on healthcare and President Obama's Affordable Care Act. Respondents to the survey were randomized into treatment and control groups. Those assigned to the treatment group heard the following prompt:

Dolores Huerta, co-founder of the United Farmworkers and a well-known activist on behalf of Latino rights and social justice, is a vocal supporter of marriage equality. She recently wrote, "As a community that has fought and continues to fight against bigotry and discrimination, we understand how dangerous it is to pick and choose who deserves equality and respect. . . . A better country for gays and lesbians is a better country for all. We're all in this together. . . . There are just as many gays and lesbian people in our communities as there are throughout the country. We too have gay and lesbian hermanos y hermanas, friends and children. Their fight is our fight for justice and equality.

Respondents randomly assigned to the control group heard the same quote, but the beginning was made anonymous, reading: "A vocal supporter of marriage equality recently wrote." All individuals were then asked two questions about their own attitudes, including their position on same-sex marriage and how they would vote on a hypothetical state ballot initiative on same-sex marriage.

Prior to launching the survey, we considered the possibility that Dolores Huerta would not be well known to all Latinos in the United States, particularly those outside of her home state of California. However, we were unable to find an appropriate quotation from another, better-known Latino leader. Rather than engage in deception (e.g., fabricating a supportive quotation from a Latino elite), we chose to clearly identify her in the prompt with the words, "co-founder of the United Farm Workers and a well-known activist on behalf of Latino rights and social justice," as noted above in the treatment script. We expected this language to bolster her effectiveness as an elite cue, triggering a shared Latino in-group identity and increasing support for marriage equality.

Overall, 46.5% of respondents said that they supported same-sex marriage while another 23% said that they supported civil unions. For the ballot measure item, 41.5% said that they would definitely vote yes and another 12.4% said that they would probably vote yes. Responses to the two questions were not always consistent but were strongly correlated. Support for marriage equality was no stronger in the treatment group than in the control group. Among those randomly assigned to hear the quotation attributed to Dolores Huerta, 47.1% said that they supported same-sex marriage, as did 45.9% of those randomly assigned to the control group. Similarly, 53.4% of respondents in the treatment group and 54.4% of respondents in the control group said that they would probably or definitely vote yes on a hypothetical ballot measure. These differences are negligible and not statistically significant (see appendix table A5.6 for details).

Revisiting our pre-survey concerns, we wondered if the effect of the elite cue could have been moderated by prior knowledge of Dolores Huerta. Although there is no direct measure of this in the survey, we hypothesized that more acculturated Latinos might be more familiar with her work. Splitting our sample between US-born and foreign-born respondents, we found evidence that this was correct. Among US-born Latino respondents to the survey, only 50% of respondents exposed to the control paragraph voiced support for marriage equality, compared to 60.5% of respondents exposed to the treatment paragraph (figure 5.4). This difference is both substantively large and statistically significant. The difference persists when splitting the sample by language of interview (English or Spanish) (see appendix table A5.6).

Is it true that US-born (more acculturated) Latinos are more likely to be familiar with Dolores Huerta? We tested this hypothesis in August 2013 with a Google Consumer Survey. The survey was limited to Google's "West" region because of Google's concern that the incidence rate for Latinos was too low (12.5%) for a national sample. We asked self-identified Latinos three questions: their nativity, an open-ended question about whom they considered to be the most important Hispanic/Latino leader in the country today, and a closed-ended question asking if they considered Dolores Huerta an important Hispanic/Latino leader. The results confirmed that US-born Latinos were more familiar with Huerta than were foreign-born Latinos (36% vs. 27%, N=209), and that she was not particularly well known overall. Huerta was not mentioned by a single respondent in response to the second, open-ended question; commonly named leaders included Sotomayor, César Chavez, and US Senator Marco Rubio (R-FL). These findings parallel those from a large (N = 5,103) Pew survey from 2013 (Lopez 2013) that asked Latinos, "In your

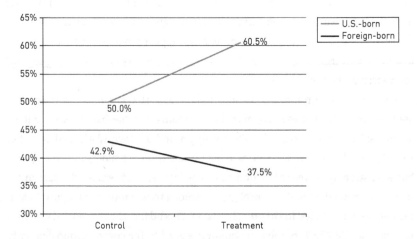

FIGURE 5.4 Latino Support for Marriage Equality, Latino Decisions Experiment, by Nativity.
Note: N = 800. Respondents are a national sample of Latino adults. Surveys were conducted in English and Spanish, April 10–22, 2013. Difference between treatment and control for US-born respondents is statistically significant at $p \leq .05$, one-tailed. See appendix 2 for question wording and additional results.

opinion, who is the most important (Hispanic/Latino) leader in the country today?" Most respondents (62%) said they didn't know, and another 9% said, "No one." The few respondents who did offer a name mentioned Sotomayor, Rubio, then-Los Angeles Mayor Antonio Villaraigosa, and US Congressman Luis Gutiérrez (D-IL).

Given these results, we again searched for supportive quotations. Despite support from Sotomayor from the Court's oral argument in the Proposition 8 case, there was no appropriate quotation available for a survey experiment. And while Chavez was an outspoken supporter of LGBT rights, marriage equality was not a prominent issue during his lifetime and thus we were similarly unable to find a supportive quotation to use in an experiment. Instead, we designed a new elite cue using the same recent statement from Huerta but added references to support from Sotomayor and Chavez. We tested the power of this new cue in a second experiment.

Experiment 4: South Texas Latinos

For this experiment, we contracted with the Survey Research Center at the University of Texas–Pan American, a well-known Latino research firm in the region, for a survey targeting Latino adults in the city of Edinburg, Texas. The elite cue paralleled the one used in the Latino Decisions experiment, but added language at the beginning of the cue to expand the list of leaders:

Hispanic leaders including Supreme Court Justice Sonya Sotomayor and civil rights activists César Chavez and Dolores Huerta . . .

In addition, the term "Latino" was replaced by the term "Hispanic" for the Texas experiment because that is the locally preferred panethnic term. The survey was in the field September 1–26, 2013, with a total of 470 completed surveys. Respondents could choose to complete the interview in either English or Spanish, a measure that roughly correlates with nativity and acculturation, although no data about nativity were collected.

Overall, we found that those hearing the script with the identity primes were more likely to voice support for marriage equality and to say that they would probably or definitely vote yes in favor of a state ballot measure approving same-sex marriage (see appendix table A5.6 for details). The strongest effect for the ethnic prime was among those conducting the survey in English, a statistically significant difference of over 12 percentage points (45.2% vs. 57.3%), as shown in figure 5.5. Given that respondents choosing to conduct the survey in English were more likely to be US-born and more likely to be familiar with the elites named in the script, this provides further support to our conclusion from the Latino Decisions survey that elite cues are more powerful among those for whom the elites are familiar. Additional multivariate analysis shows that, overall, support for marriage equality is stronger among those exposed to the identity prime script and also among individuals who

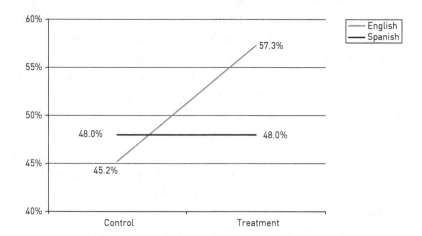

FIGURE 5.5 Latino Support for Marriage Equality, South Texas Latinos Experiment, by Language. *Note: N* = 405. Respondents are a sample of Latino adults from South Texas. Surveys were conducted in English and Spanish, September 1–26, 2013. Difference between treatment and control for English-language respondents is statistically significant at $p \leq .05$, one-tailed. See appendix 2 for question wording and additional results.

are younger, unmarried, Catholic, and who attend church less frequently. Results are slightly different for predicted support of a hypothetical ballot measure allowing for same-sex marriage. Here, support is unaffected by script or language but is also stronger among those who are younger, unmarried, Catholic, and who attend church less frequently, and also among those who identify with the Democratic Party (see appendix tables A5.7 and A5.8).

SUMMARY AND DISCUSSION

Previous studies have noted wide-ranging and powerful race-of-interviewer effects on a variety of policy opinions as well as the ability of elites to influence Black and Latino opinion. These two branches of scholarship led us to hypothesize that using same-race interviewers or ethnoracial in-group elite cues to deliver a counter-stereotypical message about marriage equality would lead Blacks and Latinos to be more likely to express support for marriage equality. Our Theory of Dissonant Identity Priming predicts that such cues will have an effect despite the lack of direct impact of same-sex marriage laws on most members of the in-group. Overall, the results of our two randomized field experiments with Black respondents support our hypotheses. Our experiments with Latino respondents also support the Theory of Dissonant Identity Priming, although to a lesser degree that reflects the weaker elite primes available.

Black interviewers in Illinois were more likely to effectively elicit statements of support for marriage equality because the racial identity of contacted individuals was primed by contact from another member of the in-group. In the wake of President Obama's announcement of support, race-of-interviewer effects faded while using him as an elite cue influenced rates of support for marriage equality. Interviewers in Illinois using the King script were no more effective than those using the control script but those in Georgia using the Obama script were notably more effective than those using the control script, even in the context of a more supportive Black community.

That our first hypothesis related to elite cues was not supported in the first experiment may reflect the reality that many well-known Black leaders at the time were opponents of same-sex marriage, including Black clergy and popular secular Blacks in the entertainment and sports industries, as well as the President of the United States. Thus, given the relative unity of Black elite opinion on the issue, a single prime was likely dismissed by many respondents as out-of-touch with their broader knowledge of Black opinion. This is consistent with how Coretta Scott King's statement was received when she made it in 1998; at the time, she was criticized by other members of the Black Civil Rights Movement for equating gay rights with civil rights. This finding is also consistent with our failure to move attitudes in the Bible Belt state of Louisiana with a single religious elite cue (see chapter 4). In the second experiment the context had changed; the cue of Obama's support for same-sex marriage was dissonant but plausible, generating the desired openness to attitudinal change.

Previous scholarship indicates that race-of-interviewer effects are driven by the desire of respondents to please or impress the interviewer. If Black respondents wanted to please the interviewer in a general opinion poll about marriage equality, particularly in 2011, they would likely express hostility to it given that was the dominant view among Blacks. In our experiments, however, the support of the interviewers is very clear, given their identification with the LGBT advocacy organizations with which we partnered. Thus, individuals contacted by Black interviewers were cued that the "correct" in-group response was support for same-sex marriage. This is evidenced by results from our experiment with Equality Illinois, where Black respondents contacted by Black callers were more likely to voice support for marriage equality. This is also evidenced to a lesser extent by results from our experiment with Georgia Equality, where Black respondents hearing a supportive cue from a well-known Black elite, President Obama, were also more likely to voice support, although here the race of the caller did not affect responses.

It is important to reiterate that respondents were *not* intentionally made aware of interviewers' race or sexual orientation—there was no explicit mention of these identities. As noted above, however, listeners are often able to use verbal cues to correctly identify the race of a caller. Consistent with existing scholarship and with our Theory of Dissonant Identity Priming, these experimental results suggest that the racial identity of interviewers and support from influential leaders can generate attitudinal shifts on controversial issues like same-sex marriage. Evidence from the November 6, 2012 vote in Maryland, where a substantial proportion (46%) of Black voters joined the majority in approving same-sex marriage, suggests such shifts may be long lasting and associated with future behavioral changes.

Latino respondents are also affected by in-group elite primes. We found that US-born Latinos exposed to a dissonant quote from Latino leader Dolores Huerta were more likely to say that they supported marriage equality. Foreign-born Latinos, however, were not affected by the elite cue, likely because they were less familiar with her and thus less likely to have their Latino in-group identity triggered by the script. In other words, only among respondents for whom the cue is activating a shared in-group identity as a Latino is the cue able to open minds to attitude change.

These results are consistent with research on Latino immigrant incorporation and the adoption of panethnic identities. Recent immigrants to the United States tend to identify as members of their national-origin group (e.g., Mexican or Dominican) more strongly than as Latinos or Hispanics. As time in the US increases, Latino immigrants are increasingly likely to adopt a panethnic identity. They are also more likely to speak English. Acculturation brings increased familiarity with US culture, the English language, and US conceptions of racial and ethnic identity. Thus the results from these two experiments are consistent with Latino immigrant acculturation research. US-born respondents in the Latino Decisions experiment and respondents more comfortable speaking in English in the South Texas experiment were more acculturated than their counterparts, and thus more likely not only to be familiar with Dolores Huerta and the history of the Farmworkers Movement but also more likely to hold a panethnic identity as a Latino (Lavariega Monforti 2014).

Attitudes about marriage equality vary significantly among ethnoracial groups in the United States. Over the last two decades, and increasingly over the last few years, whites, Blacks, and Latinos have become more likely to say that they support same-sex marriage. This rapid shift is not solely due to cohort replacement; rather, a significant proportion of individuals are changing their minds. A majority of Latinos now support marriage equality and for a time (2012 and 2013) surpassed whites in their support, confounding those who believe that Latinos are socially conservative. African Americans have become significantly more supportive over the last ten years, although only about four in 10 support marriage equality. Less is known about support for marriage equality among other ethnoracial groups. A 2012 national poll of Asian Americans put support at just 35%, with variation by national origin ranging from a high of 51% among Japanese Americans to a low of 22% among Korean and Vietnamese Americans (Ramakrishnan, Lee, and Yeung 2013). Other surveys, including Pew and Gallup, report opinions only for white, Black, and Latino Americans.

The experiments detailed in this chapter support TDIP and also the idea that some of this shift in support among Latinos and Blacks over time has been in response to elite and in-group cues. In the broader public opinion literature, numerous studies have documented that political elites have more influence over public opinion on issues with which people are less familiar. Scholarship on public opinion in Black and Latino communities also finds elite cue effects but generally limited to issues that are relevant to those communities. Here, we expand those findings to confirm that elite cues can influence Black and Latino public opinion even on issues on which individuals likely feel competent to make their own decisions and which are not considered racial or ethnic issues. Consistent with our Theory of Dissonant Identity Priming, when a counter-stereotypical in-group cue is sufficiently powerful to trigger a shared in-group identity, Black and Latino individuals are more likely to voice opinions that are in line with the received cue.

6 Come Join the Party
The Power of Partisan Elite Cues

Partisanship is a powerful influence, well established as the dominant impact on individual vote choices, issue preferences, and perceptions of party competence (Bartels 2002; Gerber and Huber 2010; Jacoby 1988). Partisan cues can influence individuals to change their evaluation of national leaders or to support or oppose proposed legislation. Just after the successful conclusion of World War II, General Dwight D. Eisenhower, the hero of the European front, was courted by both political parties to run for the presidency in the 1952 election. While earlier polls found him equally well admired among partisans on both sides of the aisle, once he declared his preference for the Republican Party, Americans quickly shifted their opinions to be more in line with their existing partisan identifications (Cotter 1983). Similarly, both major political parties courted Colin Powell, Chairman of the Joint Chiefs of Staff under Republican President George W. Bush, to run for president in the early 1990s; his standing immediately dropped among Democrats—especially African Americans—once he declared his preference for the Republican Party (Daley 1994; Stark 1993). The rapid shifts in public support that followed the partisan reveals of these two military leaders speak to the power of partisan in-group priming to generate attitudinal change.

In this chapter, we explore the effects and limits of priming party identification as a means of opening minds on the issue of marriage equality. After a brief discussion of the current partisan divide on attitudes toward LGBT individuals and rights, we review existing scholarship on partisan cues and effects. We then describe the experiments we conducted to test the power of in-group partisan primes, including a survey experiment in Virginia just prior to the 2013 gubernatorial election;

face-to-face experiments conducted with New Jersey voters entering and exiting the polls in October and November 2013; and an online experiment with a national sample. In those experiments, we tested whether partisan in-group cues can affect attitudes on the issue of marriage equality. Overall, we find that attitudes shift only when the delivered message is particularly unexpected or counter to the partisan stereotype, generating a cognitive speed bump, as predicted by our Theory of Dissonant Identity Priming.

PARTISAN CLEAVAGES ON MARRIAGE EQUALITY

Public opinion polls consistently find majorities of Democrats and Independents support marriage equality while the same is true for only a minority of Republicans. A March 2016 Pew Research Center poll found that Republican support was at just 33% compared to 70% of Democrats and 61% of Independents. Conservative Republicans were much less supportive, with only 24% in favor, compared to 55% of liberal and moderate Republicans. A number of surveys have found that support was stronger among certain subsets of Republicans such as youth and non-Tea Party members of the GOP; support for marriage equality was lowest among Republicans who are evangelical Protestants or who describe themselves as social conservatives (Benenson and Van Lohuizen 2013; Craighill and Clement 2014; Kiley 2014; Pew Research Center 2015, 2016).

The connection between same-sex marriage and partisanship is relatively clear in the public's mind as well. In 2014, the Public Religion Research Institute released a study of attitudes toward same-sex marriage and LGBT rights more generally. Among their most interesting findings was how people perceived the major parties in terms of support for marriage equality. By a significant margin (almost two to one), the Democratic Party was perceived as being friendlier than the Republican Party toward LGBT people: 70% of Americans said that the Democratic Party was friendly toward LGBT people compared to 14% who reported it as unfriendly. (The remaining 16% did not have an opinion or refused to answer.) On the other hand, only 28% of Americans reported that the Republican Party was friendly toward the LGBT community, with 54% believing it was unfriendly (18% did not have an opinion or refused to answer). LGBT Americans were as likely as Americans overall (70%) to say that the Democratic Party was friendly toward LGBT people, compared to 20% who said the party is unfriendly. Only 15% of LGBT individuals thought the Republican Party was friendly toward their community as opposed to 72% who thought the GOP was unfriendly toward LGBT people (Cox, Navarro-Rivera, and Jones 2014).

One prominent split within today's Republican Party is ideological—between those who support the conservative Tea Party movement and those who do not. Benenson and Van Lohuizen (2013) found that 47% of Republicans who opposed the Tea Party supported marriage equality, compared to 34% of Republicans neutral to the Tea Party and 13% of Republicans who supported the Tea Party. The poll also found that among the roughly 50% of Republicans who believed that people are born gay, 64% supported same-sex marriage, 61% said the Constitution provides the right to such unions, and 70% favored allowing gay and lesbian individuals to adopt (Craighill and Clement 2014). In other words, while Republicans and conservatives are generally opposed, there is a non-trivial number of Republicans who are supportive of marriage equality and other LGBT rights.

While opinion and perceptions seem to fall neatly along partisan lines, additional demographic divisions suggest conclusions should not be drawn so easily. A 2015 Pew survey confirmed that age was a significant indicator of support for same-sex marriage among Republicans. "As public support for same-sex marriage continues to grow, the gap between young and old is nowhere more striking than within the Republican coalition" (Pew Research Center 2015). Among Republicans and Republican-leaning Independents under the age of 30, 61% were supportive of marriage equality and just 35% opposed it in contrast with the 27% of support among Republicans and Independent-leaning Republicans over the age of 50. In other words, young Republicans' views were more in line with Democrats than with the majority of their own party. While there was a gap in support for marriage equality between young Democrats compared to older Democrats, even Democrats age 65 or older favor marriage equality by a margin of about two to one.

The relative liberalism of young Republicans on LGBT rights extends beyond marriage: in 2014, 26% of Republicans under the age of 30 believed that more LGBT couples raising children is a good thing, compared to 18% who said it is a bad thing for American society (and 56% who said it doesn't make a difference or they didn't know). In contrast, majorities of every older Republican age group reported that LGBT parenting is a bad thing for our country (Kiley 2014).

Partisanship and Partisan Cue Effects

A large body of scholarship examines the power of partisan identification and the degree to which it is related to individual positions on issues. While some scholars argue that an individual's partisanship represents a running tally of their choice of political party, responding to party and candidate positions (Achen 1992; Downs 1957; Fiorina 1981), others claim that party identification shapes policy preferences—that individuals change their individual policy attitudes to bring them in line with elite-level party positions (Bartels 2002; Green, Palmquist, and Schickler 2004; Layman and Carsey 2002; Miller and Shanks 1996;). In fact, scholars have at times expressed concern that citizens are *too* easily influenced to adopt the policy views of party elites rather than reaching their own conclusions based on objective information about those policies (Cohen 2003; Harrison 2016). Further, some findings have suggested that the individuals most likely to be influenced by party cues are those who are more informed and knowledgeable (Green, Palmquist, and Schickler, chapter 8; Zaller 1992).

Citizens are influenced to adopt the positions of partisan leaders when those positions are presented as consistent with citizens' underlying values (Chong and Druckman 2007a, 2007b; Fenno 1978; Jacobs and Shapiro 2000; Zaller 1992), or even just because those positions are held by politicians that they trust (Bartels 2005; Cohen 2003; Lee 2009). Panel studies have found that elites influence public opinion over time as the public becomes informed of elite policy positions or even as politicians change those positions (Abramowitz 1978; Lenz 2009, 2012; Zaller 1992). Matsubayashi (2013) found that constituents who live in House districts narrowly won by Democratic candidates then become more liberal in their opinions on government spending, government aid to Blacks, and women's equal status in society. Using a variety of panel studies that allowed him to test whether voters are leaders or followers, Lenz (2012, 19) noted that once individuals have chosen to support a candidate, they adopt that candidate's policy views: "At least on policy issues, democracy appears to be inverted: instead of politicians following the will of the people, the people seem to be following the will of politicians."

Cohen argued that individual attitudes towards policies depend "almost exclusively upon the stated position of one's own political party," even among the informed (2003, 808). Summarizing the literature on partisan cues, Bullock noted, "Cues are widely thought to be processed heuristically, but few people are motivated to scrutinize information about policies, and fewer still possess the knowledge that is typically required to evaluate arguments about policies" (2011, 497). Ordinary citizens take cues from partisan elites and extant research has shown that during times of elite polarization, partisanship plays a more prominent role in political attitude formation and decision-making (Levendusky 2009). When partisanship strongly colors the way individuals view the political world, it can create a systematic bias toward existing beliefs and can incentivize adhering to the party cues that are relatively easy to adopt. Individuals have a propensity to seek out attitudinally-congruent information that confirms prior beliefs (confirmation bias); to interpret new information that supports previous opinions as stronger and more effective (prior attitude effect); and to spend more time and energy counter-arguing and dismissing information that is incongruent with previous attitudes, regardless of its factual accuracy (disconfirmation bias) (Bartels 2002; Gelman et al. 2008; Lavine, Johnson, and Steenbergen 2012; Taber and Lodge 2006).

Other scholars claim that party affiliation and identity stem from social identity rather than an orientation toward public policy (e.g., Green, Palmquist, and Schickler 2004; Lupu 2013; Nicholson 2012). As noted in chapter 1, the groundbreaking work by Tajfel and Turner (1979) suggested that people develop their emotional and psychological affinities because of the groups with which they identify as a member, privileging others in the same in-group and being more harshly critical of those in out-groups. Iyengar, Sood, and Lelkes (2012) found that partisans' affect toward the opposing party is not strongly correlated to preferences on policy; political polarization is due more to partisan identity and distaste for the opposing side rather than policy preferences. In general, the social identity perspective holds that when partisans form attitudes on issues with clear stances from their party but additional cross-pressured cues from elites, they are more strongly influenced to remain an in-group member of their political party rather than feel torn about the specific policy being discussed. In the extreme, partisan cues can cause individuals to adopt opinions that are not consistent with their predispositions (Hovland, Janis, and Kelley 1953; Kuklinski and Hurley 1994; Rahn 1993).

Both lines of scholarship thus predict that individuals will adopt issue positions that are consistent with their partisan identification, particularly if they are strong partisans and if the cues from party elites are consistent with partisan stereotypes; less is known about cues from party elites that are *inconsistent* with partisan expectations. Given well-known partisan positions on the issue of marriage equality—generally, Democrats support it while Republicans are opposed—our Theory of Dissonant Identity Priming predicts that partisans exposed to counter-stereotypical but plausible attitudes (e.g., a Republican Party elite endorsing marriage equality) should be particularly likely to be motivated to voice support for same-sex marriage.

Political and policy cues have also been shown to be significant factors in the motivation to process information and in formation of measures of personal relevance. Political scientists have found that political actors and source cues are substantial influences on attitudes toward politics (Arceneaux 2008; Arceneaux and Kolodny 2009; Boudreau 2009; Carmines and Stimson 1989; Kuklinski and Hurley 1994; Lau and Redlawsk 2006; Lupia 1994; Sniderman, Brody, and Tetlock 1991). In particular, existing research has shown that substantive political information such as arguments for and against alternative policy proposals often holds little sway on judgments when partisan cues are present (Cohen 2003; Druckman 2001; Harrison 2016; Lavine et al. 2012).

Goren (2005) found that partisan identification is more enduring and stable than are attitudes. Over time, individual attitudes about equal opportunity, limited government, and moral tolerance were affected by partisanship; effects here are statistically significant albeit modest in size. However, attitudes about traditional family values and "new lifestyles" were not related to partisanship. Given the focus of our research, it is worth noting the specific survey items examined by Goren. Moral tolerance was measured by whether respondents agreed or disagreed with the following two items: (1) "The world is always changing and we should adjust our views of moral behavior to those changes," and (2) "We should be more tolerant of people who choose to live according to their own moral standards, even if they are very different from our own." Belief in traditional family values was measured by whether respondents agreed or disagreed with the following two items: (1) "This country would have many fewer problems if there were more emphasis on traditional family ties," and (2) "The newer lifestyles are contributing to the breakdown of our society."

Examining NES panel data for 1992–1994–1996, both Carsey and Layman (2006) and Goren (2005) found that both partisan identification and issue positions have small but statistically significant reciprocal effects on each other over time but individuals are much more likely to change their attitudes than their partisanship. While Goren examined broader attitudes, Carsey and Layman focused on specific issues such as abortion, government services and spending, and government aid to Blacks, writing, "Even on issues as divisive and emotion-laden as abortion and racial equality, there is evidence of individuals bringing their attitudes into line with their party ties" (2006, 470). These issue position shifts are most likely to occur among individuals who are aware of partisan division on the issue and find the issue to be salient. People change their minds on contentious issues because of partisan identification. In the extreme, partisan cues can short-circuit systemic processing of information about an issue, causing individuals to adopt opinions that are not consistent with their predispositions (Hovland et al. 1953; Kuklinski and Hurley 1994; Rahn 1993). The degree to which this will occur may depend on how an individual processes information: heuristically or systematically (Chaiken & Trope 1999; Petty and Cacioppo 1986).

Conflicting evidence comes from Arceneaux (2008) who found that voters may punish hypothetical candidates whose issue positions are inconsistent with partisan stereotypes, particularly on highly salient issues. Arceneaux (2008) suggested that while most partisan cues are processed heuristically, counter-stereotypical messages (i.e., messages from party elites that are inconsistent with partisan stereotypes) may inspire systematic processing. Arceneaux investigated the effect on voter evaluations of assigning counter-stereotypical views to hypothetical candidates. He found that "as the political awareness of the message recipient and the salience of the issue position increases, individuals are more likely to evaluate negatively candidates affiliated with their political party who depart from the party line" (2008, 150–151).

What we explore in this chapter is whether hearing a cue from a partisan elite causes individuals to alter their policy positions. In other words, given the general stereotype of Democrats as supporters of same-sex marriage and Republicans as opponents, what happens when Republican individuals are exposed to information about either Republican Party support or opposition? In two of the three experiments described in this chapter, participants were primed with in-group and out-group cues from real-world groups and individuals, not hypothetical candidates, using actual quotations and statements of support or opposition to LGBT rights such as marriage equality. To supplement the lack of counter-stereotypical real-world primes on the issue, we also conducted on experiment using a manufactured quotation.

Existing research provides strong support for the theory that partisan elites can shape public opinion. Broockman and Butler (2015) worked in cooperation with eight Democratic legislators in a Midwestern state to test the effect of elite opinion on public opinion: the officials altered the content of their letters to constituents and constituents were subsequently asked about those issues in an ostensibly unrelated telephone survey. Whether the letters sent to constituents merely stated positions on issues or offered supportive arguments, those receiving the letters became more supportive of those policies. Broockman and Butler concluded (2015, 28): "Elites can shape public opinion merely by announcing their positions, without paying prohibitive electoral costs for doing so among those who disagreed with them and even without making appeals to citizens' values."

We posited that partisan statements could be used to cue individuals of the positions of partisans (elite and non-elite) and to make them more likely to agree with issue positions stated by those members of their political party. Previous research on partisan frames has established that elite frames can have a powerful effect on public opinion (see Chong and Druckman 2007). Slothuus and de Vreese (2010) provided experimental evidence to support their theory that partisan frames are particularly powerful on individuals who identify with that party, on individuals who are more politically aware, and particularly on issues on which there is significant partisan conflict. Druckman, Peterson, and Slothuus (2013) found that polarized environments intensify the effect of partisan frames. Individuals are driven to cement their sense of belonging to a party (their partisan identification) through consistency with and loyalty to party opinions, and their motivation to do so is enhanced when the parties are in clear conflict on an issue and when they have a strong partisan attachment. Druckman et al. concluded from their experiments that "partisans in a polarized environment follow their party regardless of the type or strength of the argument the party makes" (2013, 74). Applied to the topic at hand, this suggests that partisans should be strongly influenced by cues from elites of their own party.

All of these existing studies constitute powerful evidence of an overarching truth: individuals are strongly influenced by partisanship, ideology, and elite partisan cues. Existing research also makes clear, however, that partisan cues are generally consistent with partisan stereotypes and that partisans are willing to punish politicians who stray from the party line, particularly on strongly-held culture war issues such as abortion. Constrained by the electoral connection, elected officials and candidates are reasonably reluctant to take counter-stereotypical positions on contentious social issues. As Rubino (2015) noted, "In the political big leagues, candidates of conviction who refuse to moderate their message or refuse to adapt to the prevailing contemporaneous political sentiment, are often abandoned at the altar by the electoral consumer."

What we are interested in here is the power of partisan elite positions to cause shifts among in-group partisans. The experiments described in this chapter tested the power of in-group partisan cues to generate attitudinal shifts on the issue of marriage equality, as predicted by TDIP. We expected these effects to be strongest when the cues were counter-stereotypical (i.e., when a Republican cue was one of support for same-sex marriage). As detailed below, there is sufficient individual-level variation on positions on the issue among Republican candidates and elected officials to allow for these experiments. At the same time, however, we were constrained by the overwhelming perception among the public described at the beginning of this chapter: that Democrats support marriage equality while Republicans are opposed. Thus, the power of dissonant identity primes is likely to be weaker than observed for other in-group cues explored in earlier chapters.

EXPERIMENTAL DESIGNS

We conducted three randomized experiments to test the power of partisan primes to open minds to attitude change on the issue of same-sex marriage. The first was a survey experiment embedded within a survey of likely Virginia voters just prior to that state's gubernatorial election and used only stereotypical cues. The second was conducted face-to-face with voters entering and exiting polling places in New Jersey during the special US Senate election of October 16, 2013 and the regular gubernatorial election just three weeks later. We manipulated the information provided in a paragraph about supporters, noting support for same-sex marriage by various well-known politicians from either the Democratic or Republican Party, randomly manipulating the partisan cue received by each voter. Our third and final partisanship experiment was conducted using Google Consumer Surveys and investigated the power of stereotypical and dissonant partisan cues with a national sample of Republican and Democratic partisans.

Given the power of partisan cues, we hypothesized partisan respondents to be more likely to be moved to say that they support or oppose marriage equality when cued that doing so was consistent with the opinion of party elites. Similar to the religious experiment in Louisiana (see chapter 4), we also hypothesized that because of overwhelming party cues on the issues about LGBT rights, partisan identity might overwhelm informational cues and thus that people would not be particularly movable given prior attitudes and the strong overall effect of partisan identity (see Harrison 2016). Given the well-known positions of the two major political parties on the issue, this means that we were testing a dissonant message when communicating Republican support to Republican individuals. To preview our findings, we found limited evidence that counter-stereotypical partisan cues can motivate increased support for marriage equality. We turn now to the details of our three experiments.

EXPERIMENT 1: VIRGINIA VOTERS

In November 2013, voters in the state of Virginia headed to the polls to elect a new governor and attorney general. Both races were hotly contested. In the governor's race, Democrat Terry McAuliffe edged out Republican Ken Cuccinelli II, 48.0% to 45.5%, in an acidly negative campaign. McAuliffe, former chair of the Democratic

National Committee and a well-known political fundraiser who had never before held elective office, offered a strikingly liberal platform. Many voters said they voted for McAuliffe in order to voice their disapproval of his opponent, Attorney General Cuccinelli, a conservative with hard-line positions on issues such as abortion and same-sex marriage and who ran on an anti-Obamacare platform and with backing from a variety of Tea Party favorites, including US Senator Marco Rubio from Florida and Wisconsin Governor Scott Walker. Some of the state's largest newspapers either refused to endorse anyone or recommended a vote for someone who wasn't even running. Turnout was about 37%, similar to the 36.1% turnout of the previous gubernatorial election in 2009.

Same-sex marriage was not a major campaign issue in 2013 but it was politically relevant in the commonwealth of Virginia. In 2006, Virginia voters approved the Marshall-Newman Amendment to the constitution by a 57%–43% margin, amending the state constitution to ban same-sex marriage. To repeal the amendment, voters would have to approve a referendum approved by two consecutive sessions of the state's legislative body, the General Assembly. On the evening of September 25, 2013 (the first night our survey was in the field), McAuliffe and Cuccinelli participated in a televised debate during which the issue of same-sex marriage was raised, in the context of ongoing legal battles over whether the state's ban violated the US Constitution. Statements by McAuliffe and Cuccinelli at that debate mirrored statements made earlier in the campaign season and included in prior media coverage of the campaign. Thus, it is likely that some attentive voters were aware of the positions of the two candidates, particularly those who had tuned in for one or more of the debates.

We used the candidates' true issue positions in our randomized field experiment. Questions were embedded in a telephone survey of registered Virginia voters that took place September 25–29, 2013, with a total of 1,001 completes. The survey included an equal number of landlines and cellphone numbers ($N = 500$ and $N = 501$, respectively), an equal number of men and women ($N = 498$ and $N = 503$, respectively), with a mean age of 52.36, and all surveys were completed in English. About 11% ($N = 110$) identified themselves as a member of the Tea Party, and about 56% ($N = 559$) were identified as likely voters. Over 70% of respondents ($N = 714$) were white, 16% ($N = 160$) were Black, fewer than 5% ($N = 46$) were Latino, fewer than 3% ($N = 27$) were Asian or Pacific Islander, and four were Native American (remaining respondents declined to provide their ethnoracial identity).

Respondents to the survey were randomly assigned to hear a statement about marriage equality that included cues from either Republican Party leaders or from Democratic Party leaders. Respondents were then asked whether they supported same-sex marriage, civil unions, or no recognition at all. Later in the survey, respondents were asked the traditional set of two questions allowing for their placement on a seven-point partisanship scale. Among the 1,001 respondents, 401 identified as Democrats or Independents leaning toward the

Democratic Party, while 449 identified as Republicans or Independents leaning toward the Republican Party. Our analysis focuses on these 850 partisans and partisan leaners.

We hypothesized that individuals hearing a cue about marriage equality from a party elite of their own party would be more likely to give responses in line with that elite cue while those hearing cues from elites from the opposing party would be more likely to give the opposite response. The scripts read as follows:

Opposition/Republican script

Many political leaders in Virginia oppose same-sex marriage, including Republican Governor Bob McDonnell and Republican Attorney General (and gubernatorial nominee) Ken Cuccinelli. How about you?

Supportive/Democratic script

Many political leaders in Virginia support same-sex marriage, including Democratic Senators Tim Kaine and Mark Warner, and Democratic candidate for governor Terry McAuliffe. How about you?

Overall, the partisan cleavage on the issue in Virginia was stark: 70.1% of Democrats responding to the survey said that they thought the state should recognize the marriages of same-sex couples, compared to just 28.8% of Republicans. Democrats who heard the supportive script with Democratic elite cues were more likely to support marriage equality than were Democrats hearing the opposition script with Republican elite cues, 72% versus 67.5%, but the difference is small and not statistically significant. We did not see a significant change among Republicans regardless of condition, reflecting the opposition to marriage equality among Republican elites (table 6.1).

Attentive readers will note that this experiment did not directly test TDIP. Constrained by the real-world political events unfolding in Virginia and therefore unable to engage in deception, we were limited to stereotypical in-group and out-group cues. Not surprisingly, the lack of dissonant cues generated negligible effects, consistent with our theory.[1]

Table 6.1 Support for Marriage Equality (%), Virginia Partisanship Experiment

	Republican Opposition Cue	Democratic Support Cue	Percentage-Point Difference (SE)	Chi-square
Democrats (N = 449)	67.47% (168/249)	72.00% (144/200)	4.53 (4.38)	1.0735 Pr = 0.300
Republicans (N = 401)	29.95 (59/197)	32.84 (67/204)	2.89 (4.65)	0.3895 Pr = 0.533

Note: Surveys collected September 25–29, 2013. Respondents are registered Virginia voters. See appendix 2 for question wording and additional results.

EXPERIMENT 2: NEW JERSEY VOTERS

We next tested the power of partisan cues in New Jersey. New Jersey voters headed to the polls twice in three weeks in the fall of 2013; faced with the need to conduct a special election to fill a seat in the US Senate and a popular Democratic candidate for that seat (then-mayor of Newark Cory Booker), Republican Governor Chris Christie chose to conduct the Senate special election on Wednesday, October 16, focusing the regular election date of Tuesday, November 5 on his candidacy for reelection. The strategy worked. On October 16, voters in the state handed Booker a solid victory over Republican Steve Lonegan, 55% to 44%, making him the first African American to represent New Jersey in the US Senate. Three weeks later, Christie cruised to victory over Democratic opponent Barbara Buono by a 60.4% to 38.1% margin.

Until just before these elections, both Booker and Christie were outspoken participants in the national debate about marriage equality—Booker as a vocal supporter and Christie as a vocal opponent. However, Christie's position shifted in the weeks in which we were in the field, reflecting ongoing court decisions. In early October 2013, the New Jersey Supreme Court issued a ruling in favor of marriage equality. Christie led the charge to stay the ruling and delay the issuing of marriage licenses to same-sex couples for several weeks, arguing that the impending decision would cause social chaos in the state. On October 10, the New Jersey Supreme Court denied all stays to marriages being performed and ordered the state to allow such marriages as of October 21. At first, Christie tried to fight the decision but when the Court ruled unanimously on October 18 that it would not grant his request to block same-sex marriages while he appealed, the writing was on the wall. As gay and lesbian couples began to wed on Monday, October 21, Christie released a memo noting, "The court has now spoken clearly as to their view of the New Jersey Constitution and, therefore, same-sex marriage is the law. The governor will do his constitutional duty and ensure his administration enforces the law as dictated by the New Jersey Supreme Court." In sum, Christie's opposition was firm during the first phase of this experiment but he shifted to a more neutral position by the second phase. His partisanship, on the other hand, remained unchanged.

Reflecting this on-the-ground political context, for our experiment we used other Republican Party elites who had been less equivocal than the candidates on the ballot. The quotations in the experiment came from elites in both political parties, including statements of support for the freedom to marry from two Republicans, former Vice President Dick Cheney and US Senator Rob Portman of Ohio, and two Democrats, President Barack Obama and former President Bill Clinton.

The experiment was conducted on site at polling places on both election days (October 16 and November 5). We targeted two voting locations: one with a predominantly Republican electorate (Bogota, NJ) and one with a predominantly

Democratic electorate (Hackensack, NJ). A team of local undergraduate student assistants administered the field experiment to voters entering and exiting polling places on each day. Some voters were exposed to the Democratic cues, some to the Republican cues, and some to a neutral cue that did not mention either party, instead attributing the statements in the partisan cues to anonymous politicians and elected officials.

A further manipulation either cued partisanship at the beginning of the survey or only asked a respondent's partisanship after collecting responses to the dependent variables. For those asked to self-identify their partisanship at the beginning of the survey, the student administering the experiment self-identified as a member of the same party, in order to further activate a shared identity and openness to agree with the partisan cue. Thus, this experimental design tests the effect of partisan cues on individuals who had been doubly primed to think about their own identity as a partisan, compared to those who had not. Our dependent variable items asked respondents if they supported marriage equality, how they would vote on a hypothetical ballot measure on marriage equality, their thermometer scale feeling toward gay men and lesbians, and their opinion of gay and lesbian parenting. We also asked respondents their sexual orientation and recorded their gender. Because we were encountering voters at their polling place, we also know that respondents were adult registered (and active) voters.

There were four possible scripts in the experiment, with the partisan identity primes as the key manipulation. At the Republican location, respondents were randomly assigned to (a) the treatment script with a statement of party positions on marriage equality and the informal conversation with the Republican canvasser or (b) an identical control script without partisan attribution and without statement of common party identification from the Republican canvasser. Similarly, at the Democratic location, respondents were randomly assigned to either (c) the treatment script with a statement of party positions on marriage equality and the informal conversation with the Democratic canvasser or (d) an identical control script without partisan attribution and without the statement of common party identification from the Democratic canvasser.

Both treatment scripts opened with a statement indicating that partisan opinions on the issue of marriage equality were in disagreement:

Democrats and Republicans fundamentally disagree on many core American political issues. One of the issues where the two parties disagree is whether gay and lesbian Americans should be able to marry.

Many (**Democrats/Republicans**) have endorsed the freedom to marry, while many (**Republicans/Democrats**) stand in the way of this freedom.

The surveys corresponded with respondent party identification to indicate support among their in-party group and opposition from the opposite party. In the

Democratic and Republican treatment scripts, respondents then heard party elite cues corresponding with their own partisan identity, reading either:

Democratic script

Several prominent Democrats have recently spoken out in favor of the freedom to marry for gay and lesbian couples. For example, Democratic President Barack Obama recently said, "I've just concluded that for me personally it is important for me to go ahead and affirm that I think same-sex couples should be able to get married." Former Democratic President Bill Clinton recently argued that bans on same-sex marriage are "contrary . . . with the principles of a nation that honors freedom, equality, and justice above all."

Republican script

Several prominent Republicans have recently spoken out in favor of the freedom to marry for gay and lesbian couples. For example, former Republican Vice President Dick Cheney once said, "Freedom means freedom for everyone. . . . I think people ought to be free to enter into any kind of union they wish. Any kind of arrangement they wish." Senator Rob Portman, Republican from Ohio, recently said, "I have come to believe that if two people are prepared to make a lifetime commitment to love and care for each other in good times and in bad, the government shouldn't deny them the opportunity to get married."

Again, in the control surveys for both the Republican and Democratic precincts, there was no mention of partisanship in the script and there was no expression of common party identification in the informal conversation with the canvasser. The control surveys utilized the same quotations as the treatment surveys but without attribution. Respondents who declined to self-identify as a partisan were randomly assigned to hear one of the four scripts and their responses are not included in our analysis.

Recall that we conducted two waves of the same exit poll survey experiment, with the first wave on October 16 and the second on November 5, 2013, and that during that short window of time, the issue of marriage equality came to the forefront in New Jersey, along with the Republican governor's shift from active opposition to tacit endorsement. This context is reflected in the results from our field experiment: there was a significant difference in results between the two waves among Republicans who received the partisan identity prime (see figures 6.1 and 6.2). Only about a quarter (27.3%) of Republican respondents in the treatment condition reported being supportive of marriage equality on October 16, compared to well over half (56.7%) on November 5. Balancing this shift was a decrease in support for civil unions, from 63.6% in October to 33.3% in November, while the percentage of Republicans believing there should be no relationship recognition remained relatively unchanged. Among Republicans, hearing a dissonant prime in a context where it was plausible provided a sufficiently powerful in-group cue to shift attitudes.[2] Overall, however, the findings from this experiment are weak.

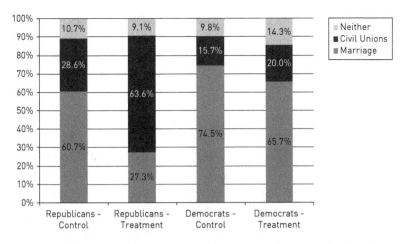

FIGURE 6.1 Republican Support for Marriage Equality, New Jersey Experiment, October 16, 2013. *Note*: N = 86 Democrats, 39 Republicans. Respondents are voters entering and exiting polling places on October 16, 2013. For Republicans, difference between treatment and control for support for civil unions is statistically significant at *p* ≤ .05, two-tailed. See appendix 2 for question wording and additional details.

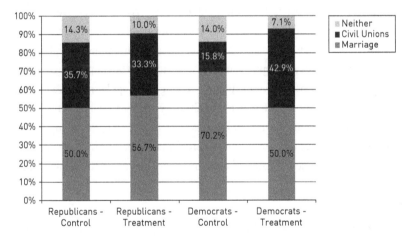

FIGURE 6.2 Republican Support for Marriage Equality, New Jersey Experiment, November 5, 2013. *Note*: N = 71 Democrats, 58 Republicans. Respondents are voters entering and exiting polling places on November 5, 2013. For Democrats, difference between treatment and control for support for civil unions is statistically significant at *p* ≤ .05, two-tailed. See appendix 2 for question wording and additional details.

EXPERIMENT 3: SENIOR PARTY SPOKESMAN

In September 2014, we ran a national Internet-based experiment, again cueing partisan identity, using a photograph and personal appeal from a purported "senior spokesman" from one of the political parties. Similar to the experiment in New Jersey, we tested the power of dissonant and non-dissonant in-group partisan cues on attitudes toward marriage equality among strong partisans, this time using a non-elite cue. To conduct the experiment, we fielded a series of Google Consumer Surveys, filtering to select only strong Republicans and strong Democrats. Respondents were shown the photo and the following prompt:

I'm James Scott, a senior **[Democratic/Republican]** spokesman. Gay marriage is consistent with our party's values and I support it. Do you?

The surveys were designed to randomly expose half of the strong Democrats to a matched prompt (with James Scott identified as a Democrat) and half to a mismatched prompt (with James Scott identified as a Republican); the same was done for the strong Republicans (matched and mismatched partisan cues). The set of surveys was in the field September 27–29, 2014, collecting 804 responses.

The results were consistent with our expectations about the power of partisan cues but only when controlling for other demographic characteristics, as shown in tables 6.2 and 6.3. Reflecting the predominant support for marriage equality among Democrats, there was no significant difference in support among Democrats between the Democratic and Republican prompts (83.7% vs. 83.6%). In other words, hearing one additional partisan cue had little effect on Democratic respondents given that this support was consistent with the predominant party view and with the average Democratic identifier. Among Republicans, however, the more unexpected cue from a Republican elite did make a difference. Respondents shown the photo referring to the spokesman as a Republican were more likely to be supportive of marriage equality than were those shown the photo referring to the spokesman as a Democrat (26.9% vs. 23.8%) and the difference is statistically significant when controlling for other variables. In sum, strong Republicans were moved to be more supportive of marriage equality—an unpopular view among strong Republicans more generally—when exposed to a cue indicating that a senior spokesman for their party was also supportive.

Table 6.2 Support for Marriage Equality (%), Senior Party Spokesman Experiment

	Democratic Prompt	Republican Prompt	Percentage-Point Difference (SE)	Chi-square
Democratic respondents (N = 403)	83.66% (169/202)	83.58% (168/201)	−0.08 (3.70)	0.0005 Pr = 0.982
Republican respondents (N = 403)	23.76 (48/202)	26.87 (54/201)	3.10 (4.34)	0.5133 Pr = 0.474

Note: Data collected online from a national sample of adults using Google Consumer Surveys. Surveys completed September 27–29, 2014. Respondents are adults who identified as strong partisans. See appendix 2 for question wording and additional results.

Table 6.3 Support for Marriage Equality, Senior Party Spokesman Experiment, Logit Models

	Democratic Respondents	Republican Respondents
Matched Partisan Prime	−.282	.429*
	(.317)	(.259)
Income Group	249	.266*
	(.217)	(.148)
Age Group	−.180*	−.239*
	(.099)	(.082)
Female	.202	.450*
	(.317)	(.081)
Urban	.915*	.172
	(.357)	(.272)
Constant	1.477*	−1.147*
	(.704)	(.516)
N	310	316
R-squared	0.0447	0.0445
Chi-square (Pr)	12.28	16.94
	(0.0312)	(0.0046)

Note: Data collected online from a national sample of adults using Google Consumer Surveys. Surveys completed September 27–29, 2014. Respondents are a national sample of adults who identified as strong partisans. Standard errors in parentheses. * = $p \leq .05$, one-tailed. Age Group is a six-category ordinal variable ranging from 1 = 18–24 to 6 = 65+; Income Group is a five-category ordinal variable ranging from 0 = −\$24,000 to 5 = \$100,000–\$149,999. Weighted regressions using weights supplied by Google Consumer Surveys.

SUMMARY AND DISCUSSION

Previous research on partisan priming has established that elite primes can have a powerful effect on public opinion, particularly with strong partisans and on issues on which there is significant partisan conflict. On the issue of marriage equality, the partisan lines are generally drawn quite clearly, with Republicans opposed and Democrats in support, and public knowledge of these party positions is strong. Applying our Theory of Dissonant Identity Priming to the issue, we hypothesized that counter-stereotypical partisan primes might be more effective than stereotypical partisan primes but also considered that the effects of partisan stances on the issue might be too strong for dissonant cues to be accepted by survey respondents.

We tested our hypotheses with three randomized experiments. The first experiment, conducted among registered voters in Virginia just prior to that state's heated gubernatorial election, used stereotypical cues rather than dissonant cues, reflecting the local electoral context. Not surprisingly, the results failed to find any evidence of attitudinal change. Democrats and Republicans exposed to cues of Democratic support or Republican opposition to marriage equality were not moved to change their levels of support for same-sex marriage. While not a test of TDIP, the results are valuable in that they confirm that consonant (i.e., non-dissonant) identity primes are unlikely to be effective.

Next, we conducted a two-part exit poll-based survey experiment in New Jersey, targeting participants in a special US Senate and a regular gubernatorial election held just three weeks apart. In this case, the issue of marriage equality was front-page news just as we were in the field, shifting the degree to which our frames were consistent with local party elite cues between the first and second elections because of shifts on the issue by Governor Chris Christie. As predicted by TDIP, this shifting context caused our primes aimed at Republicans to be seen as more plausible during the second wave, thus increasing their effectiveness.

Both real-world survey experiments priming partisanship were constrained by reality. In Virginia, given attention paid to the issue of same-sex marriage by the gubernatorial candidates, presenting respondents with counter-stereotypical primes about Democratic opposition or Republican support would have been seen as implausible rather than dissonant. In New Jersey, changing conditions during the time we were in the field, personified by Governor Chris Christie's shifting rhetoric on the issue, similarly constrained our ability to manipulate partisan cues. Partisanship is a strong identity and previous scholarship has generated evidence that partisan primes can move public opinion. These experiments, in contrast, illustrate the difficulty of generating plausible dissonant primes on an issue of significant interest and publicity. This constraint might be compared to that of finding an impartial jury in an area where there has been significant pre-trial publicity. Simply put, partisan attitudes on the issue of marriage equality were strongly predetermined in these areas by highly salient electoral politics, partisan elite cues, and judicial decisions.

Finally, moving away from the constraints of real-world politics, we conducted an online experiment with a national sample of self-identified strong Republicans and strong Democrats, exposing them to a randomly manipulated cue from an individual purporting to be a senior party spokesman, either from the same or from the opposite political party but always endorsing marriage equality. Here we found support for our Theory of Dissonant Identity Priming: among Republicans, the counter-stereotypical cue moved attitudes to be more supportive, albeit only when controlling for other variables.

To some extent, the real-world story in New Jersey parallels one from chapter 5, where the evolved position of President Barack Obama had powerful effects on Black public opinion. In New Jersey in October 2013, a poll released on the same day that Governor Christie announced that he was dropping his appeal of the state high court's ruling showed that for the first time a plurality of Republicans favored same-sex marriage (Friedman 2013). The poll, conducted from October 7 to 13, found that

49% of Republicans were in favor of same-sex marriage while 37% were opposed and further that many Republican respondents—35% of those who now said that they supported marriage equality—admitted having changed their mind on the issue. The governor had not yet dropped his appeal while the survey was in the field but those following the issue knew that the New Jersey Supreme Court had spoken. Support was even higher among New Jersey voters in early 2014 (Friedman 2014).

Given the relative low salience of marriage equality to most non-LGBT Americans and the power of partisan framing, there is considerable room for partisan effects on the issue. However, most leaders of the two major political parties in the United States continue to have opposing views on same-sex marriage and LGBT rights more broadly, making counter-stereotypical primes less available. As more Republican candidates and officials become supporters of marriage equality, rank-and-file members of the party will shift their attitudes as well.

7 Conclusion

On the Frontier of Public Opinion and LGBT Rights Research

We had three main goals for this book project: (1) to contribute to the empirical, scientific study of attitudes toward sexual orientation and gender identity and to increase the visibility of this work within mainstream political science; (2) to introduce the powerful methodology of randomized experiments—in the field, via telephone, and with online surveys—to the study of sexual orientation and gender identity; and (3) to apply the concept of pracademics, working with non-academic groups to increase our external validity and to provide scientific data to those organizations that are working on behalf of LGBT rights. We turn now to a brief review of how we have met those goals, and then to the findings from the experiments described in chapters 3–6.

Over the past few decades, support for marriage equality has surged. As recently as 1990, seven out of eight Americans disapproved of same-sex relations but by 2013, numerous polls found majorities of respondents supporting marriage equality. The shift in attitudes on this issue has been remarkably fast compared to other political and social issues. The changes cannot be attributed solely to cohort replacement (generational turnover); many people have changed their minds. Reviewing the shift in attitudes over time, Nate Silver (2015) posited: "Probably one-half to two-thirds of the rise in support for gay marriage has been a result of people changing their minds on the issue." The evidence provided in this book suggests that at least part of that shift is due to individuals finding more and more opinion leaders and peers in their in-groups voicing support.

From President Obama to National Football League Commissioner Roger Goodell, from Republican Senator Rob Portman to Pope Francis, more and more elites are openly shifting their attitudes about LGBT rights, cueing members of the public who consider those elites members of their own in-groups. At the same time, many segments of the public remain strongly opposed, notably evangelical Protestants, social conservatives, seniors, and Republicans. Our findings provide guidance to those hoping to increase support among these communities and for those hoping to shift attitudes on other contentious issues.

Social scientists have long been interested in the origins of and influences on public opinion. Even the most minimal, basic definitions of democracy require that elected officials (elites) respond to citizens' preferences (Dahl 1971; Mansbridge 2003; Pitkin 1967). Schattschneider (1960, 138) highlighted two key aspects of democracy: (a) it should be a competitive political system in which competing leaders and organizations define the alternatives of public policy and (b) the public should be active participants in the decision-making process. As Bartels (2008, 50–51) wrote, "Most liberal democratic theorists . . . assume as a matter of course that citizens do, in fact, have definite preferences and that the primary problem of democracy is to assure that a government will respond appropriately to those preferences." In sum, according to most accounts of normative democratic theory, the public has preferences and those elected to public office should follow them. Disch (2011), however, suggested that while individuals do form coherent, stable preferences, these preferences are largely based on the communication of political elites. In other words, elites may be driving preferences as well.

The shifts in public attitudes toward same-sex marriage reviewed in this book are important not just for what they teach us about how public opinion operates but because those shifts have been and continue to be influential for policymakers. Macro trends in aggregated opinions are usually remarkably stable, with attitudes on issues shifting at a glacial pace (Druckman and Leeper 2012; Page and Shapiro 1992). Attitudes on LGBT rights, however, have shifted much more quickly, as have public policies that directly affect the lives of LGBT people. There are now more Americans that strongly support marriage equality (28%) than are strongly opposed (21%); 10 years ago, strong opponents outnumbered strong supporters by a four-to-one ratio (35% vs. 9%). In other words, public opinion on this issue is anything but static.

At the same time that opinion has changed, public policy has also shifted. In 2003, Massachusetts became the first state to allow same-sex couples to obtain marriage licenses. By June 2015 (just before the Supreme Court decision in *Obergefell*), that right had expanded to 37 states, plus the District of Columbia and the territory of Guam. While many of these states adopted marriage equality through judicial decisions rather than public referenda or legislation passed by elected officials, the import of public opinion was still apparent in the decisions by many of those officials who declined to fight back against the courts.

Events in New Mexico illustrate this dynamic. For years, lawmakers in New Mexico had debated but failed to enact legislation on the issue. In December 2013, a unanimous ruling by the New Mexico Supreme Court made the state the latest to join the ranks of those allowing same-sex marriage (Santos 2013). Republican Governor Susana Martinez, who had in the past stated her opposition to marriage equality, nevertheless declined to support a move to counter the decision with a constitutional amendment, stating, "It's the law of the land. The Supreme Court has spoken" (Terrell 2014). In chapter 6, we told the story of a similar move by New Jersey Republican Governor Chris Christie. In February 2014, US Attorney General Eric H. Holder Jr. announced that state attorneys general were not obligated to defend state same-sex marriage bans if they believed those laws to be discriminatory (Apuzzo 2014). Through 2014 and 2015, as public support continued to climb, state after state embraced marriage equality. By the time the Supreme Court ruled on the issue in June 2015, a majority of the public had already been in favor for more than two years.

In this book, we have outlined a theory of identity and attitude change that helps to explain how and why these shifts are occurring, through what we call the Theory of Dissonant Identity Priming. Our work builds on existing scholarship in political psychology and political communication but with an innovative twist, bringing the science of randomized experiments to bear on the issue of how to generate attitudinal change on contentious issues like same-sex marriage, issues about which individuals often have firmly held beliefs.

We hypothesized that priming a salient shared in-group identity, through outreach from a member of that group or through exposure to quotations from elites in that group, would make individuals more likely to be open to consider the communication and thus be more open to attitude change. When a target is motivated through an activated shared in-group identity to process information, they are more likely to then undergo an attitudinal shift. We further theorized that those in-group primes would be most powerful when they were counter-stereotypical or dissonant, generating a cognitive speed bump for the recipient of the message. Our research differs from previous scholarship on identity priming and public opinion in several ways, most notably by using priming to generate attitudinal change on attitudes not related to the primed identity—for most individuals targeted in our experiments, marriage equality and other LGBT rights are not personally relevant.

We tested our theory with a variety of randomized experiments. In a variety of contexts ranging from California to Georgia, New Jersey to Wisconsin, priming a variety of identities ranging from fans of professional football to partisanship to race, we influenced respondents to be more open to approval of marriage equality. Some identities were more powerful than others: being a fan of professional hockey turned out to be a fairly weak identity in terms of influencing openness to marriage equality while identity as a football fan was more powerful. Race, particularly for African Americans, was a powerful in-group identity, as was religious identity—but not in the Bible Belt (Louisiana). Most of the experiments worked as expected while others (such as the fundraising experiment in Iowa) provided informative surprises or simply did not work at all. Overall, however, the pattern of results supports the Theory of Dissonant Identity Priming under the conditions identified in chapter 1.

Social identity theory tells us that people derive their identity from the groups to which they perceive they belong. In that identity-negotiating process, individuals make comparisons between in-groups and out-groups and they strive to hold attitudes and behave in ways that are consistent with those of other in-group members. This cements their feelings of belonging in those in-groups and leads to feelings of positive self-identity, which increases self-esteem (McClendon 2014; Tajfel 1970, 1982). Tajfel and Turner (1986) suggested that people have an in-built tendency to categorize themselves into one or more in-groups, building a part of their identity on the basis of membership in that group and enforcing boundaries with other groups. The desire to continue to clarify and to reinforce those boundaries through conformity with the attitudes and behaviors of other in-group members is what gives our Theory of Dissonant Identity Priming its power.

Identity theory is rooted in five basic principles: (1) behavior is based on an already classified world; (2) roles and positions within society are among those classifications; (3) positions in society are a key part of identity formation; (4) social positions become incorporated into our sense of identity; and (5) social behavior is heavily incumbent upon the shaping and modifying of these expectations of our positions (Rohall, Milkie, and Lucas 2014). In other words, we form our identities and make behavioral decisions based on social positions and how we see others and ourselves in those positions. Thus, individuals who hear an appeal for same-sex marriage from someone in their in-group or with a prime from an in-group elite are more likely to state that they support same-sex marriage because adopting that attitude reinforces their in-group membership. This mechanism is illustrated in the results from the experiments presented in this book.

LGBT STUDIES IN SOCIAL SCIENCE

While LGBT studies have become more common in political science (see chapter 2), it is far from an established subfield in American politics; in fact, LGBT studies are often seen as outside the purview of political science entirely. We disagree. The themes raised in an investigation of how LGBT rights have progressed in the United States highlight many of the themes common in other topics in American political studies: attitude change, public opinion, political behavior, political communication, minority rights, social identity, framing and priming, power dynamics, and institutional and extra-institutional efforts to enact social change.

It was 30 years after the pivotal, political moments at the riots at the Stonewall Inn in New York City and nearly 20 years after the assassination of Harvey Milk when Timothy E. Cook assessed the status of sexuality and LGBT rights as a meaningful part of American political science. As discussed in chapter 2, he suggested that political science was lagging far behind related fields, with academics from humanities and social science disciplines advancing important questions and finding new trends in sexuality and sexual identity over the last several decades;

in contrast, "political science was notably absent" (Cook 1999, 679). Political science has been slow to investigate sexual orientation, same-sex marriage, and gender identity in a systematic, in-depth way compared to related disciplines like sociology, psychology, history, and gender and sexuality studies. There are a variety of potential explanations for this relatively slow evolution, ranging from political and social conservatives within the discipline discouraging the inclusion of sexuality and gender identity in more traditional studies of politics to a discomfort with addressing such a taboo topic in mainstream journals and conferences. Many political scientists remain skeptical about the legitimacy and scholarly worth of LGBT political science, as reported in a recent discipline-wide survey (Novkov and Barclay 2010). As Gary Mucciaroni noted (2011, 17):

Skeptics of LGBT political studies may also suspect that the study of identity groups is political advocacy masquerading as scholarship, or that identity politics generates passions that induce scholars to color their analyses. The perception that mainly LGBT individuals study LGBT politics may also fuel suspicions of bias. All decisions that we make about what to study are political because they reveal the topics that we consider most legitimate and important to warrant examination. If our decision to study LGBT politics is a political one, so too was our neglect of it for many years.

This persistent skepticism notwithstanding, Cook provided a call to action and in the 15-plus years since his article, there has been significantly more interest in LGBT studies within political science, with Richard Vallely writing in 2012 that that silence had given way to a "buzzing and exceptionally sophisticated conversation" replete with "cutting-edge work" (2012, 316). Research on LGBT rights and politics contributes to topics integral to political science ranging from public opinion and legislative voting behavior to broader questions of social movements, interest groups, power dynamics, and discourse on rights. As noted in chapter 2, much of this work focuses on three main questions: (a) how has the LGBT movement developed and changed over the last several decades; (b) what are predictors of public support for LGBT rights; and (c) how does identifying as LGBT affect political attitudes and behaviors, both collectively and individually?

This book takes a fundamentally different approach. Rather than documenting shifts in public opinion over time and how attitudes vary among different subsets of the US public, we conducted a series of randomized experiments testing the power of primed in-group identities to generate attitudinal change. Results from those experiments in chapters 3–6 support our Theory of Dissonant Identity Priming while also highlighting important limitations and potential for future scholarship.

In chapter 3, we looked at the power of sports fan identity. This included three experiments with football fans, including two conducted via the Internet and one conducted on the sidewalks of Appleton, Wisconsin, as well as a face-to-face experiment conducted with baseball fans in San Francisco and an online experiment with fans of professional hockey. We found that despite the history of homophobia in professional sports, particularly hyper-masculine sports such as football and hockey, football fans prompted with a sports fan identity were more likely to be open to appeals to support LGBT rights when those appeals were framed as consistent with their in-group identity. The experiments with hockey fans and San Francisco Giants fans employed less dissonant (and thus less powerful) cues and did not generate attitudinal shifts. Fans of the San Francisco Giants—residents of the most liberal city in the country (according to *Forbes* magazine, see Forbes 2016)—likely viewed the statements of support from either elite cue as unremarkable. Hockey fans also tended to be more supportive, possibly because of the league's leading role in the pro-LGBT You Can Play project. In both of these contexts, strong underlying levels of support for LGBT rights weaken the effectiveness of the TDIP treatment as hypothesized in chapter 1.

In chapter 4, we explored the power of religious identity. Using a national Internet-based experiment, we found considerable evidence that individuals cued with their religious identity were more likely to voice support for marriage equality. In a follow-up telephone experiment in the Bible Belt state of Louisiana, however, where the cue was embedded in an overwhelmingly oppositional context, priming religious identity did not generate increased support. This represents the polar opposite of the constraint in the San Francisco Giants experiment. Here, opposition to LGBT rights is so strong as to make a dissonant prime not just counter-stereotypical but implausible. In other words, in the face of overwhelming cues from elites and in-group members, the treatment of a single identity prime was unlikely to be successful. While it is difficult based on just a handful of experiments to pinpoint the exact point at which a prime crosses that line from counter-stereotypical to implausible (and thus from effective to ineffective), that such a line exists is both theoretically compelling and consistent with the conclusions of other scholarship regarding affective and behavioral tipping points (Redlawsk, Civettini, and Emmerson 2010; Yin 1998).

In chapter 5, we reviewed our experiments with ethnoracial identity, finding support for the hypothesis that a shared Black or Latino identity moves individuals in those communities to be more open to the idea of marriage equality. This was particularly true when using in-group interviewers (i.e., Black interviewers talking to Black respondents), or using the cue of support from President Barack Obama, whose counter-stereotypical statement of support for same-sex marriage in 2012 had a huge impact on Black public opinion. Black support for marriage equality still lags behind that of white and Latino Americans but a dissonant in-group cue of sufficient strength—that is, from the first Black President of the United States— was powerful enough to generate attitudinal change. Among Latinos, traditionally a heavily Catholic community with less in-group national leadership on the issue, a dissonant cue from a respected in-group source also generated openness to attitude change among those familiar with the source of the elite cue. Showing the limits of our theory, less acculturated Latinos, defined using either nativity or language proficiency, were less likely to be familiar with Dolores Huerta, the in-group elite prime used in our two experiments targeting Latinos, and thus were less likely to respond as predicted by TDIP. More acculturated Latinos, in contrast, responded as predicted. As more Latino leaders become outspoken supporters of same-sex marriage and in-group primes become more numerous and familiar, we expect additional increases in Latino support.

In chapter 6, we explored the power of in-group partisan identity, including experiments with Democrats and Republicans, often embedded in electoral politics. We conducted experiments during three elections in 2013. The first experiment used stereotypical cues in a survey experiment among registered voters in Virginia, just prior to that state's gubernatorial election. We next turned our attention to the 2013 New Jersey senatorial and gubernatorial races, using exit polls and dissonant cues. Finally, we tested our theory with a national sample via an online survey experiment. These experiments were less successful, generating limited support for our theory. Our ability to provide plausible counter-stereotypical frames for these experiments was limited by the real-world political contexts in which the first two experiments were conducted. Results from the national online experiment, in contrast, were more encouraging. Here, Republicans receiving a dissonant cue (support from another Republican) were moved to be more supportive.

Returning to the point made above, plausible dissonant cues are crucial for generating attitudinal change. When cues we provided were not dissonant at all but instead mirrored the partisan rhetoric of the ongoing campaign (in Virginia), attitudes were unaffected. In contrast, in New Jersey, a dissonant prime of Republican support was effective only in the context of the second election, after Republican Governor Chris Christie backed away from his previously-strong opposition and accepted the pro-marriage equality ruling of the state Supreme Court.

Table 7.1 summarizes the results from the 14 experiments detailed in chapters 3–6. Overall, nine found statistically significant effects, most notably in the experiments priming football fan identities and ethnoracial (Black and Latino) identities. Six experiments failed to generate statistically significant effects, usually when the likelihood of finding such effects was decreased by the context (e.g., the supportive environment of San Francisco or the hostile environment of Louisiana) or the lack of appropriately dissonant frames (e.g., in the experiments linked to elections and specific candidates for office in Virginia and New Jersey).

In sum, across a wide variety of contexts and commonly held core identities, the Theory of Dissonant Identity Priming works as hypothesized, opening minds to the issue of marriage equality when the treatment primes a strong in-group identity and especially when the prime is unexpected or surprising. When the prime is excessively surprising, however, such as a religious cue in the Bible Belt, the communication fails, possibly because it is simply too dissonant to be credible.

Table 7.1 Summary of Randomized Experiments from Chapters 3–6

Chapter	Primed Identity	Target Population	Location	Shifted Attitudes
3	NFL fans	Adults	National	Yes
	NFL fans	Adults	National	Yes
	Green Bay Packers fans	Adults	Appleton, WI	Yes
	NHL fans	Adults	National	No
	San Francisco Giants fans	Adults	San Francisco, CA	No
4	Religion	Adults	National	Yes
	Religion	Adults	Louisiana	No
5	Black	Black adults	Cook County, IL	Yes
	Black	Black adults	Atlanta, GA	Yes
	Latino	Latino adults	National	Yes
	Latino	Latino adults	Edinburg, TX	Yes
6	Partisanship	Registered voters	Virginia	No
	Partisanship	Voters	New Jersey	No
	Partisanship	Adults	National	Yes

Further experiments, as always, are needed to flesh out the extent to which dissonant primes can generate attitudinal change and when those primes will be less effective.

Also absent from these studies is any evidence of the permanence of these attitudinal shifts. Respondents were asked their opinions immediately after receiving the prime; we do not know if the observed differences in opinion between those in the treatment and control groups persisted, or for how long. Research by Broockman and Kalla (2016), however, suggested that at least some of the attitudinal shifts we found may be long-lasting. In their experiments with deep canvassing—consisting of 10-minute face-to-face persuasive conversations with voters in South Florida, combined with later online surveys—increased support for non-discrimination laws to protect transgender individuals persisted for at least three months.

In addition to promoting the inclusion of sexual orientation in mainstream political science, the second aim of this book is to introduce new methodological tools to the study of political attitudes and behavior toward LGBT rights. Over the last two decades, randomized experiments have experienced a renaissance in social science. Druckman et al. (2011) noted that this growth stems from the rise of behavioralism and the influence of psychology (increasing demand for experiments) as well as methodological and technological advances that made experiments easier to conduct (increasing supply). They noted (2011, 1):

Experiments facilitate causal inference through the transparency and content of their procedures, most notably the random assignment of observations (a.k.a., subjects or experimental participants) to treatment and control groups. Experiments also guide theoretical development by providing a means for pinpointing the effects of institutional rules, preference configurations, and other contextual factors that might be difficult to assess using other forms of inference. Most of all, experiments guide theory by providing stubborn facts—that is to say, reliable information about cause and effect that inspires and constrains theory.

In this book, we have extended the use of social science experimentation to a new area of inquiry: attitudes on LGBT rights including marriage equality and how those atitudes are linked to individual identities as members of specific groups. This book thus not only strikes new ground in terms of LGBT research but also in terms of experimental political science.

Lastly, we wanted to bridge the gap between academics and practical, on-the-ground politics. Many of the experiments in the book were conducted with LGBT advocacy organizations, including Equality Illinois, Georgia Equality, Equality Maryland, and the Capital City Alliance in Louisiana. This book thus is situated within the growing field of pracademics, wherein academics cooperate with real-world groups and individuals to generate not just increases in knowledge but also real-world impacts (Gillespie and Michelson 2011). In other words, we didn't just conduct experiments of our own design and to answer our own questions, disconnected from practical politics. Instead, we interacted with organizations fighting to change attitudes on marriage equality and other LGBT rights, helping them answer questions that they had about how to succeed in their organizational and policy goals. We also used quotations and real-world events to shape our choices. Our experiment in Illinois, for example, focused on African Americans because at the time (in 2011) significant Black opposition to marriage equality was a barrier to Equality Illinois's advocacy. Our experiment in Maryland (described later in this chapter) addressed a question from an advocacy organization with a different concern: how to maintain engagement with related LGBT community needs after a state has seen advances on marriage equality legislation. We weren't just pointy-headed academics writing a book based on theories and isolated within ivory towers; we were engaging with real-world politics, thus dramatically increasing not just the external validity of our results but also providing a strong counter to critics who have recently claimed that political science is not relevant to current public policy debates (e.g., Kristof 2014). We are appreciative to those organizations who supported our work and agreed to partner with us. As mentioned earlier, we maintained control over the data and our results were not swayed or influenced by the groups with which we worked.

We encourage other social scientists to follow our lead. Reach out to groups in your area of interest and pitch them a proposal for collaboration. Emphasize how the work will both help you better understand the issue and help them in their work. We found that almost every group we approached was an enthusiastic partner; they were happy for the help and were interested in what we might be able to tell them that they could not figure out on their own—such as whether callers should come out as gay or lesbian when asking supporters for financial donations (One Iowa) or whether a message that primes religious identity can shift attitudes in the Bible Belt (Equality Louisiana). Smaller groups, in particular, are less likely to have staff on hand with the sort of experimental research skills that an academic can offer. Pracademics is also extremely valuable for academics, not just because it provides access to information and opportunities for research but because it keeps us grounded in the real world, working to improve the communities and the country in which we live. Many political scientists went into the field because they love politics. Rather than standing on the sidelines as observers, pracademics allows political scientists to be active participants in the arena they love. We hope this book will inspire other pracademics and practitioners to use the methods we describe to help move opinion forward on other important public policy issues, and we believe that they will find these methods a powerful means of doing so.

WHAT'S ON THE LGBT HORIZON?

LGBT rights are about more than marriage; in fact, many LGBT rights activists have criticized those who have fought for marriage equality as a priority, noting the relative importance of issues such as parenting laws, employment non-discrimination, bullying, hate crime legislation, homelessness among LGBT youth, and the rights of transgender and gender non-conforming (TGNC) individuals. That the fight is far from over on these issues and that expansion of marriage equality will not automatically spill over onto other LGBT rights issues is evident from related ongoing political battles. Engel (2016) posited that the federalist system of government in the United States and the diversity of LGBT rights claims means that gay and lesbian people are appropriately understood as *fragmented citizens*, as individuals whose citizenship status varies across space, time, and issue. Ongoing LGBT rights battles reflect that fragmentation.

The fight for LGBT rights also continues to include important and unfinished battles against homophobia and hate crimes. In June 2016, 49 LGBT individuals were murdered at Pulse, a gay nightclub in Orlando, Florida. Hate crimes against LGBT individuals are common, particularly violence against transgender women, LGBT people of color, and LGBT youth (NCAVP 2015). According to the Southern Poverty Law Center, LGBT individuals are more likely than members of any other group to be victimized by violent hate crime (Potok 2011). As LGBT rights advocate Gabe Ortíz wrote in a 2016 *Washington Post* op-ed, "To be gay in 2016 is still in many ways a dangerous and radical act" (Ortíz 2016).

Moscowitz (2013) argued that the focus on marriage and the use of images of gay and lesbian couples as typical middle Americans has pushed some issues (and members of the community) to the margins. Peter Staley, an AIDS and gay rights activist, wrote a column in the *Washington Post* in June 2013 entitled "Gay Marriage Is Great, but How about Some Love for the AIDS Fight." Staley noted:

During the worst years of the AIDS crisis, from 1981 to the advent of effective medications in 1996, the gay community forged a new definition of love: It encompassed traditional romantic love, but it went beyond the love between two people. Often shunned by our biological families, we created our own, complete with brothers and sisters who cared and fought for one another and elders who mentored the young. You only had to be at the 1987 meeting when ACT UP was formed—as the 52-year-old playwright Larry Kramer looked down on a packed hall of people half his age, exhorting us to fight for our lives—to know that we were about to embark on a remarkable journey together.

Today, though, we're so caught up in the giddiness of the marriage-equality movement that we've abandoned the collective fight against HIV and AIDS....

Nearly 6,000 gay men with AIDS die each year in the United States. Moreover, even well-treated HIV demands a lifetime of daily medication. Between that burden and the social stigma that unfortunately accompanies an HIV diagnosis, living with this disease can be difficult.

Yet these community health concerns have been eclipsed by advocacy and fundraising around marriage. The nation's largest gay rights groups do almost no programmatic work on HIV/AIDS. The words "HIV" and "AIDS" don't even appear in the most recent annual reports from the big three: the Human Rights Campaign (HRC), the Gay and Lesbian Alliance Against Defamation (GLAAD) and the National Gay and Lesbian Task Force (NGLTF).

Other activists have voiced similar concerns. Terry Stone of CenterLink, a national coalition of LGBT community centers, once commented that the fight for marriage equality had diverted energy and resources from less marketable causes such as rights for transgender people and HIV and AIDS issues (Crary 2013). Mara Keisling, executive director of the National Center for Transgender Equality, said in July 2013 (Crary 2013):

I am big fan of the work of the LGBT movement, but I'm really cynical about the prioritization within it. I worry about a movement that has so disproportionately prioritized marriage.... It's been a good tool for educating the rest of the public, but that's the problem—it's educating everyone else that marriage is all we care about.

The inclusion (or exclusion) of transgender issues, in particular, within the broader gay and lesbian rights struggle has been an issue of controversy for decades (Mananzala and Spade 2008). The two groups (LGB and T) are often conflated by the broader US public (Valentine 2007). In 2007, however, the last time the Employment Non-Discrimination Act came to a vote in Congress, openly-gay Representative Barney Frank (D-MA) encouraged House Democrats to remove transgender protections from the bill, claiming the change was needed to ensure passage. Frank noted at the time: "There is more resistance to protection for people who are transgender than for people who are gay, lesbian and bisexual. This is not a good fact, but ignoring bad facts is a bad way to get legislation passed" (Holland 2007).

These concerns were echoed by some of the advocacy groups with whom we spoke. In several states, they had won the fight for marriage equality but now found it increasingly difficult to raise funds and enthusiasm from their supporters in order to move forward on other issues. In other states, particularly in the South, overwhelming opposition to same-sex marriage was so strong that local LGBT rights advocates instead hoped to raise interest and activism for other issues, such as non-discrimination policies. In addition to our experiments focused on marriage equality, we also worked with those local groups to conduct pracademic research related to their organizational needs. Note that while these experiments do not test TDIP, they represent extensions of the other goals of this book: to further the use of randomized experiments as a methodology used to increase our understanding of LGBT politics and to engage in research relevant to current public policy debates.

We turn now to a description of two of those experiments. The first, conducted in cooperation with Louisiana's Capitol City Alliance, focused on support for employment non-discrimination legislation; the second, conducted in cooperation with Equality Maryland, explored how to keep members mobilized for other, post-marriage issues given that voters in that state had endorsed marriage equality in 2012.

EXPERIMENT 1: EMPLOYMENT NON-DISCRIMINATION LAWS

One LGBT rights issue on which public opinion has been relatively strong and stable, and yet public policy has stalled, is that of employment non-discrimination. As of June 2016, 21 states and the District of Columbia prohibit employment discrimination based on sexual orientation and 18 states and DC also prohibit employment discrimination based on gender identity. In addition, hundreds of companies have adopted workplace policies prohibiting workplace discrimination, including 484 (96.8%) of the Fortune 500 companies (EqualityForum.com, n.d.). Some major corporations and other employers have adopted non-discrimination policies that include gender identity but protections for transgender individuals are less popular and less widespread than for gay men and lesbians; only about two-thirds of Fortune 500 companies include specific language protecting employees from gender identity-based discrimination.

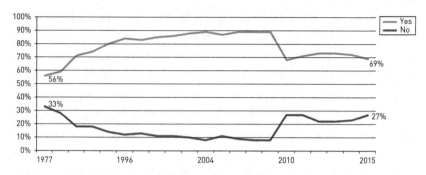

FIGURE 7.1 Support for Employment Non-discrimination Rights, 1977–2015.
Note: Question wording (1977–2010): As you may know, there has been considerable discussion in the news regarding the rights of homosexual men and women. In general, do you think homosexuals should or should not have equal rights in terms of job opportunities?

Question wording (2010–2014): Now, I'd like to get your views on some issues that are being discussed in the country today. All in all, do you strongly favor, favor, oppose, or strongly oppose . . . laws that would protect gay and lesbian people against job discrimination?

Question wording (2015): Would you favor or oppose a federal law that would prohibit discrimination against people who are gay, lesbian, bisexual, or transgender in matters of employment, housing, education, credit, jury selection, federal grants and assistance, and access to public places? This bill prohibits the discrimination on the basis of sexual orientation or gender identity in matters of employment, including the hiring, firing or promoting of employees at all privately run businesses, governments or non-profits. This bill prohibits the discrimination on matters of housing and credit and includes the buying, selling and renting of houses or apartments. This bill prohibits the discrimination on the basis of sexual orientation or gender identity in matters of access to public places, including restaurants, restrooms, gyms, retail outlets and other places open to the general public. This bill grants authority to the Attorney General to enforce this law.

Public support for LGBT employment non-discrimination laws has been strong for decades. Gallup polling on the issue dates back to 1977, when already a majority of respondents (56%) favored workplace equality. As shown in figure 7.1, support quickly spiked upward and has been at or above 80% since 1993. (Note that support shifted dramatically in 2010, reflecting a shift in the question wording used by Gallup; prior to 2010, the question asked about opportunities for LGBT individuals; in 2010, the survey question asked about laws regarding job discrimination.)

A similar trend is found in data from the American National Election Survey (ANES), which has asked a similar question since 1988: "Do you favor or oppose laws to protect homosexuals against job discrimination?" In 1988, 47% of respondents agreed; as with the Gallup Poll, support has since spiked upward. In 2012, the ANES split respondents into two groups, one half hearing the 1988 wording of the questions ("to protect homosexuals") and the other half hearing a newer question: "Do you favor or oppose laws to protect gays and lesbians against job discrimination?" Among those hearing the "gays and lesbians" version, 72% agreed; among those hearing the "homosexuals" version, 74% of respondents agreed. In sum, regardless of the particular wording used, national support for LGBT workplace non-discrimination laws is strong and increasing.

Since 1974, responding to discrimination faced by participants in the Stonewall Riots, members of Congress have considered legislation that would extend such protections to all workers; since 2004, introduced bills have been titled the Employment Non-Discrimination Act (ENDA). However, in no session of Congress has a bill been passed by both chambers, even when strongly endorsed by the president (Obama 2013). A national survey conducted in September 2013 found overwhelming support for ENDA among registered voters, defined as a federal law that protects gay men, lesbians, and transgender Americans from discrimination in the workplace. Overall, 68% of registered voters voiced support for the law, including 56% of Republicans. The same poll found that 53% of respondents supported same-sex marriage, including 34% of Republicans (Haberman 2013). The clear takeaway from these polls is that ENDA is more strongly and more widely supported than same-sex marriage and yet it does not get nearly the same level of interest from opinion leaders or the media. This is reflected in what is perhaps the most surprising finding from the September 2013 survey: that eight out of 10 voters believed it was already a federal law. As Egan noted (2014), disagreement about whether to include gender identity killed the bill when it had its most recent best chance of passage, just after the 2008 elections; control of relevant state governments by Republicans means there is little chance for expanded state-level protections in the near future.

Broad and strong national support for ENDA notwithstanding, advocacy organizations at the state level are still fighting for passage of employment non-discrimination statutes. As we conducted the research for this book, several state-level organizations expressed interest in working with us to learn how best to move public opinion on this issue. This led to a randomized field experiment with Louisiana's Capitol City Alliance (CCA) in November 2013. The experiment was conducted via email messages sent to 23,000 progressives whose contact information was on a list maintained by CCA. Respondents were randomly assigned to receive an email message containing one of the following manipulations of the key paragraph: (1) a traditional paragraph describing CCA with no additional appeal (control); (2) the addition of an appeal referring to respondents as progressives; and (3) the addition of an appeal to fairness and fair treatment of everyone, including LGBT people. Recipients of the email messages were then asked their willingness to (1) add their name to a new email list of progressive LGBT causes, (2) sign a petition supporting employment non-discrimination legislation, (3) donate money to CCA, and (4) vote in favor of a hypothetical statewide ballot initiative on marriage equality.

This experiment is different from those described in chapters 3–6; while it does not test TDIP, it represents an extension of those experiments in that it uses identity-based messaging to motivate attitudes and behavior in favor of LGBT rights. (In addition, as noted above, it pursues the second and third goals of this book: to use experiments to study LGBT rights and to engage in pracademics.) The experimental manipulation tests the power of activating an identity as a progressive against

Table 7.2 Support for Pro-LGBT Actions (%), Louisiana's Capitol City Alliance Experiment

	Control	Progressive	Difference, Progressive vs. Control (SE)	Fairness	Difference, Fairness vs. Control (SE)	Chi-square (Pr)
Willing to be added to new email list (%)	44.3 (50/113)	49.1 (54/110)	4.8 (0.236)	62.3* (66/106)	18.0 (0.004)	7.5500 (0.023)
Willing to support ENDA petition (%)	84.8 (95/112)	89.9 (98/109)	5.1 (0.127)	91.5* (98/106)	6.7 (0.038)	2.6713 (0.263)
Donated to CCA (%)	5.3 (6/113)	5.5 (6/110)	0.2 (0.480)	6.6 (7/106)	1.3 (0.341)	0.1995 (0.905)
Average donation/ contact ($)	1.64	1.23	$-0.41	1.27	$-0.37	–
Will vote yes on hypothetical ballot measure (%)	85.0 (96/113)	87.3 (96/110)	2.3 (0.309)	90.6 (96/106)	5.6 (0.104)	1.5887 (0.452)

Note: N = 329. * = sig. at $p \leq .05$, one-tailed. Surveys completed November 2013. Respondents are pro-gressives from a list maintained by CCA. Respondents who said they would probably or definitely vote yes on the hypothetical ballot measure are coded as supportive. See appendix 2 for scripts and additional details.

another theoretically powerful motivator for pro-LGBT rights behavior, the pursuit of fairness. The hypothesis motivating the experiment was that messages that triggered individual identities as progressives would be more likely to respond affirmatively to opinion questions and requests for behavior that would be considered progressive (i.e., voice support for marriage equality and be willing to sign the petition, join the email list, and donate money).

Most of the 23,000 individuals included in the experiment did not respond but the results from the 329 who did provide useful information about how CCA might move forward most effectively on the issue. As shown in table 7.2, the appeal to fairness was the most successful in encouraging people to engage in supportive behavior. When asked whether they would be willing to be added to a new email list of progressive LGBT causes, respondents in the fairness condition were most likely to say yes (62%) compared to the control condition (45%) and the progressive condition (40%) and the difference between the fairness condition and the control condition is statistically significant. When asked to sign an online petition supporting ENDA legislation, the fairness condition had the highest rate of agreement (over

91%), closely followed by the progressive paragraph (89%), both higher than the control (84%). Again, the differences between responses in the fairness condition and the control condition are statistically significant.

We did not find significant differences in donation frequency or amount between the paragraphs, reflecting the relatively low rates of donation (~5%–6%). We also found interesting differences by treatment condition on the question about a hypothetical ballot initiative. Respondents in the fairness condition were also more likely to say they would vote yes on the measure but the differences here are not statistically significant.

In sum, appeals to progressives' sense of fairness and equal treatment were the most successful in encouraging attitudes and behavior that are supportive of LGBT rights. Contrary to our hypothesis, the results suggested that appealing to folks as progressives was less effective than was appealing to their values. Further experiments are needed to better understand whether and when appeals should focus on shared identities or on shared values.

EXPERIMENT 2: TRANSGENDER EQUALITY

Another LGBT rights issue that has only more recently gained the general public's attention is transgender equality. Transgender individuals are beginning to enter public consciousness—for example, through the stories of Caitlin Jenner and imprisoned whistleblower Chelsea Manning, Laverne Cox and her character Sophia Burset on the Netflix series *Orange Is the New Black,* and through appearances of transgender individuals on popular programs like author Janet Mock on *The Colbert Report* in February 2014 and Jazz Jennings as the star of her 2015 show *I Am Jazz,* which documents her experiences as a transgender young woman. They do not, however, have nearly the visibility (or support) experienced by the gay and lesbian community. Overall, their presence on broadcast television lags far behind that of gay and lesbian characters and when they do appear, they are usually cast as sex workers or pathological killers (GLAAD 2016; Petrow 2016).

The visibility of gay men and lesbians should not be exaggerated—a Pew survey in May 2013 found that 38% of respondents could not name a single gay or lesbian entertainment or public official—but most surveys don't even include transgender individuals in their examinations of public opinion (Pew Research Center 2013). Almost nine out of 10 people in the United States (88%) say they personally know someone who is gay or lesbian and 52% have close family members or friends who are gay or lesbian (Pew 2015). The number of people who say they personally know someone who is transgender is growing rapidly, possibly in response to new focus on the issue of transgender bathroom access rights (which we discuss later in this chapter), but still lags far behind. Surveys in 2008 and late 2013 found that fewer than 10% of respondents personally knew a transgender person; by 2015, that figure had increased to 16% and by mid-2016, more than a third—35%—said that they personally know or work with someone who is transgender (GLAAD 2015; Jones, Cox, and Navarro-Rivera 2014; Miller 2016).

This familiarity matters, as noted in chapter 2. In a 2005 survey, Norton and Hayek (2013) found that individuals who had personal contact with sexual minorities had more favorable attitudes toward transgender people. Using 2011 survey data, Flores (2015) found that individuals who report being more informed about transgender people have more supportive attitudes. In addition, both studies found that individuals who report knowing someone who is gay or lesbian are also more supportive of transgender people, suggesting that positive attitudes are transferable from the former group to the latter.

Other data document the acute need for more protections for transgender individuals. According to the 2011 National Transgender Discrimination Survey, which surveyed 6,450 transgender and gender non-conforming individuals, transgender and gender non-conforming individuals face discrimination at every turn: at home, school, and work, at doctor's offices and at the hands of landlords and police officers (Grant et al. 2011). This discrimination was much more likely for people of color, especially African American transgender individuals. Transgender individuals are also much more likely than the general population to live in extreme poverty and 41% of respondents reported attempting suicide (compared to just 1.6% of the general population), with rates even higher among those who had been bullied at school, had been fired because of bias, or who were victims of physical or sexual assault.

Transgender individuals are also more likely to be homeless but are often denied access to shelter or experience harassment and even sexual assault by shelter staff and residents. They are often refused medical care or are harassed in doctors' offices or hospitals. They are regularly mistreated by police and sexually assaulted by officers. Their difficulty in obtaining documents that match their name and gender leads to difficulties in accessing employment, housing, healthcare, and travel. As gay men and lesbians are gaining acceptance, transgender individuals continue to be marginalized.

Some progress on transgender issues is being made. In 2010, the federal government extended non-discrimination laws to include transgender civilians. In June 2013, the Social Security Administration announced a new policy to make it easier for transgender people to change the gender designation on their Social Security records and thus to have their updated sex listed on their Medicare cards—a crucial victory for transgender older Americans. The year 2013 brought other important transgender victories, including protections for transgender students in several states and laws in others making it easier for individuals to legally change their names and update their birth certificates (Keisling 2013). In July 2015, California became the first state in the country to allow transgender individuals to have their preferred gender identity listed on their death certificate (Dembowsky 2015).

A zenith of support came in May 2016, when US Attorney General Loretta Lynch powerfully spoke out in favor of transgender rights, comparing their struggle to the struggle for Black civil rights and bringing some transgender activists to tears (Phillips 2016). Announcing that the Justice Department was countersuing North Carolina to stop its discriminatory bathroom law from going into effect, Lynch said:

This action is about a great deal more than just bathrooms. This is about the dignity and respect we accord our fellow citizens and the laws that we, as a people and as a country, have enacted to protect them—indeed, to protect all of us. And it's about the founding ideals that have led this country—haltingly but inexorably—in the direction of fairness, inclusion and equality for all Americans.

Following additional remarks directed at the people of North Carolina, Lynch then addressed the transgender community:

Let me also speak directly to the transgender community itself. Some of you have lived freely for decades. Others of you are still wondering how you can possibly live the lives you were born to lead. But no matter how isolated or scared you may feel today, the Department of Justice and the entire Obama Administration wants you to know that we see you; we stand with you; and we will do everything we can to protect you going forward. Please know that history is on your side. This country was founded on a promise of equal rights for all, and we have always managed to move closer to that promise, little by little, one day at a time. It may not be easy—but we'll get there together.

This support from the Obama administration is consistent with public support for transgender rights. A 2011 survey conducted by the Public Religion Research Institute found that most Americans understand what the term *transgender* means and favor transgender rights and legal protections: 69% of respondents were able to give what would be considered a correct definition of the term (Jones, Cox, and Navarro-Rivera 2014). Strong majorities (89% of respondents) agreed that "transgender people deserve the same rights and protections as other Americans" and 81% agreed that "legal protections that apply to gay and lesbian people should also apply to transgender people." Slightly weaker but still majority support for transgender protections was found in a poll conducted for the *National Journal* in December 2013. Among respondents to this survey, 66% of Americans supported ENDA to protect workers on the basis of sexual orientation, while 56% also supported protections for transgender workers (Roarty 2013).

In 2015, the issue of transgender access to bathrooms that correspond to their gender identity burst onto the national scene, culminating in the lawsuit filed by the US Department of Justice noted above. Later in this chapter, we return to the issue of bathroom access rights and the future of LGBT rights more broadly. Well before this issue commanded the nation's attention, LGBT advocacy organizations in some states, especially where the fight for marriage equality had already been won, worked for years to build support for transgender protection. Maryland is one of those states.

In November 2012, Maryland voters approved a ballot initiative in favor of marriage equality, one of three states to do so on the same day (along with Maine and Washington). These states were the first to attain marriage equality through a popular referendum rather than a court battle. It was a historic achievement, marking a decisive shift in public attitudes in the wake of the previous 33 times marriage equality had gone to the polls, losing all 33 times. Organizers at Equality Maryland, an LGBT rights organization that has been working since 1988 for equal rights for all Marylanders, was part of the coalition of groups that worked in the state on the successful 2012 ballot measure. It has also lobbied for many years for local anti-discrimination laws to include transgender protections. In the wake of the November 2012 victory, local LGBT advocacy organizations such as Equality Maryland found themselves faced with the problem of how to keep their supporters motivated to stay active and continue to fight for other issues. In particular, they hoped to keep the momentum going to bring new enthusiasm and attention to their ongoing work for transgender rights. We designed and conducted a randomized field experiment with Equality Maryland to explore this question.

The experiment was conducted in June 2013 via email messages sent to 18,000 previous Equality Maryland supporters. Individuals were randomly assigned to receive one of three versions of the email: a general statement; one appealing to respondents as progressives; or one appealing to respondents as previous supporters. As with the experiment discussed earlier in this chapter, this experiment does not test TDIP directly but represents an extension of our work, including a cue meant to trigger a shared identity as a progressive as well as a cue meant to trigger a shared identity as a supporter of Equality Maryland.

We measured three outcomes of exposure to these paragraphs: willingness to be added to a list of supporters for new issues in Maryland; willingness to sign a petition to encourage Maryland's Democratic Governor Martin O'Malley to support a transgender equality bill; and willingness to donate money to Equality Maryland. We received responses from 525 individuals, including 308 who identified as members of the LGBT community.

As shown in table 7.3, the email script sent to previous Maryland Equality supporters had significant and notable effects on respondents' willingness to agree to the various asks. The "previous supporter" treatment condition was the most successful overall, generating the highest yield of individuals willing to be added to a new email list and to sign a petition in support of a transgender rights bill but only in the first case were the differences statistically significant. It was also the most effective in terms of fundraising, garnering an average of $3.40 for each contact, but this difference is not statistically significant.

Table 7.3 Support for Pro-LGBT Actions (%), Equality Maryland Experiment

	Control Message	Progressive Message	Difference, Progressive vs. Control (SE)	Previous Supporter Message	Difference, Previous Supporter vs. Control (SE)	Chi-square (Pr)
Willing to be added to new email list (%)	58.7 (105/179)	53.7 (95/177)	−5.0 (0.171)	67.5* (115/169)	8.8. (0.045)	6.9823* (0.030)
Willing to sign transgender bill petition (%)	83.1 (148/178)	82.8 (144/174)	−0.3 (0.460)	87.0 (147/169)	4.2 (0.159)	1.4067 (0.495)
Donated to Equality Maryland (%)	7.8 (14/179)	11.3 (20/177)	3.5 (0.131)	11.2 (19/169)	3.4 (0.138)	1.5478 (0.461)
Average donation/ contact ($)	$2.74	$2.94	.20	$3.40	.66	–

Note: $N = 525$. * = sig. at $p \leq .05$, one-tailed. Surveys completed June 2013. Respondents are previous Equality Maryland supporters. See appendix 2 for scripts and additional details.

The finding is consistent with previous fundraising research and also with the theories of in-group identity reviewed in this book. When previous supporters of Maryland Equality were reminded that they had previously supported the group, it activated their in-group identity as a member of the group "people who support Maryland Equality." Activated to think of themselves as a member of that group, they were then more likely to take actions and donate financially—actions that a member of such a group would be expected to take.

In addition, respondents were asked which of six LGBT issues in Maryland they thought were important. The issues offered were generally seen as equally important, with 20% of respondents choosing LGBT teen suicide and bullying as the most important issue, followed by hate crimes legislation (18%) and parenting laws (16%). The other issues were employment non-discrimination (15%), healthcare for LGBT individuals (14%), and transgender equality (14%). There was no clear frontrunner to follow up on the success of the state's marriage equality movement but it was also very clear that much work remained to be done on a variety of LGBT rights issues.

The past two decades have seen massive progress on LGBT rights in general and marriage equality in particular. Public opinion has shifted from majority opposition to comfortable majority support and all Americans now have the legal right to marry a partner of the same sex. Significant challenges beyond marriage remain, however, and pockets of resistance to marriage equality persist in some areas of the country and among some demographic groups.

Tempering the June 2015 celebrations of the Supreme Court's ruling in favor of marriage equality was the recognition by many advocates that a gay man or lesbian could get married on Sunday and then on Monday be fired, evicted from housing, or denied credit or service for their sexual orientation (McBride 2015). The lead plaintiff in the 2015 case, Jim Obergefell, noted just days after the decision, "In many states, including my home state of Ohio and right here in Texas, you can get married but then suffer consequences. You can get married and then lose your job, lose your home and so much more because we are not guaranteed non-discrimination protections. . . . Friday's historic ruling is a victory, but it's just the beginning" (Ura 2015).

In some states, particularly those where local officials resisted extending same-sex marriage rights even when told to do so by the US Supreme Court (Texas, Louisiana, Alabama, and Mississippi), opposition to other LGBT rights is stronger and more deeply rooted. Some hint of this can be seen in resistance to the processing of spousal benefits for gay and lesbian members of the military. When the Defense of Marriage Act was declared unconstitutional in June 2013 in *Windsor* (see chapter 2), Defense Secretary Chuck Hagel ordered all branches of the military to extend federal marriage benefits to gay and lesbian spouses of members of the armed services. Six states—Georgia, Louisiana, Mississippi, Oklahoma, Texas, and West Virginia—refused to comply, citing conflict with state bans on same-sex marriage (Oppel 2013). Iowa began offering marriage licenses to same-sex couples in 2009 as the result of a decision by the state Supreme Court. A year later, three of the justices on that court lost their seats as a result, the first time an Iowa Supreme Court justice had not been retained since the retention system was adopted in 1962 (Schulte 2010).

As noted above, local officials in several states responded to the Supreme Court's June 2015 ruling with resistance rather than acceptance. Similar opposition has followed previous court rulings. Marriage equality came to Utah in December 2013 when a US district court judge threw out the marriage equality ban amendment to the state's constitution. Hundreds of same-sex couples rushed to marry, but the decision was quickly stayed awaiting appeal. Meanwhile, Utah Attorney General Sean D. Reyes issued a memo in early 2014 urging judges to reject adoption applications from same-sex couples until the issue of same-sex marriage was resolved. Under Utah state law and elsewhere, couples must be married in order to adopt. In other words, Utah officials worked not only to resist marriage rights but adoption rights as well. In the wake of the June 2015 Court decision, even as advocates celebrated the right to marry, concerns remained over adoption and other parenting issues, among others, and it was not clear how quickly those issues might be resolved.

Some Republican governors have reacted to pro-marriage equality court rulings with relative indifference, confirming their opposition to same-sex marriage but realizing the futility of continuing the fight. For example, in February 2014, when the Ninth Circuit Court of Appeals ruled that Nevada's ban on same-sex marriage was unconstitutional, Nevada's Republican governor, Brian Sandoval, agreed to withdraw from the case, saying the ban could not be legally defended. Governor Chris Christie (R-NJ) remained staunchly opposed to same-sex marriage for years, vetoing a bill approved by the New Jersey Legislature in 2012 to legalize the practice. When a trial-level judge ruled in October 2013 that the state must allow same-sex couples to wed, Christie appealed that ruling to the state Supreme Court. He eventually abandoned his appeals because the state "would have little chance of overturning them," not because his issue preferences changed. Finally, New Mexico's Republican Governor Susana Martinez was a longtime, vocal supporter of a statewide referendum to ban same-sex marriage. After the *Obergefell* ruling, she said, "I think what I said before [in opposition] was that yes, the people should have decided on it, but the Supreme Court has decided and it's now the law of the land."

Opposition continued as this book went to press, more than a year after the *Obergefell* ruling. In May 2016, the US House of Representatives passed a defense bill that would allow government contractors to discriminate against LGBT workers on religious grounds, overturning an executive order issued by President Obama in 2014 (and prompting a veto threat from the president). In March 2016, North Carolina Republicans called a special session of the legislature to pass House Bill 2, which, among other things, eliminated anti-discrimination protections for the LGBT community and legislated that in government buildings, individuals may only use restrooms and changing facilities that correspond to the sex on their birth certificate. In April 2016, Mississippi lawmakers approved legislation allowing individuals and institutions with religious objections to deny services to gay couples if doing so would violate their religious beliefs on marriage and gender, while Tennessee lawmakers approved a law making it legal for counselors to reject patients who they feel violate their "sincerely held principles," interpreted as giving counselors the ability to reject LGBT patients because of their sexual orientation and/or gender identity. Similar "religious exemption" bills were being considered in a number of states in 2016, generally in the South.

At the same time, some states are expanding their support of LGBT rights. In Maryland, where the local LGBT rights organization hoped to move on from marriage equality to transgender protection, then-Governor Martin O'Malley in May 2014 signed into law the Fairness for All Marylanders Act, which made the state the 18th to offer protection from discrimination for transgender individuals (Molloy 2014). A year later, the state legislature approved a bill with veto-proof margins that would allow transgender individuals to permanently change the name and gender noted on their birth certificates and the new governor, Republican Gary Hogan, indicated soon afterward that he would allow the bill to become law without his signature (Cox 2015; Hicks 2015).

In January 2014, California became the first state in the union to protect the right of transgender youth "to participate in sex-segregated programs, activities and facilities," such as bathrooms and sports teams, consistent with their gender identity, "irrespective of the gender listed on the pupil's records," and in July 2015 California became the first state in the union to allow transgender individuals to choose the gender identity listed on their death certificate (Dembowsky 2015; Marinucci 2014).

In the end, like many fights for equality, the fight for marriage equality for same-sex couples is progressing with some steps forward and some backward. The implementation of marriage equality policy in every state has been and will likely continue to be met with opposition. Despite pockets of resistance, however, marriage equality is rapidly advancing, spreading to states in every region of the country and increasing in popularity among almost all segments of the public.

Opponents of LGBT rights have mostly shifted their attention away from same-sex marriage and onto the right of transgender and gender non-conforming (TGNC) individuals to use the bathroom that matches their gender identity, regardless of their gender assigned at birth. Transgender activists claimed that right in 1996 as part of the International Bill of Gender Rights. Bathroom access is a widespread problem for transgender people, with 70% of respondents in a recent survey of TGNC individuals reporting that they were "denied access, verbally harassed, or physically assaulted in public restrooms" (Herman 2013, 65).

Opponents on the right see access as indecent, incompatible with privacy rights, and as giving sexual predators access to children. "Bathroom bills" that restrict access to bathrooms and locker rooms to gender assigned at birth were introduced in numerous states in 2015 and 2016. In South Dakota, a 2016 bill requiring students to use the facilities that matched their sex at birth cruised through the state legislature, winning approval in the House by a 58-10 vote and the Senate by a 20-15 vote but was vetoed by the Republican governor on March 1, 2016. The Houston Equal Rights Ordinance (HERO) gained national prominence because of its repeal in 2015. Passed by the city council in 2014, the measure banned discrimination on the basis of sexual orientation, gender identity, sex, race, color, ethnicity, national origin, age, religion, disability, pregnancy, genetic information, family, marital, and military status. Conservatives dubbed it the "bathroom ordinance" and adopted the rallying cry, "No men in women's bathrooms" to focus on the gender identity portion of the bill. The HERO ordinance was repealed in 2015 with almost 70% of the popular vote.

As mentioned above, most notable among the 2016 bathroom bills was the measure approved in North Carolina. In February 2016, the Charlotte (North Carolina) City Council approved a bill that expanded protections to LGBT residents, including a provision allowing transgender people to choose the restroom that corresponds to the gender with which they identify. North Carolina Governor Pat McCrory, a Republican and former mayor of Charlotte, claimed the restroom policy would "create major public safety issues" and vowed to correct the problem statewide. On March 23, 2016, Republicans in the North Carolina legislature heeded the governor's call, convening a special session to approve legislation to override the Charlotte ordinance. The bill, HB2, overturned all local LGBT non-discrimination ordinances statewide. Critics of the bill called it the "most anti-LGBT legislation in the nation." In protest, companies, including PayPal, that had planned to bring jobs to the state canceled their plans, and musicians such as Maroon 5, Bruce Springsteen, and Pearl Jam canceled planned concerts; government entities around the country banned public employees from using public funds to travel to the state. A report in late May 2016 estimated that HB2 had already cost the city of Charlotte $285.5 million in lost revenue (Martin 2016).

Opponents of transgender bathroom access succeeded by latching onto the idea that bill passage would lead to male sexual predators dressing as women to enter women's restrooms and commit sexual assaults. It's important to note there has not been one single instance of individuals misusing transgender access to bathrooms and locker rooms to engage in voyeurism, harassment, or sexual assault despite 17 school districts (with more than 600,000 students) with pro-transgender policies and 12 states that have bathroom access rights laws that empower transgender people to use the bathroom that matches their gender identity (Maza 2014). Instead, the rising tensions over bathroom bills had led to increased harassment against individuals perceived as transgender trying to use public restrooms, usually in the form of a transgender or gender non-conforming woman being assaulted or confronted when trying to use a public women's restroom.

CLOSING THOUGHTS

In this book, we have presented evidence that one way to open individuals' minds to reconsider attitudes on the contentious issue of marriage equality is to activate powerfully held in-group identities with counter-stereotypical cues. At the same time, the Theory of Dissonant Identity Priming is not limited to the issue of marriage equality or to LGBT rights issues more generally. The psychological mechanisms on which it is based apply to many strongly held opinions. The identities that we cued in our experiments—ethnorace, partisanship, sports fan, and religiousness—would also work to activate openness to attitude change on other issues, as would additional identities that we did not explore. We look forward to reading future descriptions of such efforts by interested scholars, particularly among those engaging in pracademics with appropriate community partners.

Opening minds to attitude change and engaging individuals with whom one disagrees on a contentious issue is all about framing the conversation as one between members of the same in-group. Instead of following the conventional good manners directive to avoid sensitive topics like politics and religion in polite company, we hope that this book will encourage readers to broach topics of interest in their everyday conversations, to spark debate and deliberation. There are many issues on which people disagree, including not just same-sex marriage and LGBT rights but also capital punishment, stem-cell research, abortion, the legalization of marijuana, and many more. As shown in our experiments, triggering a shared in-group identity among those with whom we disagree can trigger an openness to receiving and considering new information, and sometimes can change minds. Harnessing the power of in-group identities has the power to open minds to attitude change; dissonant or counter-stereotypical messages can provide cognitive speed bumps to jolt recipients into giving more attention and consideration to those messages. Combined, those dissonant in-group messages can generate increased support for equal rights and justice for all Americans. Rather than engaging in polite self-censorship, our findings suggest that individuals can help open minds by reaching out to folks with whom they share an in-group identity and starting a conversation. Rather than keeping their opinions to themselves, people can advance causes of equality and justice by turning to their fellow in-group members and saying, "Listen, we need to talk."

Appendix 1
Supplementary Tables

Table A1.1 Support for and Opposition to Marriage Equality is (%), Gallup Poll Trend, 1996–2015

	Support Same-Sex Marriage	Oppose Same-Sex Marriage
May 6–10, 2015	60	37
May 8–11, 2014	55	42
July 8–11, 2013	54	43
May 2–7, 2013	53	45
Nov 26–29, 2012	53	46
May 3–6, 2012	50	48
Dec 15–18, 2011	48	48
May 5–8, 2011	53	45
May 3–6, 2010	44	53
May 7–10, 2009	40	57
May 8–11, 2008	40	56
May 10–13, 2007	46	53
May 8–11, 2006 (new wording)	42	56
May 8–11, 2006 (old wording)	39	58
Aug 22–25, 2005	37	59
May 2–4, 2004	42	55
Feb 8–9, 1999	35	62
Mar 15–17, 1996	27	68

Note: Question wording 2006–2015: "Do you think marriages between same-sex couples should or should not be recognized by the law as valid, with the same rights as traditional marriages?" Question wording 1996–2006: "Do you think marriages between homosexuals should or should not be recognized by the law as valid, with the same rights as traditional marriages." Survey in 2006 was asked using both question wordings, in a split sample.

Source: http://www.gallup.com/poll/183272/record-high-americans-support-sex-marriage.aspx.

Table A2.1 Donation Rates, One Iowa Fundraising Experiment, Logit Models

Variable	Full Experiment			Contacted Only		
	Model 1	Model 2	Model 3	Model 1	Model 2	Model 3
Treatment Group	−.80* (.37)	−.81* (.37)	−.80* (.37)	−.57 (.39)	−.57 (.39)	−.58 (.39)
Age		.02$^+$ (.01)	.02 (.01)		.006 (.01)	.005 (.01)
Female		.02 (.37)	.06 (.38)		−.005 (.39)	.04 (.40)
Democrat		.66 (.55)	.65 (.56)		.13 (.58)	.15 (.59)
Des Moines		.50 (.36)	.46 (.37)		.24 (.38)	.19 (.39)
Voted 2008 Primary			−.35 (.45)			−.40 (.47)
Voted 2008 General			.34 (.64)			−.002 (.69)
Voted 2010 Primary			.56 (.45)			.65 (.48)
Constant	−3.45* (.21)	−5.24* (.76)	−5.46* (.90)	−1.78* (.22)	−2.31* (.81)	−2.30* (.93)
N	1,561	1,561	1,561	292	292	292
R-squared	.0151	.0406	.0465	.0107	.0143	.0231
Chi-square (Pr)	5.07 (0.0243)	13.60 (0.0184)	15.59 (0.0465)	2.29 (0.1301)	3.06 (0.6903)	4.94 (0.7640)

Note: * = p ≤ .05; $^+$ = p ≤ .10, two-tailed. Respondents are adults in Iowa who were on One Iowa's internal list of potential supporters. Surveys collected April 1–18, 2011. Standard errors in parentheses. Democrat is coded 1 = Democrat, 0 = else (includes 53 Republicans and 309 non-partisans/others).

Table A3.1 Support for Same-Sex Marriage (%), Super Bowl Experiment, by Treatment Assignment and Level of Interest in Sports

	Recycling Paragraph(A)	Anonymous Paragraph(B)	Professional Athletes Paragraph(C)	Percentage-Point Difference between Athletes and Recycling (C − A) (SE)	Percentage-Point Difference between Athletes and Anonymous (C − B) (SE)	Chi-square
	68.53% (98/143)	71.83% (102/142)	76.60% (108/141)	8.1 (5.3)	4.77 (5.2)	2.3289 (Pr = 0.312)
Sports Fan index						
Low	76.32 (58/76)	75.00 (51/68)	84.38 (54/64)	8.5 (6.8)	9.4* (7.0)	2.0059 Pr = 0.367
High	59.70 (40/67)	68.92 (51/74)	70.13 (54/77)	10.4* (8.0)	1.2 (7.5)	2.0402 Pr = 0.361
By level of interest in professional sports						
= 1 (low)	80.56 (29/36)	80.00 (24/30)	87.88 (29/33)	7.3 (8.9)	7.9 (9.3)	0.8913 Pr = 0.640
= 2	66.67 (20/30)	66.67 (18/27)	90.91 (20/22)	24.2* (11.6)	24.2* (11.7)	4.7800 Pr = 0.092
= 3	75.00 (21/28)	65.52 (19/29)	66.67 (22/33)	−8.3 (11.9)	1.1 (12.2)	0.7178 Pr = 0.698
= 4	54.17 (13/24)	68.00 (17/25)	73.08 (19/26)	18.9 (13.6)	5.1 (13.0)	2.0882 Pr = 0.352
= 5 (high)	60.00 (15/25)	77.42 (24/31)	66.67 (18/27)	6.7 (13.6)	10.8 (SE 11.9)	2.0270 Pr = 0.363

(continued)

Table A3.1 Continued

	Recycling Paragraph(A)	Anonymous Paragraph(B)	Professional Athletes Paragraph(C)	Percentage-Point Difference between Athletes and Recycling (C − A) (SE)	Percentage-Point Difference between Athletes and Anonymous (C − B) (SE)	Chi-square
			By frequency of choosing to watch sports on TV (SportsChoice)			
= 1 (never)	76.67	87.10	89.66	13.0	2.6	2.1470
	(23/30)	(27/31)	(26/29)	(9.8)	(8.4)	Pr = 0.342
= 2 (rarely)	72.09	66.67	78.79	6.7	12.1	1.3079
	(31/43)	(26/39)	(26/33)	(10.1)	(10.6)	Pr = 0.520
= 3 (sometimes)	63.26	56.76	75.68	12.5	18.9*	3.0210
	(24/38)	(21/37)	(28/37)	(10.7)	(10.9)	Pr = 0.221
= 4 (Often)	66.67	84.00	67.74	1.1	16.3	2.3790
	(14/21)	(21/25)	(21/31)	(13.5)	(11.6)	Pr = 0.304
= 5 (all the time)	54.55	70.00	63.64	9.1	6.4	0.5430
	(6/11)	(7/10)	(7/11)	(21.9)	(21.6)	Pr = 0.762
			By frequency of watching professional sports (WatchProfSports)			
1 = never	85.19	80.00	92.00	6.8	12.0	1.3688
	(23/27)	(16/20)	(23/25)	(9.0)	(10.3)	Pr = 0.504
2 = rarely	71.43	72.09	82.35	10.9	10.3	1.4490
	(30/42)	(31/43)	(28/34)	(9.9)	(9.8)	Pr = 0.485
3 = once a month	53.85	82.35	57.14	3.3	25.2*	3.5155
	(7/13)	(14/17)	(12/21)	(18.1)	(15.0)	Pr = 0.172

4 = once a week	70.00 (21/30)	68.42 (13/19)	84.00 (21/25)	14.0 (11.6)	15.6 (12.8)	1.8674 Pr = 0.393
5 = a few times per week	57.89 (11/19)	65.52 (19/29)	71.43 (20/28)	13.5 (14.3)	5.9 (12.5)	0.9227 Pr = 0.630
6 = every day (or almost every day)	50.00 (6/12)	64.29 (9/14)	50.00 (4/8)	0.00 (24.1)	14.3 (22.6)	0.6817 Pr = 0.711

Note: $N = 426$ (214 undergraduate students and 212 adult MTurk workers). Surveys completed January 28–February 3, 2013. * = $p < .05$, one-tailed. Dependent variable is support for same-sex marriage. Sports Fan index is a dichotomous variable constructed by splitting the sum of the three measures of interest in professional sports.

For level of interest, the question was "Do you consider yourself a fan of sports, either because you play a sport yourself or because you watch them, either live or on television? This can include professional sports, amateur sports, college sports, etc. How accurately does the phrase, 'I am a fan of sports' describe how you feel about them?" Clearly does not describe my feelings; Mostly does not describe my feelings; Somewhat describes my feelings; Mostly describes my feelings; or Clearly describes my feelings.

For choosing to watch sports, the question was "If you had the option of watching a sporting event or another television show (i.e. a situation comedy, reality TV, etc.), how often would you choose to watch the SPORTING EVENT over another choice?" Never, Rarely, Sometimes, Often, or All the time?

For frequency of watching sports, the question was "Some people enjoy watching professional sports like the National Football League (NFL), Major League Baseball (MLB), the National Basketball Association (NBA), or one of many other sports. What about you? How often do you watch professional sporting events?" Never, Rarely, Once a month, Once a week, A few times per week, or Every day (or almost every day).

Table A3.2 Support for Hypothetical Ballot Measure (%), Super Bowl Experiment, by Treatment Assignment and Level of Interest in Sports

	Recycling Paragraph (A)	Anonymous Paragraph (B)	Professional Athletes Paragraph (C)	Percentage-Point Difference between Athletes and Recycling (C − A) (SE)	Percentage-Point Difference between Athletes and Anonymous (C − B) (SE)	Chi-square
	62.24% (89/143)	61.27% (87/142)	70.21% (99/141)	8.0 (5.6)	8.9 (5.6)	2.9787 Pr = 0.226
Sports Fan index						
Low	73.68 (56/76)	64.71 (44/68)	76.56 (49/64)	2.9 (7.4)	11.9 (7.9)	2.5286 Pr = 0.282
High	49.25 (33/67)	58.11 (43/74)	64.94 (50/77)	15.7* (8.2)	6.8 (8.0)	3.6162 Pr = 0.164
By level of interest in professional sports						
= 1 (low)	77.78 (28/36)	70.00 (21/30)	75.76 (25/33)	−2.0 (10.3)	5.8 (11.4)	0.5512 Pr = 0.759
= 2	70.00 (21/30)	59.26 (16/27)	81.82 (18/22)	11.8 (12.3)	22.56* (13.1)	2.9201 Pr = 0.232
= 3	60.71 (17/28)	51.72 (15/29)	66.67 (22/33)	6.0 (12.5)	14.9 (12.5)	1.4445 Pr = 0.486
= 4	41.67 (10/24)	64.00 (16/25)	73.08 (19/26)	31.4* (13.5)	9.1 (13.2)	5.3803 Pr = 0.068

= 5 (high)	52.00 (13/25)	61.29 (19/31)	55.56 (15/17)	3.6 (14.1)	5.7 (13.2)	0.5050 Pr = 0.777

By frequency of choosing to watch sports on TV

= 1 (never)	80.00 (24/30)	80.65 (25/31)	75.86 (22/29)	-4.1 (11.0)	4.8 (10.8)	0.2392 Pr = 0.887
= 2 (rarely)	67.44 (29/43)	58.97 (23/39)	84.85 (28/33)	17.4* (10.0)	25.9* (10.5)	5.7984 Pr = 0.055
= 3 (sometimes)	55.26 (21/38)	40.54 (15/37)	67.57 (25/37)	12.3 (11.3)	27.0* (11.3)	5.4636 Pr = 0.065
= 4 (often)	47.62 (10/21)	68.00 (17/28)	64.52 (20/31)	16.9 (14.0)	3.5 (13.0)	2.2573 Pr = 0.323
= 5 (all the time)	45.45 (5/11)	70.00 (7/10)	36.36 (4/11)	-9.1 (21.9)	33.6 (21.6)	2.5091 Pr = 0.285

By frequency of watching professional sports

1 = never	85.19 (23/27)	75.00 (15/20)	84.00 (21/25)	-1.2 (1.2)	9.0 (12.2)	0.9149 Pr = 0.633
2 = rarely	64.29 (27/42)	60.47 (26/43)	70.59 (24/34)	6.3 (11.0)	10.1 (11.0)	0.8570 Pr = 0.651
3 = once a month	53.85 (7/13)	64.71 (11/17)	57.14 (12/21)	3.3 (18.1)	-7.6 (16.3)	0.4003 Pr = 0.819
4 = once a week	60.00 (18/30)	57.89 (11/19)	80.00 (20/25)	20.00 (12.4)	22.1 (13.8)	3.2296 Pr = 0.199

(continued)

Table A3.2 Continued

	Recycling Paragraph (A)	Anonymous Paragraph (B)	Professional Athletes Paragraph (C)	Percentage-Point Difference between Athletes and Recycling (C − A) (SE)	Percentage-Point Difference between Athletes and Anonymous (C − B) (SE)	Chi-square
5 = a few times per week	47.37 (9/19)	58.62 (17/29)	67.86 (19/28)	20.5 (15.0)	9.2 (13.0)	1.9742 Pr = 0.373
6 = every day (or almost every day)	41.67 (5/12)	50.00 (7/14)	37.50 (3/8)	−4.2 (23.5)	−12.5 (23.0)	0.3678 Pr = 0.832

Note: $N = 426$ (214 undergraduate students and 212 adult MTurk workers). Surveys completed January 28–February 3, 2013. * = $p < .05$, one-tailed. Dependent variable is support for a hypothetical ballot measure for marriage equality. Sports Fan index is a dichotomous variable constructed splitting the sum of the three measures of interest in professional sports. For level of interest, the question was "Do you consider yourself a fan of sports, either because you play a sport yourself or because you watch them, either live or on television? This can include professional sports, amateur sports, college sports, etc. How accurately does the phrase, 'I am a fan of sports' describe how you feel about them?" Clearly does not describe my feelings; Mostly does not describe my feelings; Somewhat describes my feelings; Mostly describes my feelings; or Clearly describes my feelings.

For choosing to watch sports, the question was "If you had the option of watching a sporting event or another television show (i.e. a situation comedy, reality TV, etc.), how often would you choose to watch the SPORTING EVENT over another choice?" Never, Rarely, Sometimes, Often, or All the time?

For frequency of watching sports, the question was "Some people enjoy watching professional sports like the National Football League (NFL), Major League Baseball (MLB), the National Basketball Association (NBA), or one of many other sports. What about you? How often do you watch professional sporting events?" Never, Rarely, Once a month, Once a week, A few times per week, or Every day (or almost every day).

Table A3.3 Support for Non-Discrimination Statement (%), Michael Sam / Roger Goodell Experiment

	Control (Anonymous)	Treatment (Roger Goodell)	Percentage-Point Difference (SE)	Chi-square
All (N = 811)	38.53% (168/436)	38.67% (145/375)	0.13 (3.43)	0.0015 Pr = 0.969
Football Fans (N = 409)	45.67% (95/208)	50.25% (101/201)	4.58 (4.9)	0.8575 Pr = 0.354
Non-Football Fans (N = 402)	32.02% (73/228)	25.29 (44/174)	−6.76 (4.6)	2.1664 Pr = 0.141

Note: The survey experiment was in the field February 18–20, 2014. N = 811. The fan question read: "On a scale of one to five, how interested are you in professional football?" Responses (randomly reversed): not interested at all; slightly interested; moderately interested; very interested; extremely interested. Football Fans are those who replied "extremely interested;" non-fans replied "not interested at all."

Table A3.4 Support for Non-Discrimination Statement, Michael Sam / Roger Goodell Experiment, Logit Models

	Non-Football Fans	Football Fans
Treatment	−934* (.261)	.165 (.217)
Age Group	−.079 (.080)	−.082 (.070)
Female	−.191 (.259)	−.248 (.231)
Income Group	−.082 (.176)	−.180 (.155)
Constant	−.155 (.567)	.608 (.465)
N	302	349
R-squared	0.042	0.010
Chi-square (Pr)	15.80 (0.0033)	4.72 (0.3174)

Note: The survey experiment was in the field February 18–20, 2014. N = 811. * = $p \leq .05$, two-tailed. Standard errors in parentheses. Age Group is a six-category ordinal variable ranging from 1 = 18–24 to 6 = 65+; Income Group is a five-category ordinal variable ranging from 0 = $0–$24,000 to 5 = $100,000–$149,999.

Table A3.5 Support for Marriage Equality (%), Green Bay Packers Experiment

	Control (Jay-Z)	Treatment (LeRoy Butler)	Percentage-Point Difference (SE)	Chi-square
All (N = 306)	62.67% (94/150)	69.23% (108/156)	6.56 (5.42)	1.4686 Pr = 0.226
Packers Fans (N = 111)	63.16 (36/57)	77.78 (42/54)	14.62* (8.65)	2.8371 Pr = 0.092
Non-Packers Fans (N = 195)	62.37 (58/93)	64.71 (66/102)	2.34 (6.93)	0.1151 PR = 0.734

Note: N = 306. Respondents are adults in Appleton, Wisconsin. Surveys completed October 19–November 12, 2014. The fandom question read: "Thinking specifically now about the Green Bay Packers, which of the following best describes how you feel about the team? (a) I'm a huge fan (b) I'm somewhat of a fan (c) I'm not much of a fan or (d) I'm not at all a fan." * = $p \le .05$, one-tailed.

Table A3.6 Support for Marriage Equality, Green Bay Packers Experiment, Logit Models

	Non-Packers Fans	Packers Fans
Treatment (LeRoy Butler)	.069 (.331)	1.317* (.553)
Age	.001 (.013)	−.088** (.022)
Female	−.399 (.343)	−1.033* (.528)
Renter	−.683 (.373)	−.745 (.555)
Education	−.138 (.160)	.186 (.224)
Republican	−1.793** (.430)	−2.007* (.856)
Other PID	−1.250** (.415)	−.466 (.575)
Constant	2.490** (.724)	4.107** (1.088)
N	188	108
R-squared	0.119	0.267
Chi-square (Pr)	29.27 (0.0001)	35.44 (0.0000)

Note: N = 306. Respondents are adults in Appleton, Wisconsin. Surveys completed October 19–November 12, 2014. * = $p \le .05$, ** = $p \le .01$, two-tailed. Standard errors in parentheses. Female is coded 0 = male, 1 = female; renter is coded 0 = own home, 1 = Renter; Education is an ordinal variable coded from 1 = less than high school diploma to 7 = graduate/professional degree; Republican and Other PID are dummy variables for partisanship (Democrats are the omitted category).

Table A3.7 Support for Marriage Equality, Hockey Experiment, Logit Models

	Non-Hockey Fans	Hockey Fans
Treatment	−.078	.025
	(.251)	(.235)
Age Group	−.165*	−.274*
	(.076)	(.077)
Female	.257	.770*
	(.251)	(.241)
Income Group	−.073	−.048
	(.184)	(.158)
Constant	.395	1.224*
	(.555)	(.488)
N	270	337
R-squared	0.0168	0.0547
Chi-square (Pr)	6.22	24.16
	(0.1835)	(0.0001)

Note: Data collected online from a national sample of adults using Google Consumer Survey product. Surveys completed February 21–26, 2014. * = $p \leq .05$, two-tailed. Standard errors in parentheses. Age Group is a six-category ordinal variable ranging from 1 = 18–24 to 6 = 65+; Income Group is a five-category ordinal variable ranging from 0 = $0–$24,000 to 5 = $100,000–$149,999. Weighted using weights supplied by Google Consumer Surveys.

Table A4.1 Support for LGBT Rights (%), SocialSci Experiment

	Control	Treatment	Percentage-Point	Chi-square
	(Anonymous Citizen)	(Rev. Lawrence)	Difference (SE)	
Percentage supporting marriage equality				
Secular respondents (N = 250)	92.0% (115/125)	89.6% (112/125)	−2.4 (3.7)	0.4310 Pr = 0.512
Religious respondents (N = 250)	51.2 (64/125)	62.4 (78/125)	11.2* (6.25)	3.1951 Pr = 0.074
Percentage would vote yes on hypothetical ballot measure				
Secular respondents (N = 250)	92.8 (116/125)	93.6 (117/125)	0.8 (3.2)	0.0631 Pr = 0.802
Religious respondents (N = 250)	55.2 (69/125)	69.6 (87/125)	14.4* (6.1)	5.5237 Pr = 0.019

(continued)

Table A4.1 Continued

	Control (Anonymous Citizen)	Treatment (Rev. Lawrence)	Percentage-Point Difference (SE)	Chi-square
		Percentage approving of gay and lesbian parenting		
Secular respondents (N = 250)	91.2 (114/125)	94.4 (118/125)	3.2 (3.3)	0.9579 Pr = .328
Religious respondents (N = 250)	63.2 (79/125)	72.8 (91/125)	9.6* (5.9)	2.6471 Pr = 0.104

Note: N = 500. Surveys were completed May 17–28, 2013. * = p ≤ .05, two-tailed.

Table A4.2 Support for LGBT Rights, SocialSci Experiment, Logit Models

	A. Support for Same-Sex Marriage	B. Support for Hypothetical Ballot Measure	C. Support Gay and Lesbian Parenting
Treatment	−.461 (.457)	−.213 (.541)	.210 (.512)
Religiousness	−.477* (.090)	−.529* (.101)	−.361* (.092)
Religious *Treatment	1.140* (.531)	1.185* (.611)	.441 (.590)
Age	−.024* (.009)	−.020* (.010)	−.022* (.010)
Education	.092 (.089)	.101 (.097)	.227* (.095)
Female	−.165 (.257)	−.131 (278)	.314 (.270)
Partisanship	−.419* (.068)	−.460* (.074)	−.262* (.069)
Fundamentalist Christian	−.841* (.204)	−.936* (.213)	−.943* (.199)
Constant	5.067* (.712)	5.512* (.788)	3.560* (.688)
Chi-square	175.91* (.000)	183.86* (.000)	130.25* (.000)
N	500	500	500
R-squared	0.306	0.347	0.263
Chi-square (Pr)	175.91 (0.0000)	183.86 (0.0000)	130.25 (0.0000)

Note: Surveys were completed May 17–28, 2013. * = p ≤ .05, two-tailed. Standard errors in parentheses. Religiousness is coded 1 = extremely secular to 7 = extremely religious. The interaction term, Religious* Treatment, interacts a dichotomized religiousness variable with assignment to the treatment paragraph. Partisanship is coded 1 = strong Democrat to 7 = strong Republican, Education is coded 1 = less than high school diploma to 7 = doctoral or professional degree.

Table A4.3 Support for LGBT Rights (%), Louisiana Experiment, by Script

	Control	Treatment	Percentage-Point Difference (SE)	Chi-square
Script A				
% Supporting marriage equality (N = 138)	26.47% (18/68)	24.29% (17/70)	2.2 (7.5)	0.0870 Pr = 0.768
% would vote yes on ballot measure (N = 143)	37.50 (27/72)	29.58 (21/71)	−7.9 (7.9)	1.0062 Pr = 0.316
% approving of gay and lesbian parenting (N = 140)	46.48 (33/71)	49.28 (34/69)	2.8 (8.5)	0.1097 Pr = 0.741
% supporting ENDA (N = 142)	67.61 (48/71)	70.42 (50/71)	2.8 (7.8)	0.1317 Pr = 0.717
Script B				
% supporting marriage equality (N = 132)	21.54 (14/65)	20.90 (14/67)	−0.6 (7.2)	0.0082 Pr = 0.928
% would vote yes on ballot measure (N = 138)	26.87 (18/67)	29.58 (21/71)	2.7 (7.7)	0.1250 Pr 0.724
% approving of gay and lesbian parenting (N = 140)	50.75 (34/67)	47.89 (34/71)	−2.9 (8.6)	0.1127 Pr = 0.737
% supporting ENDA (N = 142)	61.76 (42/68)	66.20 (47/71)	4.4 (8.2)	0.2963 Pr = 0.586

Note: Respondents are adults in Louisiana who are members of a religious household. Surveys were collected February 4–27, 2014.

Table A5.1 Support for Marriage Equality (%), Pew Surveys, by Ethnorace, 2006–2016

	Whites	Blacks	Latinos
2006	35%	25%	31%
2007	38	26	32.5
2008	41	26	34
2009	37	29	39
2010	44	30	41
2011	49	36	46.5
2012	49	40	52
2013	51	38	56
2014	54	43	52
2015	59	41	56
2016	57	42	56

Note: Data from Pew Research Center polls, aggregated by year, compiled by the authors. See http://www.pewforum.org/2016/05/12/changing-attitudes-on-gay-marriage/, http://www.pewresearch.org/fact-tank/2013/06/19/latinos-changing-views-of-same-sex-marriage/. Additional data provided by Mark Hugo Lopez, Director of Hispanic Research, Pew Research Center.

Table A5.2 Black Support for Marriage Equality (%), Equality Illinois Experiment

	Control	Treatment	Percentage-Point Difference (SE)	Chi-square
All (N = 285)	28.39% (44/155)	26.92% (35/130)	1.46 (5.34)	0.0756 Pr = 0.783
Non-Black Callers (N = 148)	26.25 (21/80)	23.53 (16/68)	2.72 (7.19)	0.1451 Pr = 0.703
Black Callers (N = 137)	30.67 (23/75)	30.65 (19/62)	0.02 (7.97)	0.0000 Pr = 0.998

Note: Respondents are adult African-Americans living in Cook County, Illinois. Interviews were conducted April–June 2011. The dependent variable asked, "[*Name*], can I add you to our list of supporters of marriage equality?" See appendix 2 for question wording and additional results.

Table A5.3 Black Support for Marriage Equality, Equality Illinois Experiment, Logit Models

	Model 1	Model 2
Coretta Scott King Script	.043 (.295)	−.087 (.395)
Black Interviewer	1.023* (.368)	.890* (.452)
King Script * Black Interviewer	–	.309 (.622)
Female Interviewer	.949* (.406)	.987* (.416)
Interviewer Age	.066* (.026)	.068* (.027)
LGBT Interviewer	1.087* (.428)	1.048* (.435)
Constant	−4.092* (1.063)	−4.107 (1.066)
N	285	285
R-squared	0.0349	0.0356
Chi-square (Pr)	11.73 (0.0386)	11.98 (0.0624)

Note: $N = 285$. * = $p \le .05$, two-tailed. Standard errors in parentheses. Respondents are adult African Americans living in Cook County, Illinois. Interviews were conducted April–June 2011. The dependent variable asked, "[*Name*], can I add you to our list of supporters of marriage equality?"

Table A5.4 Black Support for Marriage Equality (%), Georgia Equality Experiment

	Control	Treatment	Percentage-Point Difference (SE)	Chi-square
All (N = 183)	27.59% (24/87)	37.50% (36/96)	9.91 (6.95)	2.0355 Pr = 0.154
Non-Black Callers (N = 82)	28.12 (9/32)	34.0 (17/50)	5.88 (10.65)	0.3110 Pr = 0.577
Black callers (N = 101)	27.27 (15/55)	41.3 (19/46)	14.03 (9.43)	2.2085 Pr = 0.137

Note: Respondents are adult African Americans living in Atlanta, Georgia. Interviews were conducted July–September 2012. The dependent variable asked, "[Name], can I add you to our list of supporters of marriage equality?" * = $p \leq .05$, two-tailed.

Table A5.5 Black Support for Marriage Equality, Georgia Equality Experiment, Logit Models

	Model 1	Model 2
Obama Script	.676* (.341)	.751 (.618)
Black Interviewer	−.072 (.343)	−.011 (.538)
Obama Script * Black Interviewer	–	−.119 (.808)
Female Interviewer	−.794* (.404)	−.824 (453)
Interviewer Age	.013 (.012)	.014 (.012)
LGBT Interviewer	−.119 (.363)	−.153 (.431)
Constant	−1.133 (.574)	−1.150* (.587)
N	183	183
R-squared	0.0292	0.0292
Chi-square (Pr)	6.75 (0.2398)	6.77 (0.3424)

Note: Respondents are adult African Americans living in Atlanta, Georgia. Interviews were conducted July–September 2012. The dependent variable asked, "[Name], can I add you to our list of supporters of marriage equality?" * = $p \leq .05$, two-tailed.

Table A5.6 Latino Support for Marriage Equality (%), Latino Decisions Experiment, by Treatment Group and Nativity

	Support for marriage equality			
	Control	*Treatment*	*Percentage-Point Difference (SE)*	*Chi-square*
All respondents (N = 800)	45.89% (184/401)	47.12% (188/399)	1.23 (3.53)	0.1221 Pr = 0.727
US-born respondents (N = 335)	50.0 (84/168)	60.48 (101/167)	10.48* (5.42)	3.7192 Pr = 0.054
Foreign-born respondents (N = 465)	42.92 (100/233)	37.5 (87/232)	−5.42 (4.55)	1.4196 Pr = 0.233
English-language interviews (N = 393)	51.98 (105/202)	58.64 (112/191)	6.66 (5.02)	1.7602 Pr = 0.185
Spanish-language interviews (N = 407)	39.7 (79/199)	36.54 (76/208)	−3.16 (4.82)	0.4307 Pr—0.512
	Support for hypothetical ballot measure			
All respondents (N = 800)	54.36% (218/401)	53.38% (213/399)	−0.98 (3.53)	0.0774 Pr = 0.781
US-born respondents (N = 335)	59.52 (100/168)	64.67 (108/167)	5.15 (5.31)	0.9425 Pr = 0.332
Foreign-born respondents (N = 465)	50.64 (118/233)	45.26 (105/232)	−5.39 (4.64)	1.3507 Pr = 0.245
English-language interviews (N = 393)	62.38 (126/202)	66.49 (127/191)	4.12 (4.84)	0.7252 Pr = 0.394
Spanish-language interviews (N = 407)	46.23 (92/199)	41.35 (86/208)	−4.89 (4.93)	−0.9862 Pr = 0.321

Note: N = 800. Respondents are a national sample of Latino adults. Surveys were conducted in English and Spanish, April 10–22, 2013. * = $p \leq .05$, one-tailed.

Table A5.7 Latino Support for Marriage Equality (%), South Texas Experiment, by Script and Language of Interview

	Control	Treatment	Percentage-Point Difference (SE)	Chi-square
Support for marriage equality				
All respondents (N = 405)	46.53% (94/202)	52.71% (107/203)	6.17 (4.97)	1.5442 Pr = 0.214
English-language interviews (N = 207)	45.19 (47/104)	57.28 (59/103)	12.09* (6.93)	3.0270 Pr = 0.082
Spanish-language interviews (N = 198)	47.96 (47/98)	48.0 (48/100)	0.04 (7.14)	0.0000 Pr = 0.995
Support for hypothetical ballot measure				
All respondents (N = 398)	55.33 (109/197)	58.21 (117/201)	2.88 (4.98)	0.3360 Pr = 0.562
English-language interviews (N = 207)	55.55 (55/99)	57.41 (62/108)	1.85 (6.93)	0.0721 Pr = 0.788
Spanish-language interviews (N = 191)	55.1 (54/98)	59.14 (55/93)	4.04 (7.20)	0.3175 Pr = 0.573

Note: $N = 405$. Respondents are a sample of Latino adults from South Texas. Surveys were conducted in English and Spanish, September 1–26, 2013. * = $p \leq .05$, one-tailed.

Table A5.8 Latino Support for Marriage Equality, South Texas Latinos Experiment, Logit Models

	Support for Marriage Equality	Support for Ballot Measure
Treatment	.264	.196
	(.228)	(.224)
English	−.048	−.111
	(.231)	(.227)
Female	−.026	.396
	(.260)	(.260)
Education	−.009	−.075
	(.097)	(.098)
Age Group	−.162*	−.168*
	(.071)	(.071)
Married	−.810*	−.856*
	(.237)	(.237)
Democrat	.188	.362
	(.236)	(.233)
Catholic	.715*	1.111*
	(.246)	(.242)
Church Attendance	−.291*	−.368*
	(.104)	(.104)
Income Group	.228*	.129
	(.084)	(.083)
Constant	.390	.616
	(.492)	(.476)
N	365	388
R-squared	0.1073	0.1324
Chi-square (Pr)	54.31	71.00
	(0.0000)	(0.0000)

Note: N = 405. Respondents are a sample of Latino adults from South Texas. Surveys were conducted in English and Spanish, September 1–26, 2013. Standard errors in parentheses. * = $p \leq .05$, two-tailed. Education is an ordinal variable coded 0 = less than a high school diploma to 3 = college graduate+. Age Group is an ordinal variable with seven categories coded 1 = 18–29, 2 = 30–39, 3 = 40–49, 4 = 50–59, 5 = 60–69, 6 = 70–79, and 7 = 80+. Income Group is an ordinal variable with six categories ranging from 1 = less than $10K to 6 = more than $100K. Church Attendance is an ordinal variable coded 0 = never to 4 = all of the time.

Table A6.1 Support for Marriage Equality [%], Virginia Experiment

	Strong Democrats	Weak Democrats	Leaning Democrats	Independents	Leaning Republicans	Weak Republicans	Strong Republicans	All
Republican Opposition Cue, All Voters	66.43% (93/140)	61.02% (36/59)	78.00% (39/50)	59.62% (31/52)	33.33% (25/75)	30.95% (13/42)	26.25% (21/80)	51.81% (258/498)
Republican Opposition Cue, Likely Voters	77.65 (66/85)	69.23 (18/26)	69.23 (18/26)	69.23 (18/26)	24.39 (10/41)	29.17 (7/24)	24.07 (13/54)	53.19 (150/282)
Democratic Support Cue, All Voters	71.43 (75/105)	68.09 (32/47)	77.08 (37/48)	40.91 (18/44)	38.46 (25/65)	53.19 (25/47)	18.48 (17/92)	51.12 (229/448)
Democratic Support Cue, Likely Voters	80.56 (58/72)	93.33 (14/15)	86.36 (19/22)	64.71 (11/17)	40.00 (18/45)	45.45 (10/22)	15.15 (10/66)	54.05 (140/259)

Note: $N = 1,001$. Surveys collected September 25–29, 2013 among registered Virginia voters.

Table A6.2 Support for Marriage Equality and Civil Unions (%), New Jersey Experiments

	Control	Treatment	Percentage-Point Difference (SE)	Chi-square
Marriage equality, October 16, 2013				
Democrats (N = 86)	74.51 (38/51)	65.71 (23/35)	8.80 (10.04)	0.7787 Pr = 0.378
Republicans (N = 39)	60.71 (17/28)	27.27 (3/11)	−33.44 (17.41)	3.5351 Pr = 0.060
Civil unions, October 16, 2013				
Democrats (N = 86)	15.69 (8/51)	20.00 (7/35)	4.31 (8.41)	0.2682 Pr = 0.605
Republicans (N = 39)	28.57 (8/28)	63.64 (7/11)	35.06* (16.81)	4.1026 Pr = 0.043
Marriage equality, November 5, 2013				
Democrats (N = 71)	70.18 (40/57)	50.00 (7/14)	−20.18 (14.11)	2.0446 Pr = 0.153
Republicans (N = 58)	50.00 (14/28)	56.67 (17/30)	6.67 (13.31)	0.2587 Pr = 0.611
Civil unions, November 5, 2013				
Democrats (N = 71)	15.79 (9/57)	42.86 (6/14)	27.07* (11.91)	4.9418 Pr = 0.026
Republicans (N = 58)	35.71 (10/28)	33.33 (10/30)	−2.38 (12.71)	0.0363 Pr = 0.849

Note: * = $p \leq .05$, two-tailed. Respondents are voters exiting polling places.

Appendix 2
List of Scripts for 17 Randomized Experiments in This Book

1. Chapter 2, One Iowa Experiment
2. Chapter 3, Super Bowl Experiment
3. Chapter 3, Michael Sam / Roger Goodell Experiment
4. Chapter 3, Green Bay Packers Experiment
5. Chapter 3, NHL Experiment
6. Chapter 3, San Francisco Giants Experiment
7. Chapter 4, SocialSci.com Experiment
8. Chapter 4, Equality Louisiana Experiment
9. Chapter 5, Equality Illinois Experiment
10. Chapter 5, Georgia Equality Experiment
11. Chapter 5, Latino Decisions Experiment
12. Chapter 5, South Texas Experiment
13. Chapter 6, Virginia Experiment
14. Chapter 6, New Jersey Experiment
15. Chapter 6, National Partisanship Experiment
16. Chapter 7, Equality Maryland Experiment
17. Chapter 7, Capital City Alliance Experiment

CHAPTER 2

(1) One Iowa Experiment Script

[INTRO]

Hi! Is [*first name*] available? My name is [*your name*] and I'm a volunteer with One Iowa, the statewide organization fighting to protect the freedom to marry for gay and lesbian couples in Iowa. How are you? [*Listen and respond*]

For an entire year we have been working hard to stop anti-equality radicals from pushing a discriminatory amendment to the Iowa constitution in 2010. Our hard work paid off, the Legislature has adjourned, and the amendment never even made it to the floor for debate. Isn't that great? [*Listen and respond*]

Unfortunately, anti-equality forces are more frustrated, angry, and desperate than ever before. They are launching a half million dollar campaign to kick out fair minded legislators so they will have the votes they need to write discrimination into our constitution next year. That's not surprising, is it? [*Listen and respond*]

We are ramping up our volunteer outreach so that we will have supporters all around the state ready to defend key legislative seats up for grabs this November. Does that make sense? [*Listen and respond*]

[TREATMENT PARAGRAPH, NOT READ TO CONTROL GROUP]

As a (*gay man, lesbian, bisexual individual, transgendered individual, straight ally*) I remember being incredibly proud to be an Iowan when our Supreme court ruled in favor of equal rights and I'm concerned about the effect rolling back equality in Iowa will have on me and our community.

That's why I'm volunteering with One Iowa tonight. Our team just isn't big enough to put up real fights where the opposition is targeting.

We are recruiting concerned volunteers like you to help us reach out to One Iowa supporters and ask them to take action. Will you make it a priority to join us next _____ for our phone bank so we can build a big enough team to win in November.

- [If YES, go to DETAILS]
- [If NO or MAYBE, go to PROBLEM-SOLVING]

One final thing before I let you go. [*Name*], One Iowa is working hard to raise enough funds to counter their $500,000 campaign to roll back equality in Iowa. We're really excited about the support we're getting from our friends and allies because we cannot let their lies and dirty tricks go unanswered. Will you support equality in Iowa by investing $150 in the campaign tonight? That's one dollar for each seat in the legislature.

[if NO to $150] That's ok. I hear you. While millionaires are funding the opposition, we are proud to be doing this the grassroots way. They spent $90,000 on a SINGLE special election for House District 90 last year. A lot of people are feeling great about a symbolic $90 contribution to get us out into every corner of the state to build more support. Can we count on you for $90?

[if NO to $90] No problem. I really would like to find a level that works for you! When everyone who cares about equality for LGBT people gives what they can it really adds up. That's why even more people are doing $43.09 in honor of the April 3rd, 2009 Supreme Court decision. Sounds like that might fit better in your budget.

[IF YES FOR ANY AMOUNT]

Great, thank you so much! I just need to get some information from you.

[Confirm Name, Confirm Billing Address, Ask for Credit Card Information]

[*Read back amount and thank them for their time and their support!*]

[*If insist on paying by mail, make note on pledge form and we send a form in the mail*]

[DETAILS]

Do you have a pen and paper handy to write down the address of our meeting place?

[Address and any land markers] 500 E. Locust Street, 3rd Floor. (Intersection of E. 5th and Locust in the East Village)

[Parking information] Street parking is 1 cent per minute up to 6:00PM (Free on Saturday/Sunday) or there is a FREE parking ramp on the corner of E. 6th and Pennsylvania next to the Capital Building.

We need this phase of the campaign to be the very biggest. Will you bring a friend or family member with you? Who?
Do you have any questions? Okay, great. If you think of anything you can call _____ at _____. Thanks so much.

[PROBLEM SOLVING]
I definitely hear that you care. What's holding you back from joining us _____?

- *If Busy:* I hear that. It sounds like you have a lot going on. Spring is a busy season for all of us. April 3rd is the one year anniversary of the unanimous Supreme Court decision and anti-equality groups and candidates are working hard to make gay and lesbian families a political wedge issue in the coming election. They will do ANYTHING to take these rights away. Have you seen that in the news? In order to make sure we will get to celebrate the 5th anniversary of marriage equality in 2014, we need your help to stop them right now. Will you move around whatever you have going on to make *this* a priority?
- *If Vague, Unsure:* The only way we can win is by getting supporters who rarely vote out to the polls. We have lost marriage equality in 35 states across the country. We don't want Iowa to be next, right? To make sure that doesn't happen, we need you to volunteer. Will you make it a priority to join us for this one shift.
- *If Scared/Nervous:* I'm curious, have you ever done something like this before? I was definitely nervous my first time. Lots of people have never done anything like this before. But folks are being so moved by the campaign that they're trying it out for the first time. Our coaches will help you have a good experience. How does that sound. Will you give it a try.
- *If still NO:* Ok. I'm so sorry I won't see you _____ [date] at the _____ [action]. Will you join us on _____ instead.
- *Troubleshoot with your volunteer. . .*

CHAPTER 3

(2) Super Bowl Experiment

Please choose one of the choices below. You will be randomly assigned to a short paragraph on one issue in American politics.

[A, B, C, D, E]

**(Random assignment takes place at this point, not as a result of the response to the previous question; the initial question leads respondents to believe the survey isn't solely about one issue).*

[CONTROL]

Recycling is the process of separating, collecting, and remanufacturing or converting used or waste products into new materials. The recycling process involves a series of steps to produce the new products. Recycling helps extend the life and usefulness of something that has already served its initial purpose by producing something that is useable. Almost everything we see around us can be recycled- batteries, biodegradable waste, clothing, electronics, garments, glass, metals, paper, plastics, and a lot more. Recycling has a lot of benefits and importance not only to us humans but also to our planet as a whole.

[TREATMENT GROUPS]

Introduction

Americans fundamentally disagree on many core political issues. One of the issues where people disagree is whether gay and lesbian Americans should be able to marry. Many individuals have endorsed gay marriage while many others are opposed.

[PROFESSIONAL ATHLETES CONDITION]

Please read the following paragraph carefully before moving on to the next page.

Brendon Ayanbadejo, All-Pro Linebacker for the Baltimore Ravens in the National Football League, supports gay marriage. He recently said, "Right now it's the time for gay rights and it's time for them to be treated equally and for everybody to be treated fairly, in the name of love." Sean Avery, forward for the New York Rangers pro hockey team, recently said, "I'm a New Yorker for marriage equality. I treat everyone the way I expect to be treated and that applies to marriage. Committed couples should be able to marry the person they love." Chris Kluwe, punter for the Minnesota Vikings and another supporter, recently wrote that gay marriage would make gays "full-fledged American citizens just like everyone else, with the freedom to pursue happiness and all that entails."

[ANONYMOUS CONDITION]

Please read the following paragraph carefully before moving on to the next page.

One supporter of gay marriage recently said, "Right now it's the time for gay rights and it's time for them to be treated equally and for everybody be treated fairly, in the name of love." Another supporter recently said, "I'm a New Yorker for marriage equality. I treat everyone the way I expect to be treated and that applies to marriage. Committed couples should be able to marry the person they love." Another supporter recently wrote that gay marriage would make gays "full-fledged American citizens just like everyone else, with the freedom to pursue happiness and all that entails."

Do you think gay and lesbian people: (1) should be able to get legally married; (2) should be able to enter into a legal partnership similar to but not called marriage; or (3) should not have legal recognition given to their gay and lesbian relationships.

[No legal recognition for gay and lesbian relationships, Get married, Enter into a similar legal partnership (i.e. a civil union) but not marriage]

In general, what do you think is more important: protecting the environment, even at the risk of curbing economic growth, OR maintaining a prosperous economy, even if the environment suffers to some extent?

[Protecting the environment even at the risk of curbing economic growth, Maintaining a prosperous economy, even if the environment suffers to some extent]

On a scale from 0 to 100, how do you feel toward gay and lesbian Americans? 0 means very unfavorable, and 100 means very favorable. Fifty means neither unfavorable nor favorable. Of course, you can use any number between zero and 100.

[sliding thermometer scale]

Do you consider yourself a fan of sports, either because you play a sport yourself or because you watch them, either live or on television? This can include professional sports, amateur sports, college sports, etc. How accurately does the phrase, "I am a fan of sports" describe how you feel about them?

[Clearly does not describe my feelings, Mostly does not describe my feelings, Somewhat describes my feelings, Mostly describes my feelings, Clearly describes my feelings]

Many believe that children are safest and healthiest in a family with a mother and a father. Others feel that children are safest and healthiest in a household full of love of commitment, regardless of whether there is a mother and father. (This includes families with two mothers or two fathers). What about you? Are you against or in favor of gay and lesbian couples being parents, whether through adoption or some other means?

[Strongly against, Somewhat against, Undecided, Somewhat in favor, Strongly in favor]

Would you vote for or against a law that would increase taxes on cigarettes by one dollar per pack to fund research on lung cancer?

[Definitely vote no, Probably vote no, Undecided, Probably vote yes, Definitely vote yes]

Gay marriage is often an issue at the state level. Suppose your state had a ballot initiative in the 2014 election where you could vote on a law that would allow gay marriage/marriage equality. How would you vote on such a measure? Note: a "yes" vote would mean allowing gay marriage' a "no" vote would mean not allowing gay marriage.

[Definitely vote no, Probably vote no, Undecided, Probably vote yes, Definitely vote yes]

If you had the option of watching a sporting event or another television show (i.e. a situation comedy, reality TV, etc.), how often would you choose to watch the SPORTING EVENT over another choice?

[Never, Rarely, Sometimes, Often, All of the time]

In which state do you currently reside? [drop-down menu]

In what year were you born? [drop-down menu]

What is your gender? [Male, Female]

Some people enjoy watching professional sports like the National Football League (NFL), National Hockey League (NHL), the National Basketball Association (NBA), or one of many other sports. What about you? How often do you watch professional sporting events?

[Never, rarely, Once a month, Once a week, A few times per week, Every day (or almost every day)]

Generally speaking, do you consider yourself to be a Republican, a Democrat, and Independent, or something else?

[Republican, Democrat, Independent, Something else]

[IF INDEPENDENT OR SOMETHING ELSE] Do you think of yourself as closer to the Republican Party, to the Democratic Party, or equally close to the Republican Party and Democratic Party?

[Closer to the Republican Party, Closer to the Democratic Party, Equally close to both Democratic Party and Republican Party]

[IF REPUBLICAN OR DEMOCRAT] How strong is your identification to the partisanship choice you just made?

[Very weak, Weak, Somewhat weak, Somewhat strong, Strong, Very strong]

Would you like to be entered into a contest to win a $100 gift card to Amazon.com? If so, you will need to provide a valid e-mail address so we can contact you if you win.

[e-mail address collected here]

Thank you very much for your participation in this survey! We truly value your time and appreciate your help. If you have any questions, please contact bharrison@u.northwestern.edu. Thank you!

(3) Michael Sam / Roger Goodell Experiment

Screening question:

On a scale of one to five, how interested are you in professional football?

Responses (randomly reversed):

1) not interested at all
2) slightly interested
3) moderately interested
4) very interested
5) extremely interested

[Sample restricted to those who answered 1 or 5]

[CONTROL]

A corporate CEO recently said discrimination based on sexual orientation is inconsistent with modern values. Do you agree?

[TREATMENT]

NFL's Roger Goodell recently said discrimination based on sexual orientation is inconsistent with NFL values. Do you agree?

Responses (randomly reversed):

1) strongly disagree
2) somewhat disagree
3) neither agree nor disagree
4) somewhat agree
5) strongly agree

(4) Green Bay Packers Experiment

[*NOTE: Paper surveys used to collect data included photos of Jay-Z and Leroy Butler, shown to the left side of question #4.]

1. If you had the option of watching a sporting event or another television show (i.e. a situation comedy, reality TV, etc.), how often would you choose to watch the SPORTING EVENT over another choice? (check one)[Never, Rarely, Sometimes, Often, All of the time]

2. Some people enjoy watching professional sports like the National Football League (NFL), Major League Baseball (MLB), the National Basketball Association (NBA), or one of many other sports. What about you? How often do you watch professional sporting events? (check one)[Never, Rarely, Once a month, Once a week, A few times per week, Every day (or almost every day)]
3. Thinking specifically now about the Green Bay Packers, which of the following best describes how you feel about the team? (check one)[I'm a huge fan, I'm somewhat of a fan, I'm not much of a fan, I'm not at all a fan]

[CONTROL]

4. Rapper and music producer Jay-Z (seen in the photo on the left) supports same-sex marriage. What do you think? Should gays and lesbian individuals (check one):

Be able to get married, Be able to enter into a legal partnership similar to but not called marriage (such as a domestic partnership or civil union), Have no legal recognition given to their relationships]

[TREATMENT]

4. Green Bay Packers Hall of Famer LeRoy Butler (seen in the photo on the left) supports same-sex marriage. What do you think? Should gays and lesbian individuals (check one):

[Be able to get married, Be able to enter into a legal partnership similar to but not called marriage (such as a domestic partnership or civil union), Have no legal recognition given to their relationships]

5. Gay marriage is often an issue at the state level. Suppose Wisconsin had a ballot initiative in an upcoming election where you could decide the issue gay marriage once and for all. How would you vote on such a measure?
   [Definitely vote no, Probably vote no, Undecided, Probably vote yes, Definitely vote yes]
6. Many believe that children are safest and healthiest in a family with a mother and a father. Others feel that children are safest and healthiest in a household full of love of commitment, regardless of whether there is a mother and father. (This includes families with two mothers or two fathers). What about you? Do you think gay and lesbian couples should be able to be parents, whether through adoption or some other means? (check one)
   [Definitely against, Probably against, Undecided, Probably support, Definitely support]
7. Which of the following best describes your racial and ethnic identity? (check all that apply)
   [White/Caucasian, Black/African American, Latino/Hispanic, Asian American, Native American, Pacific Islander, Other _____]
8. Do you own or rent your home? (check one) [Own, Rent]
9. What is the highest level of education you have completed? (check one)
   [Less than high school diploma, High school diploma or GED, Some college, Bachelors degree, Masters degree, Doctoral or Professional degree (JD, MD, PhD)]
10. Generally speaking, do you consider yourself to be (check one)
    [Republican, Democrat, Independent, Other: _____]
11. What is your current relationship status? (check one)
    [Single, never married, Married, Civil Union, Divorced, Separated, Widowed, Living with partner]
12. Are you a parent? (check one) [Yes, No]
13. What is your gender? (check one) [Male, Female]

14. What year were you born? _____
15. What is your sexual orientation and/or gender identity? (check one)
    [Straight/heterosexual, Gay/lesbian/queer, Other: _____]

Thank you for your time! Please return this completed survey to receive your gift card.

(5) Hockey Experiment

Screening question: on a scale of one to five, how interested are you in professional hockey?

Responses (randomly reversed):

1) not interested at all
2) slightly interested
3) moderately interested
4) very interested
5) extremely interested

[Sample restricted to those who answered 1 or 5]

[CONTROL]

A recent survey found that a large majority of respondents support same sex marriage. How about you?

[TREATMENT]

A recent ESPN survey found that a large majority of NHL players support same sex marriage. How about you?

Responses: (order varied randomly)

1) yes, I support same-sex marriage
2) no, but I support civil unions
3) no, I oppose same-sex marriage

(6) San Francisco Giants Experiment

[*NOTE: Paper surveys used to collect data included photos of David Hasselhoff and Matt Cain, shown to the left side of question #1. See page 63.]

[CONTROL]

1. In the photo on the left, actor David Hasselhoff is showing his opposition to Prop 8, the 2008 initiative that banned same-sex marriage in California and is currently being reviewed by the U.S. Supreme Court. What do you think the photo is supposed to mean? (check one)
   [Hasselhoff opposed Prop 8 and supports gay marriage, Hasselhoff supported Prop 8 and opposes gay marriage]

[TREATMENT]

1. In the photo on the left, San Francisco Giants Pitcher Matt Cain is showing his opposition to Prop 8, the 2008 initiative that banned same-sex marriage in California and is currently being reviewed by the U.S. Supreme Court. What do you think the photo is supposed to mean? (check one)
   [Matt Cain opposed Prop 8 and supports gay marriage, Matt Cain supported Prop 8 and opposes gay marriage]

2. Do you think gay and lesbian individuals (check one)
[Should be able to get married, Should be able to enter into a legal partnership (such as a civil union) similar to but not called marriage, Should have no legal recognition given to their relationships]

3. On a scale from 0 to 100, how do you feel toward gay and lesbian Americans? _____
0 means very unfavorable, and 100 means very favorable. Fifty means neither unfavorable nor favorable. Of course, you can use any number between zero and 100.

4. Gay marriage is often an issue at the state level. Suppose your state had a ballot initiative in an upcoming election where you could vote on a law that would allow gay marriage. How would you vote on such a measure? Note: a "yes" vote would mean allowing gay marriage; a "no" vote would mean not allowing gay marriage. (check one)
[Definitely vote no, Probably vote no, Undecided, Probably vote yes, Definitely vote yes]

5. Many believe that children are safest and healthiest in a family with a mother and a father. Others feel that children are safest and healthiest in a household full of love of commitment, regardless of whether there is a mother and father. (This includes families with two mothers or two fathers). What about you? Do you think gay and lesbian couples should be able to be parents, whether through adoption or some other means? (check one)
[Definitely against, Probably against, Undecided, Probably support, Definitely support]

6. If you had the option of watching a sporting event or another television show (i.e. a situation comedy, reality TV, etc.), how often would you choose to watch the **SPORTING EVENT** over another choice? (check one)
[Never, Rarely, Sometimes, Often, All of the time]

7. Some people enjoy watching professional sports like Major League Baseball (MLB), the National Football League (NFL), the National Basketball Association (NBA), or one of many other sports. What about you? How often do you watch professional sporting events? (check one)
[Never, Rarely, Once a month, Once a week, A few times per week, Every day (or almost every day)]

8. Thinking specifically now about the San Francisco Giants, which of the following best describes how you feel about the team? (check one)
[I'm a huge fan, I'm somewhat of a fan, I'm not much of a fan, Go Marlins!]

9. Which of the following best describes your racial and ethnic identity? (check all that apply)
[White/Caucasian, Black/African American, Latino/Hispanic, Asian American, Native American, Pacific Islander, Other _____]

10. Do you own or rent your home? (check one) [Own, Rent]

11. What is the highest level of education you have completed? (check one)
[Less than high school diploma, High school diploma or GED, Some college, Bachelors degree, Masters degree, Doctoral or Professional degree (JD, MD, PhD)]

12. Generally speaking, do you consider yourself to be (check one)
[Republican, Democrat, Independent, Other: _____]

13. What is your current relationship status? (check one)
[Single, never married, Married, Civil Union, Divorced, Separated, Widowed, Living with partner]

14. Are you a parent? (check one) [Yes, No]

15. What is your gender? (check one) [Male, Female]

16. What year were you born? _____

17. What is your sexual orientation and/or gender identity? (check one)
[Straight/heterosexual, Gay/lesbian/queer, Other: _____]

Thank you for your time! Please return this completed survey to receive your $5 gift card.

CHAPTER 4

(7) SocialSci.com Experiment

1. Please choose one of the choices below. You will be randomly assigned to one short paragraph on a public policy issue. We'll ask you a few questions after you finish reading it.

[A, B, C, D, E]

**(Random assignment takes place at this point, not as a result of the response in the previous question; the initial question leads respondents to believe the survey isn't solely about one issue).

[CONTROL]

In a recent newspaper op-ed, a citizen wrote, "It seems to me, therefore, that one might easily judge that even if we do not believe that gay marriage ever could or should be allowed in the church, we could live with a provision that allows civil marriage of gay and lesbian couples. Personally, however, I would go farther than that ... we could come to recognize the total, exclusive, permanent, interpersonal commitment of gay and lesbian couples as a part of the sacrament of matrimony."

[TREATMENT]

Reverend Richard T. Lawrence recently told members of his church, "It seems to me, therefore, that one might easily judge that even if we do not believe that gay marriage ever could or should be allowed in the church, we could live with a provision that allows civil marriage of gay and lesbian couples. Personally, however, I would go farther than that ... we could come to recognize the total, exclusive, permanent, interpersonal commitment of gay and lesbian couples as a part of the sacrament of matrimony."

2. What do you think? Should gay and lesbian individuals (1) be able to get legally married; (2) be able to enter into a legal partnership similar to but not called marriage (such as civil unions); or (3) have no legal recognition given to their relationships?
   [Be able to get legally married, Be able to enter into a legal partnership similar to but not called marriage (such as civil unions), Have no legal recognition given to their relationships]
3. Would you vote for or against a law that would increase taxes on cigarettes by one dollar per pack to fund research on lung cancer?
   [Definitely vote no, Probably vote no, Undecided, Probably vote yes, Definitely vote yes]
4. In general, what do you think is more important: protecting the environment, even at the risk of curbing economic growth, OR maintaining a prosperous economy, even if the environment suffers to some extent?
   [Protecting the environment even at the risk of curbing growth/Maintaining a prosperous economy, even if the economic growth environment suffers to some extent]
   Please answer the following questions about hypothetical ballot initiatives.
5. Would you vote for or against a law that would require all voters to display state-issued photo identification at the polls before voting?
   [In favor of a law requiring photo ID to vote, Against a law requiring photo ID to vote]

6. Many believe that children are safest and healthiest in a family with a mother and a father. Others feel that children are safest and healthiest in a household full of love of commitment, regardless of whether there is a mother and father. (This includes families with two mothers or two fathers). What about you? Do you think gay and lesbian couples should be able to be parents, whether through adoption or some other means?
   [Definitely against, Probably against, Undecided, Probably support, Definitely support]

7. Gay marriage is often an issue at the state level. Suppose your state had a ballot initiative in the 2014 election where you could vote on a law that would allow gay marriage/marriage equality. How would you vote on such a measure? Note: a "yes" vote would mean allowing gay marriage; a "no" vote would mean not allowing gay marriage.
   [Definitely vote no, Probably vote no, Undecided, Probably vote yes, Definitely vote yes]

8. Under current law, utility companies in some states are required to get at least 10% of their energy from renewable resources like wind or solar power by 2020. Would you vote for or against a law that would increase that amount to 20% by 2020?
   [Definitely vote no, Probably vote no, Undecided, Probably vote yes, Definitely vote yes]

9. On a scale from 0 to 100, how do you feel toward gays and lesbians? 0 means very unfavorable, and 100 means very favorable. Fifty means neither unfavorable nor favorable. Of course, you can use any number between zero and 100.
   [slider between 0–100]

10. What is your gender? [Male, Female]

11. Generally speaking, would you describe your political views as very liberal, liberal, moderate, conservative, or very conservative?
    [Very liberal, Liberal, Moderate, Conservative, Very conservative]

12. Which of the following categories best describes your employment status?
    [Employed, working 1–39 hours per week, Employed, working 40 + hours per week, Not employed, looking for work, Not employed, not looking for work, Retired, Full-time Student, Disabled, not able to work]

13. Which of the following best describes your racial and ethnic identity (you can choose more than one)? (Check all that apply).
    [White/Caucasian, Black/African American, Latino/Hispanic, Asian American, Native American, Pacific Islander, Other _____]

14. What is the highest level of education you have completed? (check one)
    [Less than high school diploma, High school diploma or GED, Some college, 2-year college degree, 4-year college degree, Masters degree, Doctoral degree, Professional degree (JD, MD)]

15. Generally speaking, do you consider yourself to be a Republican, a Democrat, an Independent, or something else?
    [Republican, Democrat, Independent, Something else]

16. [If Independent or Something else] Do you think of yourself as closer to the Republican Party, the Democratic Party, or equally close to the Republican Party and Democratic Party?
    [Closer to the Republican Party, Closer to the Democratic Party, Equally close to both the Democratic and Republican Parties]

17. [If Republican/Democrat] Would you consider yourself a strong (Republican/Democrat) or a weak (Republican/Democrat)?
    [Strong, Weak]

18. What is your current relationship status?
    [Single, never married, Married, Civil Union, Divorced, Separated, Widowed, Living with partner]

19. In which state do you currently reside? [drop-down list of U.S. States and Territories]

20. What is your sexual orientation or sexual identity?
    [Homosexual (gay/lesbian/queer), Bisexual, Transgender, Heterosexual or straight]

21. What year were you born? [1900–1995]
22. In most states in the U.S., people cannot vote in an election unless they fill out a government form to "register to vote." Are you currently registered to vote in the state where you live now, or are you not registered to vote there?

    Registered to vote, Not registered to vote, No registration needed (North Dakota resident)]

(8) Louisiana Experiment

Hi, my name is [NAME], may I please speak with [CITIZEN].

Hi, [CITIZEN], my name is [NAME] and I'm calling from [Louisiana State University/ Equality Louisiana].

[GROUP A]

[CONTROL]

Forty community groups recently signed a letter to members of the U.S. Senate that stated the following: "As a nation, we cannot tolerate arbitrary discrimination against millions of Americans just because of who they are. Lesbian, gay, bisexual and transgender (LGBT) people should be able to earn a living, provide for their families and contribute to our society without fear that who they are or who they love could cost them a job."

[TREATMENT]

Forty faith groups including [religion as listed on sheet] recently signed a letter to members of the U.S. Senate that stated the following: "As a nation, we cannot tolerate arbitrary discrimination against millions of Americans just because of who they are. Lesbian, gay, bisexual and transgender (LGBT) people should be able to earn a living, provide for their families and contribute to our society without fear that who they are or who they love could cost them a job."

[GROUP B]

[CONTROL]

A citizen recently wrote an article in a national magazine about his belief that same-sex marriage is consistent with Jesus' teachings. He wrote, "When we refuse to make room for gay people to live in loving, stable relationships, we consign them to lives of loneliness, secrecy and fear . . . Christ-like love calls us to go beyond tolerance to want for the other the same respect, freedom and equality one wants for oneself."

[TREATMENT]

Evangelical Pastor Steve Chalke recently wrote an article in *Christianity Magazine* about his belief that same-sex marriage is consistent with Jesus' teachings. He wrote, "When we refuse to make room for gay people to live in loving, stable relationships, we consign them to lives of loneliness, secrecy and fear . . . Christ-like love calls us to go beyond tolerance to want for the other the same respect, freedom and equality one wants for oneself."

2. What do you think? Should gay and lesbian individuals (1) be able to get legally married; (2) be able to enter into a legal partnership similar to but not called marriage (such as civil unions); or (3) have no legal recognition given to their relationships?
[Should be able to get married, Should be able to enter into a legal partnership such as a civil union, No legal recognition]

3. Would you support a law in Louisiana that would prohibit discrimination in hiring and employment on the basis of sexual orientation or gender identity by civilian, nonreligious employers?
[Definitely against, Probably against, Undecided, Probably support, Definitely support]

4. Many believe that children are safest and healthiest in a family with a mother and a father. Others feel that children are safest and healthiest in a household full of love of commitment, regardless of whether there is a mother and father. (This includes families with two mothers or two fathers). What about you? Do you think gay and lesbian couples should be able to be parents, whether through adoption or some other means?
[Definitely against, Probably against, Undecided, Probably support, Definitely support]

5. Gay marriage is often an issue at the state level. Suppose your state had a ballot initiative in the 2014 election where you could vote on a law that would allow marriage equality. How would you vote on such a measure? A "yes" vote would mean allowing gay marriage; a "no" vote would mean not allowing gay marriage.[Definitely against, Probably against, Undecided, Probably support, Definitely support]

6. On a scale of 1 to 7, where 1 is "not religious at all" (extremely secular) and 7 is "extremely religious", how would you describe your religious identity?
[Extremely secular, Somewhat secular, Slightly secular, Neither secular nor religious, Slightly religious, Somewhat religious, Extremely religious]

7. What is your present religion, if any? Are you Protestant, Roman Catholic, Mormon, Orthodox such as Greek or Russian Orthodox, Jewish, Muslim, Buddhist, Hindu, atheist, agnostic, something else, or nothing in particular?
[Protestant, Roman Catholic, Mormon (Church of Jesus Christ of Latter-day Saints/ LDS), Orthodox (Greek, Russian, or some other orthodox church), Jewish (Judaism), Muslim (Islam), Buddhist, Hindu, Atheist (do not believe in God), Agnostic (not sure if there is a God), Something else, Nothing in particular, Spiritual but not religious (VOL)]

8. [**IF PROTESTANT**] As far as your present religion, what denomination or church, if any, do you identify with most closely? Just stop me when I get to the right one. Are you Baptist, Methodist, Lutheran, Presbyterian, Pentecostal, Episcopalian or Anglican, nondenominational or independent church, something else or none in particular?
[Baptist, Methodist, Lutheran, Presbyterian, Pentecostal, Episcopalian or Anglican, Just a Protestant, Just a Christian, Something else, None in particular]

9. Do you think of yourself as a Christian or not? [Yes, No]

10. [**IF CHRISTIAN in at least one of the questions above**] Would you describe yourself as a "born-again" or evangelical Christian, or not? [Yes, No, Don't Know/Refused]

11. Aside from weddings and funerals, how often do you attend religious services... more than once a week, once a week, once or twice a month, a few times a year, seldom, or never? [More than once a week, Once a week, Once or twice a month, A few times a year, Seldom, Never, Don't Know/Refused]

12. How important is religion in your life—very important, somewhat important, not too important, or not at all important?
[Very important, Somewhat important, Not too important, Not at all important]

Thank you very much for your time. Goodbye!

CHAPTER 5

(9) Equality Illinois Experiment

Hi! Is *[first name]* available? My name is *[your name]*. I'm a volunteer with Equality Illinois, the statewide organization working to secure and protect rights for individuals of all sexual orientations and identities.

[CONTROL]

On June 1, a new statewide law will allow civil unions. While this is an important step toward equality, civil unions are not the same as marriage. We want to keep fighting to ensure marriage equality for all residents of Illinois. We believe that everyone should be allowed to marry, regardless of sexual orientation.

[TREATMENT]

On June 1, a new statewide law will allow civil unions. While this is an important step toward equality, civil unions are not the same as marriage. Coretta Scott King once said that she stood with gay and lesbian people just as they stood with her husband in places like Selma and Montgomery. We want to keep fighting to ensure marriage equality for all residents of Illinois. We believe that everyone should be allowed to marry, regardless of sexual orientation.

(NAME), can I add you to our list of supporters for marriage equality? [LISTEN & RESPOND; if possible, make note of their response]

We sometimes like to be able to contact our supporters through e-mail. We do not send e-mails more than 1–2 times per week but it's important to be able to stay in touch. Would you be willing to give me your e-mail address?

- [If YES]. Great! Thank you very much. Can you spell that for me? [CONFIRM SPELLING].
- [IF MAYBE, offer www.eqil.org for more information]
- [If NO]: I understand. [If possible, make note of their explanation.]

(NAME), Equality Illinois is celebrating its 20th anniversary in 2011. Now more than ever, we need to reach out to our friends who agree these issues are important, especially to fight back against the anti-equality campaigns to deny equal rights in Illinois. Will you support your friends and neighbors in their fight for the equal right to marry in Illinois by investing $20 in the campaign tonight?

- [if NO to $20] No problem. I really would like to find a level that works for you! When everyone who cares about equality gives what they can, it really adds up. That's why even more people are doing a donation of $10. Would you be willing to donate $10 to support us?
- [If no to $10]. OK, I understand. Is there an amount that would be better for your budget?

[If YES, go to NEXT SECTION]

- [IF MAYBE, offer www.eqil.org for more information.]
- [If NO]: I understand. [If possible, make note of their explanation.]

[IF YES FOR ANY AMOUNT]

Great, thank you so much! I just need to get some information from you.

[Confirm Name, Confirm Billing Address, Ask for Credit Card Information]

[*Read back amount and thank them for their time and their support!*]

[*If insist on paying by mail, make note on pledge form and we will send a form in the mail*]

One last thing, (NAME). We are recruiting concerned volunteers like you to help us reach out to Equality Illinois supporters and ask them to take action. Will you make it a priority to join us next _____ for our phone bank so we can build momentum for our equality campaign?

- [If YES, go to DETAILS]
- [If NO or MAYBE, go to PROBLEM-SOLVING]

[DETAILS]

Do you have a pen and paper handy to write down the address of our meeting place?

[Address and any land markers] XXXX North Halsted Street (near the intersection of North Halsted and Roscoe Streets in the Lakeview neighborhood).

[Travel information] We are very accessible by bus and by train. The nearest El stop is the Belmont Red Line stop, only a few blocks away from our headquarters. The (BUS NUMBER) bus stops almost right outside our front door.

We need this phase of the campaign to be the very biggest. Will you bring a friend or family member with you? Who? Do you have any questions? Okay, great. If you think of anything you can call Joey McDonald at 773-xxx-xxxx. Thanks so much. [GO TO THANK YOU]

[PROBLEM-SOLVING]

I definitely hear that you care. What's holding you back from joining us _____?

- *If Busy:* I hear that. It sounds like you have a lot going on. Spring is a busy season for all of us. We have a lot to be thankful for, with civil unions starting June 1. The problem is, anti-equality groups and candidates are working hard to deny equal rights to gay and lesbian families in Illinois. They will do ANYTHING to take these rights away. Have you seen that in the news? Will you move around whatever you have going on to make *this* a priority?
- *If Vague, Unsure:* The only way we can win is by getting supporters who rarely speak up on important issues like this one. Currently, only 5 states across the country allow for marriage equality. We want that to happen in Illinois, right? To make sure that can happen, we need you to volunteer. Will you make it a priority to join us for this one shift?
- *If Scared/Nervous:* I'm curious, have you ever done something like this before? I was definitely nervous my first time. Lots of people have never done anything like this before. But folks are being so moved by the campaign that they're trying it out for the first time. Our coaches will help you have a good experience. How does that sound? Will you give it a try?
- *If still NO:* Ok. I'm so sorry I won't see you _____ [date] at the _____ [action]. Will you join us on _____ instead?
- *If possible, make note of their reasoning for not agreeing to volunteer.*

**(NAME), thank you very much for your time tonight and for your support for marriage equality in Illinois. Have a good evening! **

(10) Georgia Equality Experiment

Hi! Is *[first name]* available? My name is *[your name]*. I'm a volunteer with Georgia Equality, the statewide organization working to secure and protect rights for individuals of all sexual orientations and identities.

[CONTROL]

We want to keep fighting to ensure marriage equality for all residents of Georgia. We believe that everyone should be allowed the freedom to marry, regardless of sexual orientation.

[TREATMENT]

We want to keep fighting to ensure marriage equality for all residents of Georgia. We believe that everyone should be allowed the freedom to marry, regardless of sexual orientation. As you may know, President Obama recently announced his support for gay marriage, saying, "I've just concluded that for me personally it is important for me to go ahead and affirm that I think same-sex couples should be able to get married."

(NAME), can I add you to our list of supporters for marriage equality? [LISTEN & RESPOND; if possible, make note of their response]
We sometimes like to be able to contact our supporters through e-mail. We do not send e-mails more than 1–2 times per week but it's important to be able to stay in touch. Would you be willing to give me your e-mail address?

- [If YES]. Great! Thank you very much. Can you spell that for me? [CONFIRM SPELLING].
- [IF MAYBE, offer www.georgiaequality.org for more information]
- [If NO]: I understand. [If possible, make note of their explanation.]

(NAME), Georgia Equality was started in 1995 to advance fairness, freedom, safety and opportunity for Georgia's LGBT communities. Now more than ever, we need to reach out to our friends who agree these issues are important, especially to fight back against the anti-equality campaigns to deny equal rights in Georgia. Will you support your friends and neighbors in their fight for the equal right to marry in Georgia by investing $20 in the campaign tonight?

[if NO to $20] No problem. I really would like to find a level that works for you! When everyone who cares about equality gives what they can, it really adds up. That's why even more people are doing a donation of $10. Would you be willing to donate $10 to support us? [If no to $10]. OK, I understand. Is there an amount that would be better for your budget?

- [If YES, go to NEXT SECTION]
- [IF MAYBE, offer www.georgiaequality.org for more information.]
- [If NO]: I understand. [If possible, make note of their explanation.]

[IF YES FOR ANY AMOUNT] Great, thank you so much! I just need to get some information from you. [Confirm Name, Confirm Billing Address, Ask for Credit Card Information]

[*Read back amount and thank them for their time and their support!*]

[*If insist on paying by mail, make note on pledge form and we will send a form in the mail*]

(NAME), thank you very much for your time tonight and for your support for marriage equality in Georgia. Have a good evening!**

(11) Latino Decisions Experiment

[NOTE: These items were embedded in a larger survey. All callers were fully bilingual.]

[CONTROL, ENGLISH]

A vocal supporter of marriage equality recently wrote, "As a country that has fought and continues to fight against bigotry and discrimination, we understand how dangerous it is to pick and choose who deserve equality and respect . . . A better country for gays and lesbians is a better country for all. We're all in this together . . . There are many LGBT people throughout the country. We have gay and lesbian brothers and sisters, friends and children. Their fight is our fight for justice and equality."

[CONTROL, SPANISH]

Una seguidora vocal de la igualdad en el matrimonio recientemente escribió, "Como un país que ha peleado y continua peleando en contra de la intolerancia y la discriminación, entendemos lo peligroso que es escoger y elegir quien merece igualdad y respeto . . . Un mejor país para los homosexuales y las lesbianas es un mejor país para todos. Todos estamos en esto juntos . . . Hay tantas personas LGBT a través del país. Tenemos hermanos y hermanas homosexuales y lesbianas, amigos e hijos. Su lucha es nuestra lucha por la justicia e igualdad."

[TREATMENT, ENGLISH]

Dolores Huerta, co-founder of the United Farm Workers and a well-known activist on behalf of Latino rights and social justice, is a vocal supporter of marriage equality. She recently wrote, "As a community that has fought and continues to fight against bigotry and discrimination, we understand how dangerous it is to pick and choose who deserve equality and respect . . . A better country for gays and lesbians is a better country for all. We're all in this together . . . There are just as many LGBT people in our communities as there are throughout the country. We too have gay and lesbian hermanos y hermanas, friends and children. Their fight is our fight for justice and equality."

[TREATMENT, SPANISH]

Dolores Huerta, co-fundadora de la Unidad de Trabajadores Agrícolas y una activista reconocida en nombre de los derechos de los Latinos y la justicia social, es una seguidora vocal de la igualdad en el matrimonio. Ella recientemente escribió, "Como una comunidad que ha peleado y continua peleando en contra de la intolerancia y la discriminación, entendemos lo peligroso que es escoger y elegir quien merece igualdad y respeto . . . Un mejor país para los homosexuales y las lesbianas es un mejor país para todos. Todos estamos juntos en esto . . . Hay tantas personas LGBT en nuestras comunidades como lo hay a través del país. Nosotros también tenemos hermanos y hermanas homosexuales y lesbianas, amigos e hijos. Su lucha es nuestra lucha por la justicia e igualdad."

1. What do you think? Should gay and lesbian individuals (1) be able to get legally married; (2) be able to enter into a legal partnership similar to but not called marriage (such as civil unions); or (3) have no legal recognition given to their relationships?
   [Be able to get legally married, Be able to enter into a legal partnership similar to but not called marriage, Have no legal recognition given to their relationships, Don't know, Refused]

Qué piensa usted? Deberían los individuos homosexuales y lesbianas (1) poder casarse legalmente; (2) poder entrar en una vida conyugal legal similar a pero no llamada matrimonio (como una unión civil); o (3) no tener el reconocimiento legal a sus relaciones?

[Poder casarse legalmente, Poder entrar en una vida conyugal similar a pero no llamada matrimonio, No tener el reconocimiento legal a sus relaciones, No sabe, Rehusó]

2. Gay marriage is often an issue at the state level. Suppose your state had a ballot initiative in the 2013 election where you could vote on a law that would allow gay marriage/marriage equality. How would you vote on such a measure? A "yes" vote would mean allowing gay marriage; a "no" vote would mean not allowing gay marriage.

[Definitely yes, Probably yes, Probably no, Definitely no, Don't know, Refused]

El matrimonio homosexual es frecuentemente un tema a nivel estatal. Supongamos que su estado tuviera una votación iniciativa en la elección del 2013, en donde usted pudiera votar por una ley que permitiera los matrimonios homosexuales/igualdad del matrimonio. Como votaría usted en tal medida? Un voto "si" significaría permitir el matrimonio homosexual, un "no" significaría no permitirse el matrimonio homosexual.

[Definitivamente si, Probablemente si, Probablemente no, Definitivamente no, No sabe, Rehusó]

(12) South Texas Experiment

[NOTE: These items were embedded in a larger survey. All callers were fully bilingual.]

[CONTROL ENGLISH]

Many leaders in this country have long supported equal rights for gays and lesbians, including gay marriage. One recently wrote, "As a country that has fought and continues to fight against bigotry and discrimination, we understand how dangerous it is to pick and choose who deserve equality and respect.... We have gay and lesbian brothers and sisters, friends and children. Their fight is our fight for justice and equality."

[CONTROL, SPANISH]

Muchos líderes en este país han apoyado durante mucho tiempo la igualdad de derechos para homosexuales y lesbianas, como el matrimonio homosexual. Uno de ellos escribió recientemente: "Como un país que ha luchado y sigue luchando contra la intolerancia y la discriminación, entendemos lo peligroso que es legir quien merece igualdad y respeto.... Tenemos hermanos gays y lesbianas y hermanas, amigos y niños. Su lucha es nuestra lucha por la justicia y la igualdad."

[TREATMENT, ENGLISH]

Latino leaders including Supreme Court Justice Sonya Sotomayor and civil rights activists César Chavez and Dolores Huerta, co-founders of the United Farm Workers, have long supported equal rights for gays and lesbians, including gay marriage. Huerta recently wrote, "As a community that has fought and continues to fight against bigotry and discrimination, we understand how dangerous it is to pick and choose who deserve equality and respect.... We have gay and lesbian hermanos y hermanas, friends and children. Their fight is our fight for justice and equality."

[TREATMENT, SPANISH]

Líderes hispanos, incluyendo la Justicia Sonia Sotomayor de la Corte Suprema y activistas de los derechos civiles César Chávez y Dolores Huerta, co-fundadores de la Unión de

Campesinos, han apoyado durante mucho tiempo la igualdad de derechos para homosexuales y lesbianas, como el matrimonio homosexual. Huerta escribió recientemente: "Como una comunidad que ha luchado y sigue luchando contra la intolerancia y la discriminación, entendemos lo peligroso que es elegir quien merece igualdad y respeto....Disponemos de gays y lesbianas Hermanos y hermanas, amigos y niños. Su lucha es nuestra lucha por la justicia y la igualdad."

1. What do you think? Should gay and lesbian couples (a) be able to get legally married, (b) be able to enter into a legal partnership similar to but not called marriage, such as civil unions, or (c) have no legal recognition given to their relationships? [Response order randomly reversed]

Qué piensa usted? Deberían los individuos homosexuales y lesbianas (1) poder casarse legalmente; (2) poder entrar en una vida conyugal legal similar a pero no llamada matrimonio (como una unión civil); o (3) no tener el reconocimiento legal a sus relaciones?

2. Gay marriage is often an issue at the state level. Suppose Texas had a ballot initiative in the November 2013 election where you could vote on a law that would allow gay marriage. How would you vote on such a measure? A "yes" vote would mean allowing gay marriage; a "no" vote would mean not allowing gay marriage.
[Definitely yes, Probably yes, Probably no, Definitely no] [Response order randomly reversed]

El matrimonio homosexual es frecuentemente un tema a nivel estatal. Supongamos que su estado tuviera una votación iniciativa en la elección del 2013, en donde usted pudiera votar por una ley que permitiera los matrimonios homosexuales/igualdad del matrimonio. Como votaría usted en tal medida? Un voto "sí" significaría permitir el matrimonio homosexual, un "no" significaría no permitirse el matrimonio homosexual. [Definitivamente sí, Problamente sí, Problamente no, Definitivamente no]

(13) Virginia Experiment

[Note: These items were embedded in a larger survey; respondents were randomly assigned to answer only one of these questions]

[OPPOSE SCRIPT]

Many political leaders in Virginia oppose same-sex marriage, including Republican Governor Bob McDonnell and Republican Attorney General (and gubernatorial nominee) Ken Cuccinelli. How about you?

[Full marriage, Civil unions, Neither]

[SUPPORT SCRIPT]

Many political leaders in Virginia support same-sex marriage, including Democratic Senators Tim Kaine and Mark Warner, and Democratic candidate for governor Terry McAuliffe. How about you?

[Full marriage, Civil unions, Neither]

(14) New Jersey Experiment

[CONTROL GROUPS]

PLEASE LISTEN TO THE FOLLOWING PARAGRAPH CLOSELY:

[DEMOCRATIC CONTROL]

Several prominent politicians have recently spoken out *in favor* of the freedom to marry for gay and lesbian couples in the United States. For example, one elected official said, "I've just concluded that for me personally it is important for me to go ahead and affirm that I think same-sex couples should be able to get married." Another politician recently argued that bans on same-sex marriage are "contrary...with the principles of a nation that honors freedom, equality, and justice above all."

[REPUBLICAN CONTROL]

Several prominent politicians have recently spoken out in favor of the freedom to marry for gay and lesbian couples in the United States. For example, one once said "Freedom means freedom for everyone.... I think people ought to be free to enter into any kind of union they wish. Any kind of arrangement they wish." Another politician recently said, "I have come to believe that if two people are prepared to make a lifetime commitment to love and care for each other in good times and in bad, the government shouldn't deny them the opportunity to get married."

[TREATMENT GROUPS]

1. Which of the following best describes your party identification? Do you consider yourself:
   [A strong Republican, A weak Republican, A strong Democrat, A weak Democrat, Independent leaning Democratic, Independent leaning Republican, Something else (e.g. Green Party, Libertarian Party, etc.]

[DEMOCRATIC TREATMENT GROUP]

[IF DEMOCRAT OR INDEPENDENT LEANING DEMOCRATIC]: "Oh, great. Me too!"

[IF REPUBLICAN, INDEPENDENT LEANING REPUBLICAN, or ANYTHING ELSE]: "Great, thank you!"

PLEASE LISTEN TO THE FOLLOWING PARAGRAPH CLOSELY: Several prominent Democrats have recently spoken out *in favor* of the freedom to marry for gay and lesbian couples. For example, Democratic President Barack Obama recently said, "I've just concluded that for me personally it is important for me to go ahead and affirm that I think same-sex couples should be able to get married." Former Democratic President Bill Clinton recently argued that bans on same-sex marriage are "contrary...with the principles of a nation that honors freedom, equality, and justice above all."

[REPUBLICAN TREATMENT GROUP]

[IF REPUBLICAN OR INDEPENDENT LEANING REPUBLICAN]: "Oh, great. Me too!"

[IF DEMOCRAT or ANYTHING ELSE]: "Great, thank you!"

PLEASE LISTEN TO THE FOLLOWING PARAGRAPH CLOSELY: Several prominent Republicans have recently spoken out *in favor* of the freedom to marry for gay and lesbian couples. For example, former Republican Vice President Dick Cheney once said, "Freedom means freedom for everyone.... I think people ought to be free to enter into any kind of union they wish. Any kind of arrangement they wish." Senator Rob Portman, Republican from Ohio, recently said, "I have come to believe that if two people are prepared to make a lifetime commitment to love and care for each other in good times and in bad, the government shouldn't deny them the opportunity to get married."

2. Do you think gay and lesbian people (check one)

[Should be able to get married, Should be able to enter into a legal partnership (such as a civil union) similar to but not called marriage, Should have no legal recognition given to their relationships]

3. On a scale from 0 to 100, how do you feel toward gay and lesbian Americans? 0 means very unfavorable, and 100 means very favorable. Fifty means neither unfavorable nor favorable. Of course, you can use any number between zero and 100. _____

4. Gay marriage is often an issue at the state level. Suppose your state had a ballot initiative in an upcoming election where you could vote on a law that would allow gay marriage. How would you vote on such a measure? Note: a "yes" vote would mean allowing gay marriage; a "no" vote would mean not allowing gay marriage. (check one)
   [Definitely vote no, Probably vote no, Undecided, Probably vote yes, Definitely vote yes]

5. Many believe that children are safest and healthiest in a family with a mother and a father. Others feel that children are safest and healthiest in a household full of love of commitment, regardless of whether there is a mother and father. (This includes families with two mothers or two fathers). What about you? Do you think gay and lesbian couples should be able to be parents, whether through adoption or some other means? (check one)
   [Definitely against, Probably against, Undecided, Probably support, Definitely support]

6. Which of the following best describes your racial and ethnic identity? (check all that apply)
   [White/Caucasian, Black/African American, Latino/Hispanic, Asian American, Native American, Pacific Islander, Other _____]

7. Do you own or rent your home? (check one) [Own, Rent]

8. What is the highest level of education you have completed? (check one)
   [Less than a high school diploma, High school diploma or GED, Associates degree, some college, Bachelors degree, Masters degree, Doctoral or Professional Degree (JD, MD, PhD)

9. [CONTROL GROUPS ONLY] Generally speaking, do you consider yourself to be (check one)
   [A strong Republican, A weak Republican, A strong Democrat, A weak Democrat, Independent leaning Democratic, Independent leaning Republican, Something else (e.g. Green Party, Libertarian Party, etc.]

10. What is your current relationship status? (check one)[Single, never married, Married, Civil Union, In a committed relationship, Separated, Widowed, Living with partner, Divorced]

11. Are you a parent? (check one) [Yes, No]

12. What is your gender? (check one) [Male, Female]

13. What year were you born? _____

14. What is your sexual orientation and/or gender identity? (check one)[Straight/heterosexual, Bisexual, Gay/lesbian, queer, Asexual, Other: _____]

Thank you for your time! To thank you, please accept a $2 gift card to Dunkin Donuts.

(15) National Partisanship Experiment

Screening question:
Do you think of yourself as a member of a political party?

1) I strongly identify as a Republican
2) I lean towards the Republican Party
3) I strongly identify as a Democrat
4) I lean towards the Democratic Party
5) No, I don't

[Sample restricted to those who answered 1 or 3]

[Script randomly assigned to match or conflict with respondent's stated partisanship]

[*NOTE: Both versions of the item below included a personal photo of the husband of one of the authors, shown to the left side of the question.]

I'm James Scott, a senior [Democratic/Republican] spokesman. Gay marriage is consistent with our party's values and I support it. Do you?

1) Yes I support same-sex marriage

2) No, I don't support same-sex marriage

(16) Equality Maryland Experiment

[EMAIL]

We are e-mailing to thank you for all of your support as we fought for marriage equality in the state of Maryland. Thanks to you, gay, lesbian, bisexual, and transgender Marylanders have more rights than ever before.

We know, however, that we are only at the beginning of our fight for true equality. **We would like to hear from you about where you think we might go from here.**

Please click on this link to take you to a short survey and be entered into a raffle to win a $100 gift card to Amazon.com. Thank you for your support and for your feedback!

[SURVEY]

1. What do you think are the *most* important issues facing the LGBT community? Please rank the issues below in order of importance (1 being most important and so on).

   [Transgender Equality, Parenting laws, Employment non-discrimination, Health care for LGBT individuals, Hate crimes legislation, LGBT teen suicide and bullying]

2. As an LGBT individual, have you ever experienced discrimination based on your sexual orientation?

   [Yes, No, I am not LGBT]

[IF YES] Please briefly describe your experiences of discrimination for being an LGBT individual in the box below.

3. Now that marriage equality has been won in the state of Maryland, what are the three issues facing the LGBT community that you think should be addressed *first*?

   [open-ended]

4. *Please read the following paragraph carefully before moving on to the next page.*

   Equality Maryland lobbies in Annapolis and across the state to create equal protection under the law for LGBT Marylanders and their families; to eliminate prejudice and discrimination based on sexual orientation and gender identity through outreach, education, research, community organizing, training and coalition building; and to utilize our Political Action Committee (PAC) to elect fair minded candidates.

   Though marriage equality is now the law of Maryland, the fight for full equality is *far* from finished. They need to raise money to fight long-standing battles in Maryland in new ways like transgender equality, and new battles such as the equal application of marriage equality laws for all LGBT Marylanders and advocating for young and older LGBT Marylanders.

[PROGRESSIVE TREATMENT ONLY]

We know that you are a progressive Marylander and someone who understands the value of championing progressive causes. We are asking for your continued support as we continue to work for the rights of the LGBT communities in Maryland.

[PREVIOUS SUPPORTER TREATMENT ONLY]

We know that you are a progressive Marylander and someone who understands the value of championing progressive causes. We are asking for your continued support as we continue to work for the rights of the LGBT communities in Maryland.

At the end of the survey, you will be able to get more information about these important issues that Equality Maryland is fighting for on behalf of all LGBT people within the state and to support their efforts in the state of Maryland.

5. Would you be willing to be added to a *new* list of supporters to receive news and alerts about LGBT issues in Maryland like transgender equality? [Yes, No]

[IF YES] Please enter your email to be added to a list of NEW supporters to receive information about LGBT issues in Maryland like transgender equality and application of marriage laws. Please make sure to enter your full e-mail address (i.e. johnsmith@ gmail.com).

NOTE: Your e-mail will never be sold or given to any other organization and you will have the option to opt out of future e-mails if you choose.

6. Would you be willing to sign an online petition to ask Governor O'Malley to pass a transgender anti-discrimination law? [Yes, No]

[IF YES] Please enter your e-mail to receive ONE notice of how to sign the petition to urge the Maryland General Assembly to pass a transgender anti-discrimination law.

7. Will you continue your support of Equality Maryland as they fight the next set of battles? Any amount can help us make our state a more fair and free place to live. There are new issues now that we have won the freedom to marry in Maryland and your support can keep the fight going strong.

Can you pledge to make a donation? You will receive a follow-up email with instructions on how to donate. The process is quick and easy! Equality Maryland would appreciate any amount you can give.

[$5, $15, $25, $50, $75, $100, $500, No thank you, I would not like to pledge to donate at this time.]

[IF PLEDGE AMOUNT SELECTED] Thank you for your generosity! We appreciate your support.

Please enter your e-mail to receive instructions on how to process the donation. The process is quick and easy.

8. What year were you born? [1900–2006]

9. What is your gender? Do you identify as:
   [Male, Female, Gender non-conforming, Trans*, Transsexual, Intersex]

10. Generally speaking, would you describe your political views as very progressive, progressive, moderate, conservative, or very conservative?
    [Very Progressive, Progressive, Moderate, Conservative, Very Conservative]

11. Which of the following best describes your racial and ethnic identity? You can choose more than one—check all that apply.
    [White or Caucasian, Black or African American, Hispanic or Latino(a), Asian American, American Indian, Pacific Islander, Other]

12. What is your current relationship status?
    [Single, never married, Married without children, Married with children, Civil Union, Divorced, Separated, Widowed, Living with partner]

13. Generally speaking, do you consider yourself to be a Republican, a Democrat, an Independent, or something else?
    [Republican, Democrat, Independent, Something else]

[If Independent or Something else] Do you think of yourself as closer to the Republican Party, the Democratic party, or equally close to the Republican Party and Democratic Party?

[Closer to the Republican Party, Closer to the Democratic Party, Equally close to both Democratic Party and Republican Party]

[If Democrat or Republican] How strong is your identification to the partisanship choice you just made?

[Very Weak, Weak, Somewhat Weak, Somewhat strong, Strong, Very strong]

14. Would you like to be entered into a contest to win a $100 gift card to Amazon.com? If so you will need to provide a valid e-mail address so we can contact you if you win.

[Yes, I will provide my e-mail address to be notified if I win, No thank you, I decline to enter the contest]

[IF YES] Please enter your e-mail address below so we can contact you if you win the $100 gift card to Amazon.com. Be sure to enter your full e-mail address; for example, bsmith@ gmail.com

Thank you very much for your participation in this survey! We truly value your time and appreciate your help. If you have any questions, please contact bharrison@wesleyan.edu. Thank you!

(17) Capital City Alliance Experiment

1. In what state do you currently reside? (Please select the state you consider your PRIMARY state of residence). [drop-down menu of U.S. states and territories]
2. What do you think are the *most* important issues facing the lesbian, gay, bisexual, transgender, and queer (LGBTQ) community in your state? Please rank the issues below in order of importance (1 being most important and so on).

[Transgender Equality, Parenting laws, Employment non-discrimination, Health care for LGBT individuals, Hate crimes legislation, LGBT teen suicide and bullying, Marriage Equality]

3. As an LGBT individual, have you ever experienced discrimination based on your sexual orientation? [Yes, No, I am not LGBT]

[IF YES] If you would like to share, please briefly describe your experiences of discrimination for being an LGBT individual in the box below.

4. What are three most important issues facing the LGBT community where you are?

[First priority, Second priority, Third priority]

5. *Please read the following paragraph carefully before moving on to the next page.*

As you may know, the Capital City Alliance is an organization in Louisiana with a civic purpose rather than political one. CCA strives to be involved in all aspects of community life, including governmental processes that affect the Baton Rouge Community, particularly those that impact the lives of the community's gay, lesbian, bisexual and transgender citizens. Their goal is to improve the quality of life for lesbian, gay, bisexual, and transgender (LGBT) people and their allies in greater Baton Rouge and around the state of Louisiana through education, communication, advocacy, and community building.

CCA works closely with other progressive organizations in Baton Rouge, across the state, and nationally to achieve our mission and goals.

[CONTROL]

We are asking for your continued support as we continue to work for the rights of the LGBT communities in Louisiana and beyond.

[PROGRESSIVE TREATMENT]

We know that you are a progressive and someone who understands the value of championing PROGRESSIVE causes. We are asking for your continued support as we continue to work for the rights of the LGBT communities in Louisiana and beyond.

[FAIRNESS TREATMENT]

We know that you are someone who values FAIRNESS and fair treatment for all people, regardless of sexual orientation and/or gender identity. We are asking for your continued support as we continue to work for the rights of the LGBT communities in Louisiana and beyond.

At the end of the survey, you will be able to get more information about these important issues that CCA is fighting for on behalf of all LGBT people within the state and to support their efforts.

6. Would you be willing to be added to a *new* list of supporters to receive news and alerts about LGBT issues in Louisiana like employment non-discrimination for LGBT people, legislation to help stop bullying and teen suicide, and equality for transgender people? [Yes, No]

   [IF YES] Please enter your e-mail to be added to a list of NEW supporters to receive information about LGBT issues in Louisiana. Please make sure to enter your full e-mail address (i.e. johnsmith@gmail.com).

   NOTE: Your e-mail will never be sold or given to any other organization and you will have the option to opt out of future e-mails if you choose.

7. Under current law, a person can be fired from a job- public or private- for no reason other than they are a gay, lesbian, bisexual, or transgender person.

   Would you be willing to sign a petition to urge Louisiana's state legislators to support new legislation outlawing this kind of employment discrimination against LGBT people?

   [IF YES] Please enter your e-mail to receive ONE notice of how to sign the petition to urge the passage of an employment non-discrimination agreement (ENDA).

8. Will you continue your support of the Capital City Alliance as they fight the next set of battles? Any amount can help make our state and our country a more fair and free place to live. Your support can keep the fight going strong.

   Can you pledge to make a donation? You will receive a follow-up e-mail with instructions on how to donate. The process is quick and easy! CCA would appreciate any amount you can give.

   [$5, $15, $25, $50, $75, $100, $500, No thank you, I would not like to pledge to donate at this time.]

   [IF PLEDGE AMOUNT SELECTED] Thank you for your generosity! We appreciate your support.

   Please enter your e-mail to receive instructions on how to process the donation. The process is quick and easy.

9. Gay marriage is often an issue at the state level. Suppose your state had a ballot initiative in the 2014 election where you could vote on a law that would allow gay marriage/marriage equality. How would you vote on such a measure?

   Note: a "yes" vote would mean allowing gay marriage a "no" vote would mean not allowing gay marriage.

   [Definitely vote no, Probably vote no, Undecided, Probably vote yes, Definitely vote yes]

10. What year were you born? [1900–2006]

11. What is your gender? Do you identify as:

    [Male, Female, Gender non-conforming, Trans*, Transsexual, Intersex]

12. What is your sexual orientation?

    [Gay, Lesbian, Bisexual, Queer, Asexual, Pansexual, Questioning, Heterosexual]

13. Generally speaking, would you describe your political views as very progressive, progressive, moderate, conservative, or very conservative?

    [Very Progressive, Progressive, Moderate, Conservative, Very Conservative]

14. Which of the following best describes your racial and ethnic identity? You can choose more than one—check all that apply.

    [White or Caucasian, Black or African American, Hispanic or Latino(a), Asian American, American Indian, Pacific Islander, Other]

15. What is your current relationship status?

    [Single, never married, Married without children, Married with children, Civil Union, Divorced, Separated, Widowed, Living with partner]

16. Generally speaking, do you consider yourself to be a Republican, a Democrat, an Independent, or something else?

    [Republican, Democrat, Independent, Something else]

    [If Independent or Something else] Do you think of yourself as closer to the Republican Party, the Democratic party, or equally close to the Republican Party and Democratic Party?

    [Closer to the Republican Party, Closer to the Democratic Party, Equally close to both Democratic Party and Republican Party]

    [If Democrat or Republican] How strong is your identification to the partisanship choice you just made?

    [Very Weak, Somewhat Weak, Somewhat strong, Very strong]

17. Would you like to be entered into a contest to win a $100 gift card to Amazon.com? If so you will need to provide a valid e-mail address so we can contact you if you win.

    [Yes, I will provide my e-mail address to be notified if I win, No thank you, I decline to enter the contest]

    [IF YES] Please enter your e-mail address below so we can contact you if you win the $100 gift card to Amazon.com. Be sure to enter your full e-mail address; for example, bsmith@gmail.com

Thank you very much for your participation in this survey! We truly value your time and appreciate your help. If you have any questions, please contact bharrison@wesleyan.edu. Thank you!

Notes

CHAPTER 1

1. These shifts are documented in Gallup Polls tracking polls (Gallup Poll 1975, 2012; Gallup Poll Trends 2016).

2. A number of previous field experiments have been used to explore how best to increase charitable giving. Miller and Krosnick (2004) found that appeals to donate to an abortion rights group that included a "policy change threat" message were more likely to result in monetary donations than were appeals that included a "policy change opportunity" message. Frey and Meier (2004) found that individuals are more likely to contribute when informed that a majority of other individuals have already done so; Shang and Croson (2009) found that individuals are influenced by information about how much others have contributed. Karlan and List (2007) found that the rate and amount of giving are positively influenced when large matching gifts are available.

CHAPTER 3

1. Wearing hats and clothing with the Principle 6 campaign logo or the wording of Principle 6 did not technically violate Olympic rules and yet was clearly a statement of support for LGBT rights. In possibly the strongest rebuke of Russia's stance against LGBT freedoms, President Obama skipped the Games entirely but included three openly LGBT athletes, Billie Jean King, Caitlin Cahow, and Brian Boitano, in the official US Olympic delegation.

2. Because interest in sports was measured post-treatment, there is a small possibility that responses were influenced by the treatment, i.e., that some respondents in the treatment group who were previously opposed to marriage equality reported less interest in sports and that those previously supportive reported more interest. We chose to ask interest in sports post-treatment so as not to have any priming of sports identity other than the treatment paragraph.

3. Consistent with these findings, we also found the Athletes cue was most effective among those who reported they would choose to watch sports often or all of the time and among those who reported heavy viewership of sporting events, compared to those reporting less interest in watching sports and those less likely to watch sporting events. For additional details see appendix tables A3.1 and A3.2.

4. For additional details, see appendix tables A3.3 and A3.4.

5. In contrast to the experiment conducted just before the 2013 Super Bowl, in this experiment, interest in sports was measured pre-treatment rather than post-treatment in order to minimize the possibility of the treatment influencing respondents' reported interest in sports.

6. As one reviewer of this experiment put it, "Looking for homophobes in San Francisco to nudge towards tolerance, particularly among those who can apparently afford to attend

a baseball game at AT&T Park, is like looking for punk rockers at an *Up With People* revival."

CHAPTER 4

1. Several studies have found that the effect of religious priming is dependent on the degree of religiosity of the participant (Carpenter and Marshall 2009; Gervais and Norenzayan 2012; Horton, Rand, and Zeckhauser 2010; McKay et al. 2011; Paciotti et al. 2011; and Shariff and Norenzayan 2007). At the same time, priming religious identity can motivate individuals to behave in ways that they believe are consistent with their religious beliefs rather than generating prosocial behavior. For example, it may cause individuals to focus on the transcendent goal of personal salvation rather than on empathy (Rokeach 1969). Blogowska and Saroglou (2011) found that the religiosity of high fundamentalists caused them to extend less prosociality to targets who threatened their values. Barker and Bearce (2012) found that believers in Christian end-times theology—those who believe the planet has a relatively short life expectancy—are less likely to support policies designed to curb global warming than are other Americans. Various scholars have found that those who believe in the inerrancy of the Bible are also less likely to support environmental protection (see Djupe and Calfano 2014).

2. Across three experiments, Gervais and Norenzayan (2012) found that priming religious individuals to think about God increased their public self-awareness as well as their socially-desirable response. Religious participants who were primed to think about God were more likely to give socially-desirable answers compared to non-religious participants and religious participants in the control condition. Ben-Nun Bloom, Arikan, and Courtemanche (2015) found that priming religious identity increases opposition to immigrants when the religion or ethnicity of immigrants is perceived as constituting membership in an out-group. Among more religious participants, religious dissimilarity between the participants and the immigrant group generates even stronger anti-immigrant sentiments. Finally, Van Tongeren et al. (2013) posited that priming religion among religious individuals should decrease existential anxiety, helping them manage existential concerns and thus decrease their defensiveness to members of out-groups. In contrast, priming religion among non-religious individuals should increase those concerns and increase defensiveness.

3. Robinson (2010) exposed evangelical Protestants who are members of the Christian Right political movement to dissonant messages on immigration and capital punishment, either attributing the message to an in-group religious leader (a Catholic) or an out-group religious leader (a mainline Protestant). Here Catholics were considered in-group members because Evangelicals agree with Catholic positions on abortion and the family; mainline Protestants, in contrast, were considered out-group members because of their political differences on such issues. Participants responded with more tolerance to the cross-cutting message attributed to a member of their in-group, and became more intolerant when the message was attributed to an out-group member. Djupe and Calfano (2014) exposed individuals associated with the Family First PAC in southwestern Ohio to mailings that included a mock newspaper article. Some versions of the article included an anti-marriage equality statement from a pastor, noting that same-sex marriage was a threat to family values; some included a statement from a law professor claiming courts were unlikely to force states to recognize same-sex marriages, some included both statements, and some included neither. Djupe and Calfano found that low-information respondents were easily swayed by the elite statements and were more likely to follow the in-group cue (the pastor) when both were presented. High-information respondents

tended to be less influenced by the elite cues, but were more likely to follow the out-group cue (the professor) when both were presented.

4. Most respondents who claimed a religious affiliation were Christians, but the sample included small numbers of adherents of other religions as well, including Judaism, Islam, and Hinduism.

5. See appendix table A4.1 for additional details.

6. See appendix table A4.2.

7. See appendix table A4.3 for additional details.

CHAPTER 5

1. Huerta earned the nickname "Dragon Lady" from growers with whom she battled in her work as a leader of the United Farmworkers Union, referring to her ability to speak "with fire" as she negotiated for the rights of farm workers.

CHAPTER 6

1. For additional details, see appendix table A6.1. Similar results are obtained with multiple regression models controlling for other variables (not shown).

2. See appendix table A6.1 for additional details.

References

Abrajano, Marisa. 2010. "Are Blacks and Latinos Responsible for the Passage of Proposition 8? Analyzing Voter Attitudes on California's Proposal to Ban Same-Sex Marriage in 2008." *Political Research Quarterly* 63, 4: 922–932.

Abramowitz, Alan I., and Kyle L. Saunders. 1998. "Ideological Realignment in the US Electorate." *Journal of Politics* 60, 3: 634–652.

Achen, Christopher H. 1992. "Social Psychology, Demographic Variables, and Linear Regression: Breaking the Iron Triangle in Voting Research." *Political Behavior* 14, 3: 195–211.

Adkins, Jeremie. 2013. "Op-ed: What Happened When I Met Dave Kopay." *Advocate*, August 29. http://www.advocate.com/commentary/2013/08/29/op-ed-what-happened-when-i-met-dave-kopay.

Aldrich, John H. 1995. *Why Parties? The Origin and Transformation of Political Parties in America*. Chicago: University of Chicago Press.

Allport, Gordon W. 1954. *The Nature of Prejudice*. New York: Doubleday.

Amichai-Hamburger, Yair, and Katelyn Y. A. McKenna. 2006. "The Contact Hypothesis Reconsidered: Interacting via the Internet." *Journal of Computer-Mediated Communication* 11, 3: 825–843.

Anderson, Eric. 2005. *In the Game: Gay Athletes and the Cult of Masculinity*. Albany: State University of New York Press.

Apuzzo, Matt. 2014. "Holder Sees Way to Curb Bans on Gay Marriage." *New York Times*, February 25, A1. http://www.nytimes.com/2014/02/25/us/holder-says-state-attorneys-general-dont-have-to-defend-gay-marriage-bans.html.

Apsler, Robert, and David O. Sears. 1968. "Warning, Personal Involvement, and Attitude Change." *Journal of Personality and Social Psychology* 9, 2: 162–166.

Arceneaux, Kevin. 2008. "Can Partisan Cues Diminish Democratic Accountability?" *Political Behavior* 30, 2: 139–160.

Arceneaux, Kevin, and Robin Kolodny. 2009. "Educating the Least Informed: Group Endorsements in a Grassroots Campaign." *American Journal of Political Science* 53, 4: 755–770.

Ashmore, Richard D., and Frances K. Del Boca. 1981. "Conceptual Approaches to Stereotypes and Stereotyping." In *Cognitive Processes in Stereotyping and Intergroup Behavior*, edited by David L. Hamilton, 1–35. New York: Psychology Press.

Bargh, John A., and Roman D. Thein. 1985. "Individual Construct Accessibility, Person Memory, and the Recall-Judgment Link: The Case of Information Overload." *Journal of Personality and Social Psychology* 49, 5: 1129–1146.

Barker, David C., and David H. Bearce. 2012. "End-Times Theology, the Shadow of the Future, and Public Resistance to Addressing Global Climate Change." *Political Research Quarterly* 66, 2: 267–279.

Barra, Allen. 2013. "Actually, Jason Collins Isn't the First Openly Gay Man in a Major Pro Sport." *Atlantic.com*, May 2. http://www.theatlantic.com/entertainment/archive/2013/05/actually-jason-collins-isnt-the-first-openly-gay-man-in-a-major-pro-sport/275523/.

Barreto, Matt. 2007. "¡Sí Se Puede! Latino Candidates and the Mobilization of Latino Voters." *American Political Science Review* 101, 3: 425–441.

Bartels, Larry M. 2002. "Beyond the Running Tally: Partisan Bias in Political Perceptions." *Political Behavior* 24, 2: 117–150.

Bartels, Larry M. 2005. "Homer Gets A Tax Cut: Inequality and Public Policy in the American Mind." *Perspectives on Politics* 3, 1: 15–31.

Bartels, Larry M. 2008. *Unequal Democracy: The Political Economy of the New Gilded Age.* Princeton, NJ: Princeton University Press.

Barth, Jay, L. Marvin Overby, and Scott H. Huffmon. 2009. "Community Context, Personal Contact, and Support for an Anti-gay Rights Referendum." *Political Research Quarterly* 62, 2: 355–365.

Barton, Bernadette C. 2012. *Pray the Gay Away: The Extraordinary Lives of Bible Belt Gays.* New York: New York University Press.

Baumeister, Roy, Isabelle M. Bauer, and Stuart A. Lloyd. 2010. "Choice, Free Will, and Religion." *Psychology of Religion and Spirituality* 2, 2: 67–82.

Baunach, Dawn M. 2012. "Changing Same-Sex Marriage Attitudes in America from 1988 through 2010." *Public Opinion Quarterly* 76, 2: 364–378.

Beltrán, Cristina. 2010. *The Trouble with Unity: Latino Politics and the Creation of Identity.* New York: Oxford University Press.

Bennett-Smith, Meredith. 2013. "Chris Culliver, 49ers Cornerback, Says Gay Players Not Welcome on NFL Team." *Huffington Post*, January 30. http://www.huffingtonpost.com/2013/01/30/chris-culliver-49ers-cornerback-gay-players-not-welcome-in-nfl_n_2584762.html.

Ben-Nun Bloom, Pazit, Gizem Arikan, and Marie Courtemanche. 2015. "Religious Social Identity, Religious Belief, and Anti-immigration Sentiment." *American Political Science Review* 109, 2: 203–221.

Bergan, Daniel E. 2012. "Partisan Stereotypes and Policy Attitudes." *Journal of Communication* 62, 6: 1102–1120.

Bettencourt, Ann B., Mark Manning, Lisa Molix, Rebecca Schlegel, Scott Eidelman, and Monica Biernat. 2016. "Explaining Extremity in Evaluation of Group Members: Meta-Analytic Tests of Three Theories." *Personality and Social Psychology Review* 20, 1: 49–74.

Bishin, Benjamin J., Thomas J. Hayes, Matthew B. Incantalupo, and Charles Anthony Smith. 2016. "Opinion Backlash and Public Attitudes: Are Political Advances in Gay Rights Counterproductive?" *American Journal of Political Science* 60, 3: 625–648.

Bond, Jon R., and Richard Fleisher. 2001. "The Polls: Partisanship and Presidential Performance Evaluations." *Presidential Studies Quarterly* 31, 3: 529–540.

Boudreau, Cheryl. 2009. "Closing the Gap: When Do Cues Eliminate Differences between Sophisticated and Unsophisticated Citizens?" *Journal of Politics* 71, 3: 964–976.

Bowler, Shaun, and Gary Segura. 2011. *The Future Is Ours: Minority Politics, Political Behavior, and the Multiracial Era of American Politics.* Washington, DC: CQ Press.

Brandt, Eric, ed. 1999. *Dangerous Liaisons: Blacks, Gays, and the Struggle for Equality.* New York: New Press.

Branton, Regina, Ana Franco, and Robert Wrinkle. "¿Quién Apoya Qué? The Influence of Acculturation and Political Knowledge on Latino Policy Attitudes." In *Latino Politics en Sciencia Política: The Search for Latino Identity and Racial Consciousness*, edited by Tony Affigne, Evelyn Hu DeHart, and Marion Orr, 115–131. New York: New York University Press.

Brewer, Marilynn B. 1991. "The Social Self: On Being the Same and Different at the Same Time." *Personality and Social Psychology Bulletin* 17, 5: 475–482.

Brewer, Mark D. 2005. "The Rise of Partisanship and the Expansion of Partisan Conflict within the American Electorate." *Political Research Quarterly* 58, 2: 219–229.

Brewer, Paul R. 2003. "Values, Political Knowledge, and Public Opinion about Gay Rights." *Public Opinion Quarterly* 67, 2: 173–201.

Brewer, Paul R. 2008. *Value War: Public Opinion and the Politics of Gay Rights*. Lanham, MD: Rowman & Littlefield.

Broockman, David E. and Daniel M. Butler. 2015. "The Causal Effects of Elite Position-Taking on Voter Attitudes: Field Experiments with Elite Communication." *American Journal of Political Science*. doi: 10.1111/ajps.12243.

Broockman, David, Josh Kalla, and Peter Aronow. 2015. "Irregularities in LaCour (2014)." http://web.stanford.edu/~dbroock/broockman_kalla_aronow_lg_irregularities.pdf.

Brown, Rupert, James Vivian, and Miles Hewstone. 1999. "Changing Attitudes through Intergroup Contact: The Effects of Group Membership Salience." *European Journal of Social Psychology* 29, 56: 741–764.

Brydum, Sunnivie. 2015. "Southern Baptists Ready to Defy Supreme Court on Marriage Equality." *Advocate*, June 17. http://www.advocate.com/politics/religion/2015/06/17/southern-baptists-ready-defy-scotus-supreme-court-marriage-equality.

Bullock, John G. 2011. "Elite Influence on Public Opinion in an Informed Electorate." *American Political Science Review* 105, 3: 496–515.

Burke, Daniel. 2015. "Mormon Church Backs LGBT Rights—with One Condition." *CNN*, January 28. http://www.cnn.com/2015/01/27/us/mormon-church-lgbt-laws/.

Burstein, Paul. 2003. "The Impact of Public Opinion on Public Policy: A Review and an Agenda." *Political Research Quarterly* 56, 1: 29–40.

Cacioppo, John T., Gary C. Berntson, and Barbara L. Andersen. 1991. "Psychophysiological Approaches to the Evaluation of Psychotherapeutic Process and Outcome." *Psychological Assessment* 3, 30: 321–336.

Calvert, Randall L. 1985. "The Value of Biased Information: A Rational Choice Model of Political Advice." *Journal of Politics* 47, 2: 530–555.

Camp, Bayliss J. 2008. "Mobilizing the Base and Embarrassing the Opposition: Defense of Marriage Referenda and Cross-Cutting Electoral Cleavages." *Sociological Perspectives* 51, 4: 713–733.

Campbell, David E., and J. Quin Monson. 2008. "The Religion Card: Gay Marriage and the 2004 Election." *Public Opinion Quarterly* 72, 3: 399–419.

Carmines, Edward G., and James A. Stimson. 1989. *Issue Evolution: Race and the Transformation of American Politics*. Princeton, NJ: Princeton University Press.

Carpenter, Thomas P., and Margaret A. Marshall. 2009. "An Examination of Religious Priming and Intrinsic Religious Motivation in the Moral Hypocrisy Paradigm." *Journal for the Scientific Study of Religion* 48, 2: 386–393.

Carsey, Thomas M., and Geoffrey C. Layman. 2006. "Changing Sides or Changing Minds? Party Identification and Policy Preferences in the American Electorate." *American Journal of Political Science* 50, 2: 464–477.

Casey, Logan. 2016. "Emotional Agendas: Disgust and the Dynamics of LGBT Politics." Ph.D. dissertation, University of Michigan.

Chaiken, Shelly, and Yaacov Trope. 1999. *Dual-Process Theories in Social Psychology*. New York: Guilford Press.

Chalke, Steve. 2013. "The Bible and Homosexuality: Part One." *Christianity Magazine*. http://www.premierchristianity.com/Featured-Topics/Homosexuality/The-Bible-and-Homosexuality-Part-One.

Chauncey, George. 2004. *Why Marriage? The History of Today's Debate over Gay Equality.* New York: Basic Books.

Chong, Dennis, and James N. Druckman. 2007a. "Framing Theory." *Annual Review of Political Science* 10: 103–126.

Chong, Dennis, and James N. Druckman. 2007b. "A Theory of Framing and Opinion Formation in Competitive Elite Environments." *Journal of Communication* 57, 1: 99–118.

Citrin, Jack, and Matthew Wright. 2009. "Defining the Circle of We: American Identity and Immigration Policy." *The Forum* 7, 3: Article 6.

Cizmar, Anne M., and Geoffrey C. Layman. 2009. "What Makes an Issue Easy? The Impact of Party, Group, and Policy Cues on Attitudes toward Abortion." Working Paper. University of Notre Dame.

CNN. 2012. "Fast Facts: Same-Sex Marriage." May 31. http://www.cnn.com/2012/05/31/us/ff-same-sex-marriage/.

Cohen, Cathy J. 1999. *The Boundaries of Blackness: AIDS and the Breakdown of Black Politics.* Chicago: University of Chicago Press.

Cohen. Geoffrey L. 2003. "Party over Policy." *Journal of Personality and Social Psychology* 85, 5: 808–822.

Coleman, John J. 1997. "The Decline and Resurgence of Congressional Party Conflict." *Journal of Politics* 59, 1: 165–184.

Collie, Melissa P., and John Lyman Mason. 2000. "The Electoral Connection between Party and Constituency Reconsidered: Evidence from the U.S. House of Representatives, 1972–1994." In *Continuity and Change in House Elections,* edited by D. W. Brady, J. F. Cogan, and M. P. Fiorina, 211–234. Stanford, CA: Stanford University Press.

Connelly, Marjorie. 2012. "Support for Gay Marriage Growing, but U.S. Remains Divided." *New York Times,* December 7. http://www.nytimes.com/2012/12/08/us/justices-consider-same-sex-marriage-cases-for-docket.html?_r=0.

Cook, Timothy E. 1999. "The Empirical Study of Lesbian, Gay, and Bisexual Politics: Assessing the First Wave of Research." *American Political Science Review* 93, 3: 679–692.

Cotter, Cornelius P. 1983. "Eisenhower as Party Leader." *Political Science Quarterly* 98, 2: 255–283.

Cotter, Patrick R., Jeffrey Cohen, and Philip B. Coulter. 1982. "Race-of-Interviewer Effects in Telephone Interviews." *Public Opinion Quarterly* 46, 2: 278–284.

Cottingham, Marci D. 2012. "Interaction Ritual Theory and Sports Fans: Emotion, Symbols, and Solidarity." *Sociology of Sport Journal* 29, 2: 168–185.

Cox, Erin. 2015. "Legislature Approves New Birth Certificates for Transgender People." *Baltimore Sun,* April 8. http://www.baltimoresun.com/news/maryland/politics/blog/bal-legislature-approves-new-birth-certificates-for-transgender-people-20150408-story.html.

Craig, Maureen A., and Jennifer A. Richeson. 2014. "Discrimination Divides across Identity Dimensions: Perceived Racism Reduces Support for Gay Rights and Increases Anti-gay Bias." *Journal of Experimental Social Psychology* 55: 169–174.

Craighill, Peyton M., and Scott Clement. 2014. "Support for Same-Sex Marriage Hits New High; Half Say Constitution Guarantees Right." *Washington Post,* March 5. http://www.washingtonpost.com/politics/support-for-same-sex-marriage-hits-new-high-half-say-constitution-guarantees-right/2014/03/04/f737e87e-a3e5-11e3-a5fa-55f0c77bf39c_story.html.

Crary, David. 2013. "Some Gay-Rights Activists Regret Focus on Marriage." *San Jose Mercury News* (AP story), July 18. http://www.mercurynews.com/breaking-news/ci_23686416/some-gay-rights-activists-regret-focus-marriage.

Cross, William E., Jr. 1991. *Shades of Black: Diversity in African-American Identity.* Philadelphia: Temple University Press.

Dahl, Robert A. 1971. *Polyarchy.* Chicago: University of Chicago Press.

Daley, Steve. 1994. "Powell's Aura Continuing to Brighten." *Chicago Tribune,* September 22. http://articles.chicagotribune.com/1994-09-22/news/9409220250_1_gen-colin-powell-gop-presidential-ticket-republicans.

Davis, Darren W. 1997a. "The Direction of Race of Interviewer Effects among African-Americans: Donning the Black Mask." *American Journal of Political Science* 41, 1: 309–322.

Davis, Darren W. 1997b. "Nonrandom Measurement Error and Race of Interviewer Effects among African Americans." *Public Opinion Quarterly* 61, 1: 187–207.

Davis, Darren W., and Brian D. Silver. 2003. "Stereotype Threat and Race of Interviewer Effects in a Survey on Political Knowledge." *American Journal of Political Science* 47, 1: 33–45.

Davis, R. E., M. P. Couper, N. K. Janz, C. H. Caldwell, and K. Resnicow. 2010. "Interviewer Effects in Public Health Surveys." *Health Education Research* 25, 1: 14–26.

David, Stephen, and Bob G. Knight. 2008. "Stress and Coping among Gay Men: Age and Ethnic Differences." *Psychology and Aging* 23, 1: 62–69.

Dawson, Michael C. 1994. *Behind the Mule: Race and Class in African-American Politics.* Princeton, NJ: Princeton University Press.

Dawson, Michael C. 2001. *Black Visions: The Roots of Contemporary African-American Political Ideologies.* Chicago: University of Chicago Press.

Dembowsky, April. 2015. "California Gives Transgender People Right to Determine Sex Listed on Death Certificate." *KQED News,* June 22. http://ww2.kqed.org/stateofhealth/2015/06/22/new-bill-would-give-transgender-people-more-control-over-death-certificates/.

Demby, Gene. 2012. "More Blacks in North Carolina Approve of Same-Sex Marriage since Obama's Announcement: Poll." *Huffington Post,* May 17. http://www.huffingtonpost.com/2012/05/17/blacks-north-carolina-gay-marriage_n_1524678.html.

Denison, Erik, and Alistair Kitchen. 2015. *Out on the Fields.* May 10. http://www.outon-thefields.com.

DiMaggio Paul, John Evans, and Bethany Bryson. 1996. "Have Americans' Social Attitudes Become More Polarized?" *American Journal of Sociology* 102, 3: 690–755.

Disch, Lisa. 2011. "Toward a Mobilization Conception of Democratic Representation." *American Political Science Review* 105, 1: 100–114.

Djupe, Paul A., and Brian R. Calfano. 2014. *God Talk: Experimenting with the Religious Causes of Public Opinion.* Philadelphia: Temple University Press.

Donadio, Rachel. 2013. "On Gay Priests, Pope Francis Asks, 'Who Am I to Judge?'" *New York Times,* July 30, A1. http://www.nytimes.com/2013/07/30/world/europe/pope-francis-gay-priests.html.

Doosje, Bertjan, Naomi Ellemers, and Russell Spears. 1995. "Perceived Intragroup Variability as a Function of Group Status and Identification." *Journal of Experimental Social Psychology* 31, 5: 410–436.

Downs, Anthony. 1957. *An Economic Theory of Democracy.* New York: HarperCollins.

Druckman, James N. 2001. "On the Limits of Framing Effects: Who Can Frame?" *Journal of Politics* 63, 4: 1041–1066.

Druckman, James N. 2003. "The Power of Television Images: The First Kennedy-Nixon Debate Revisited." *Journal of Politics* 65, 2: 559–571.

Druckman, James N. 2012. "The Politics of Motivation." *Critical Review* 24, 2: 199–216.

Druckman, James N., and Toby Bolsen. 2011. "Framing, Motivated Reasoning, and Opinions about Emergent Technologies." *Journal of Communication* 61, 4: 659–688.

Druckman, James N., Jordan Fein, and Thomas J. Leeper. 2011. "Framing and Biased Information Search." Paper presented at the Annual Meeting of the American Political Science Association, Seattle.

Druckman, James N., Donald P. Green, James H. Kuklinski, and Arthur Lupia, eds. 2011. *Cambridge Handbook of Experimental Political Science*. New York: Cambridge University Press.

Druckman, James N., Cari Lynn Hennessy, Kristi St. Charles, and Jonathan Weber. 2010. "Competing Rhetoric over Time." *Journal of Politics* 72, 1: 136–148.

Druckman, James N., and Justin W. Holmes. 2004. "Does Presidential Rhetoric Matter? Priming and Presidential Approval." *Presidential Studies Quarterly* 34, 4: 755–778.

Druckman, James N., and Thomas J. Leeper. 2012. "Is Public Opinion Stable? Resolving the Micro/Macro Disconnect in Studies of Public Opinion." *Daedalus* 141, 4: 50–68.

Druckman, James N., and Arthur Lupia. 2000. "Preference Formation." *Annual Review of Political Science* 3, 1: 1–24.

Druckman, James N., and Kjersten R. Nelson. 2003. "Framing and Deliberation: How Citizens' Conversations Limit Elite Influence. *American Journal of Political Science* 47, 4: 729–745.

Druckman, James N., Erik Peterson, and Rune Slothuus. 2013. "How Elite Polarization Affects Public Opinion." *American Political Science Review* 107, 1: 57–79.

Eagly, Alice H., and Shelly Chaiken. 1995. "Attitude Strength, Attitude Structure, and Resistance to Change." In *Attitude Strength: Antecedents and Consequences*, edited by Richard E. Petty and Jon A. Krosnick, 413–432. New York: Psychology Press.

Edmiston, John. 2002. "What Does the Bible Say about Same Sex Marriage?" http://christiananswers.net/q-eden/edn-f018.html.

Egan, Patrick J. 2010. *Findings from a Decade of Polling on Ballot Measures Regarding the Legal Status of Same-Sex Couples*. Report prepared for the Evelyn and Walter Haas, Jr. Fund. June 15. http://www.nyu.edu/about/news-publications/news/2010/06/15/campaigns-on-same-sex-marriage-ballot-measures-fail-to-move-voters.html.

Egan, Patrick J. 2014. "More Gay People Can Now Get Legally Married. They Can Still Be Legally Fired." *Washington Post*, October 6. http://www.washingtonpost.com/blogs/monkey-cage/wp/2014/10/06/more-gay-people-can-now-get-legally-married-they-can-still-be-legally-fired/.

Egan, Patrick J., and Kenneth Sherrill. 2005. "Marriage and the Shifting Priorities of a New Generation of Lesbians and Gays." *PS: Political Science & Politics* 38, 2: 229–232.

Egan, Patrick J., and Kenneth Sherrill. 2009. *California's Proposition 8: What Happened, and What Does the Future Hold?* Washington, DC: National Gay and Lesbian Task Force. www.ncsu.edu/stud_affairs/glbt/pdfs/Prop%208%20Report.pdf.

Egan, Patrick J., Nathaniel Persily, and Kevin Wallsten. 2008. "Gay Rights." In *Public Opinion and Constitutional Controversy*, edited by Nathaniel Persily, Jack Citrin, and Patrick J. Egan, 234–266. New York: Oxford University Press.

Eisenbach, David. 2006. *Gay Power: An American Revolution*. New York: Carroll & Graff.

Ellison, Christopher G., Gabriel A. Acevedo, and Aida I. Ramos-Wada. 2011. "Religion and Attitudes toward Same-Sex Marriage among U.S. Latinos." *Social Science Quarterly* 92, 1: 35–56.

Engel, Stephen M. 2001. *The Unfinished Revolution: Social Movement Theory and the Gay and Lesbian Movement*. New York: Cambridge University Press.

Engel, Stephen M. 2012. "Frame Spillover: Media Framing and Public Opinion of a Multifaceted LGBT Rights Agenda." *Law and Social Inquiry* 38, 2: 403–441.

Engel, Stephen M. 2016. *Fragmented Citizens: The Changing Landscape of Gay and Lesbian Lives.* New York: New York University Press.

EqualityForum.com. N.d. http://www.equalityforum.com/fortune500.

Erikson, Robert S., Michael MacKuen, and James A. Stimson. 2002. *The Macro Polity.* New York: Cambridge University Press.

Eskridge, William, Jr. 1999. *Gaylaw: Challenging the Apartheid of the Closet.* Cambridge, MA: Harvard University Press.

ESPN. 2007. "Retired NBA Star Hardaway Says He Hates 'Gay People.'" *ESPN.com,* February 16. http://sports.espn.go.com/nba/news/story?id=2766213.

ESPN. 2012. "Political Confidential: Anonymous Athletes Give Views." *ESPN.com*, October 11. http://espn.go.com/nfl/story/_/id/8465169/anonymous-athletes-give-views-presidential-election-social-issues-sports-gambling-espn-magazine.

Ewers, Justin. 2008. "California Same-Sex Marriage Initiative Campaigns Shatter Spending Records." *U.S. News,* October 29. http://www.usnews.com/news/national/articles/2008/10/29/california-same-sex-marriage-initiative-campaigns-shatter-spending-records.

Family Research Council. N.d. "What You Need to Know about Marriage—Questions and Answers Driving the Debate." http://www.frc.org/brochure/what-you-need-to-know-about-marriage-questions-and-answers-driving-the-debate.

Faulk, Kent. 2015. "Alabama Supreme Court First in Nation to Defy Federal Court Gay Marriage Order." *AI.com,* March 6. http://www.al.com/news/birmingham/index.ssf/2015/03/alabama_supreme_court_alone_in.html.

Fenno, Richard F. 1978. *Home Style: Members in Their Districts.* Boston, MA: Little & Brown.

Fetner, Tina. 2008. *How the Religious Right Shaped Lesbian and Gay Activism.* Minneapolis: University of Minnesota Press.

Fields, Liz. 2013. "Judge Orders Colorado Bakery to Cater for Same-Sex Weddings." *ABC News,* December 7. http://abcnews.go.com/US/judge-orders-colorado-bakery-cater-sex-weddings/story?id=21136505.

Fiorina, Morris P. 1981. *Retrospective Voting in American Elections.* New Haven, CT: Yale University Press.

Fiorina, Morris P., Samuel J. Abrams, and Jeremy C. Pope. 2005. *Culture War and the Myth of a Polarized America.* New York: Pearson Longman.

First Amendment Center. 2013. "State of the First Amendment: 2013." July 16. http://www.firstamendmentcenter.org/madison/wp-content/uploads/2013/07/SOFA-2013-final-report.pdf.

Flores, Andrew R. 2015. "Attitudes toward Transgender Rights: Perceived Knowledge and Secondary Interpersonal Contact." *Politics, Groups, and Identities* 3, 3: 398–416.

Forbes. 2016. "The Most and Least Conservative Cities in America." http://www.forbes.com/pictures/gfii45img/most-liberal-no-1/.

Ford, Zack. "Judge to Anti-gay Florist: Religion Is Not An Excuse to Defy Anti-discrimination Laws." *Thinkprogress.org,* February 19. http://thinkprogress.org/lgbt/2015/02/19/3624626/washington-florist-loses-religious-freedom-anti-gay-discrimination/.

Fraga, Luis R., John A. Garcia, Rodney E. Hero, Michael Jones-Correa, Valerie Martinez-Ebers, and Gary M. Segura. 2011. *Latinos in the New Millennium: An Almanac of Opinion, Behavior, and Policy Preferences.* New York: Cambridge University Press.

Frey, Bruno S., and Stephan Meier, S. 2004. "Social Comparisons and Pro-social Behavior: Testing 'Conditional Cooperation' in a Field Experiment." *American Economic Review* 94, 5: 1717–1722.

Friedman, Matt. 2013. "Poll Finds Strong Support for Gay Marriage in N.J., Including among Republicans." *NJ.com,* October 21. http://www.nj.com/politics/index.ssf/2013/10/poll_even_nj_republicans_support_gay_marriage.html.

Friedman, Matt. 2014. "Clinton Leads Christie in NJ, Virginia, NY, New 2016 polls Show." *NJ.com*, March 4. http://www.nj.com/politics/index.ssf/2014/03/clinton_leads_christie_in_nj_virginia_ny_new_2016_polls_show.html.

Funk, Cary, and Jessica Martínez. 2014. "Fewer Hispanics Are Catholic, So How Can More Catholics Be Hispanic?" Pew Research Center, May 7. http://www.pewresearch.org/fact-tank/2014/05/07/fewer-hispanics-are-catholic-so-how-can-more-catholics-be-hispanic/.

Gallup Poll. 1975. July. iPOLL Databank, Roper Center for Public Opinion Research, University of Connecticut. http://www.ropercenter.uconn.edu/data_access/ipoll/ipoll.html.

Gallup Poll. 2012. September. iPOLL Databank, Roper Center for Public Opinion Research, University of Connecticut. http://www.ropercenter.uconn.edu/data_access/ipoll/ipoll.html.

Gallup Poll Trends. 2016. http://www.gallup.com/poll/1606/death-penalty.aspx, http://www.gallup.com/poll/1576/abortion.aspx, http://www.gallup.com/poll/21814/evolution-creationism-intelligent-design.aspx.

Garcia, Gilbert. 2015. "Joaquin Castro Sees Latino Support for Same-Sex Marriage." *San Antonio Express News*, March 12. http://www.expressnews.com/news/news_columnists/gilbert_garcia/article/Joaquin-Castro-sees-Latino-support-for-same-sex-6131191.php.

Garcia, John A. 2012. *Latino Politics in America: Community, Culture, and Interests*. Lanham, MD: Rowman & Littlefield.

García Bedolla, Lisa. 2009. *Latino Politics*. Cambridge, UK: Polity.

García Bedolla, Lisa, and Melissa R. Michelson. 2012. *Mobilizing Inclusion: Transforming the Electorate through Get-Out-the-Vote Campaigns*. New Haven, CT: Yale University Press.

Garretson, Jeremiah J. 2015. "Exposure to the Lives of Lesbians and Gays and the Origin of Young People's Greater Support for Gay Rights." *International Journal of Public Opinion Research* 27, 2: 277–288.

Gates, Henry Louis, Jr. 1999. "Blacklash?" In *Dangerous Liaisons: Blacks, Gays, and the Struggle for Equality*, edited by Eric Brandt, 25–30. New York: New Press.

Gaudio, Rudolf P. 1994. "Sounding Gay: Pitch Properties in the Speech of Gay and Straight Men." *American Speech* 69, 1: 30–57.

Gelman, Andrew, Jeffrey Lax, and Justin Phillips. 2010. "Over Time, a Gay Marriage Groundswell." *New York Times*, August 21. http://www.nytimes.com/2010/08/22/week-inreview/22gay.html.

Gelman, Andrew, David Park, Boris Shor, Joseph Bafumi, and Jeronimo Cortina. 2008. *Red State, Blue State, Rich State, Poor State: Why Americans Vote the Way They Do*. Princeton, NJ: Princeton University Press.

Gerber, Alan S., James G. Gimpel, Donald P. Green, and Daron R. Shaw. 2011. "How Large and Long-Lasting Are the Persuasive Effects of Televised Campaigns? Results from a Randomized Field Experiment." *American Political Science Review* 105, 1: 135–150.

Gerber, Alan S., and Donald P. Green. 2012. *Field Experiments: Design, Analysis, and Interpretation*. New York: Norton.

Gerber, Alan S., and Gregory A. Huber. 2010. "Partisanship, Political Control, and Economic Assessments." *American Journal of Political Science* 54, 1: 153–173.

Gerber, Alan S., Neil Malhotra, Conor M. Dowling, and David Doherty. 2010. "Publication Bias in Two Political Behavior Literatures." *American Politics Research* 38, 4: 591–613.

Gervais, Will M., and Ara Norenzayan. 2012. "Like a Camera in the Sky? Thinking about God Increases Public Self-Awareness and Socially Desirable Responding." *Journal of Experimental Social Psychology* 48, 1: 298–302.

Ghavami, Negin, and Kerri L. Johnson. 2011. "Comparing Sexual and Ethnic Minority Perspectives on Same-Sex Marriage." *Journal of Social Issues* 67, 2: 394–412.

Ghaziani, Amin. 2008. *The Dividends of Dissent: How Conflict and Culture Work in Lesbian and Gay Marches on Washington.* Chicago: University of Chicago Press.

Gigerenzer, Gerd, and Peter M. Todd. 1999. *Simple Heuristics That Make Us Smart.* New York: Oxford University Press.

Gilreath, Shannon. 2011. *The End of Straight Supremacy: Realizing Gay Liberation.* New York: Cambridge University Press.

Gillespie, Andra, and Melissa R. Michelson. 2011. "Participant Observation and the Political Scientist: Possibilities, Priorities, and Practicalities." *PS: Political Science & Politics* 44, 2: 261–265.

GLAAD. 2015. "Number of Americans Who Report Knowing a Transgender Person Doubles in Seven Years, according to New GLAAD Survey." September 17. http://www.glaad.org/releases/number-americans-who-report-knowing-transgender-person-doubles-seven-years-according-new.

GLAAD. 2016. "Victims or Villains: Examining Ten Years of Transgender Images on Television." http://www.glaad.org/publications/victims-or-villains-examining-ten-years-transgender-images-television.

Goodbread, Chase. 2014. "NFL Commissioner Roger Goodell Welcomes Michael Sam." *NFL.com,* February 12. http://www.nfl.com/news/story/0ap2000000325478/article/nfl-commissioner-roger-goodell-welcomes-michael-sam.

Goodstein, Laurie. 2012. "Episcopalians Approve Rite to Bless Same-Sex Unions." *New York Times,* July 11, A15. http://www.nytimes.com/2012/07/11/us/episcopalians-approve-rite-to-bless-same-sex-unions.html.

Goodstein, Laurie. 2013. "Defrocking of Minister Widens Split over Gays." *New York Times,* December 20, A16. http://www.nytimes.com/2013/12/20/us/methodist-pastor-defrocked-over-gay-marriage-service.html.

Goodstein, Laurie. 2015. "Largest Presbyterian Denomination Gives Final Approval for Same-Sex Marriage." *New York Times,* March 18, A13. http://www.nytimes.com/2015/03/18/us/presbyterians-give-final-approval-for-same-sex-marriage.html.

Goren, Paul. 2005. "Party Identification and Core Political Values." *American Journal of Political Science* 49, 4: 881–896.

Grack, Christine, and Charles L. Richman. 1996. "Reducing General and Specific Heterosexism through Cooperative Contact." *Journal of Psychology and Human Sexuality* 8, 4: 59–68.

Grant, Jaime M., Lisa A. Mottet, Justin Tanis, Jack Harrison, Jody L. Herman, and Mara Keisling. 2011. *Injustice at Every Turn: A Report of the National Transgender Discrimination Survey.* Washington, DC: National Center for Transgender Equality and National Gay and Lesbian Task Force. http://www.thetaskforce.org/downloads/reports/reports/ntds_full.pdf.

Green, Donald P., and Alan S. Gerber. 2002. "The Downstream Benefits of Experimentation." *Political Analysis* 10, 4: 394–402.

Green, Donald P., Bradley Palmquist, and Eric Schickler. 2004. *Partisan Hearts and Minds: Political Parties and the Social Identities of Voters.* New Haven, CT: Yale University Press.

Gregory, Anne. 2004. "Rethinking Homophobia in Sports: Legal Protections for Gay and Lesbian Athlete and Coaches." *DePaul Journal of Sports Law and Contemporary Problems* 2, 2: 264–292.

Haberman, Maggie. 2013. "Poll: Big Support for Anti-discrimination Law." *Politico,* September 30. http://www.politico.com/story/2013/09/poll-big-support-for-anti-discrimination-law-97540.html.

Haider-Markel, Donald P. 2007. "Representation and Backlash: The Positive and Negative Influence of Descriptive Representation." *Legislative Studies Quarterly* 32, 1: 107–133.

Haider-Markel, Donald P. 2010. *Out and Running: Gay and Lesbian Candidates, Elections, and Policy Representation.* Washington, DC: Georgetown University Press.

Haider-Markel, Donald P., and Mark R. Joslyn. 2008. "Beliefs about the Origins of Homosexuality and Support for Gay Rights: An Empirical Test of Attribution Theory." *Public Opinion Quarterly* 72, 2: 291–310.

Hall, Deborah L., David C. Matz, and Wendy Wood. 2010. "Why Don't We Practice What We Preach? A Meta-analytic Review of Religious Racism." *Personality and Social Psychology Review* 14, 1: 126–139.

Hamilton, David L. 1988. "Causal Attribution Viewed from an Information-Processing Perspective." In *The Social Psychology of Knowledge*, edited by Daniel Bar-Tal and Arie W. Kruglanski, 359–385. New York: Cambridge University Press.

Hamilton, David L., and Steven J. Sherman. 1996. "Perceiving Persons and Groups." *Psychological Review* 103, 2: 336–355.

Han, Hahrie C. 2009. "Does the Content of Political Appeals Matter in Motivating Participation? A Field Experiment on Self-Disclosure in Political Appeals." *Political Behavior* 31, 1: 103–116.

Hansen, Susan B. 2014. *The Politics of Sex: Public Opinion, Parties, and Presidential Elections.* New York: Routledge.

Hargreaves, Jennifer, and Eric Anderson. 2014. "Sport, Gender and Sexuality: Surveying the Field." In *Routledge Handbook of Sport, Gender and Sexuality*, edited by Hargreaves and Anderson, 3–18. New York: Routledge.

Harrison, Brian F. 2016. "Bully Partisan or Partisan Bully? Partisanship, Elite Polarization and U.S. Presidential Communication." *Social Science Quarterly* 97, 2: 418–438.

Harrison, Brian F., and Melissa R. Michelson. 2012. "Not That There's Anything Wrong with That: The Effect of Personalized Appeals on Marriage Equality Campaigns." *Political Behavior* 34, 2: 325–344.

Harrison, Brian F., and Melissa R. Michelson. 2015. "God and Marriage: The Impact of Religious Identity Priming on Attitudes toward Same-Sex Marriage." *Social Science Quarterly* 96, 5: 1411–1423.

Harrison, Brian F. and Melissa R. Michelson. 2016. "More than a Game: Football Fans and Marriage Equality." *PS: Political Science & Politics* 49, 4: 782–787.

Hastie, Reid. 1984. "Causes and Effects of Causal Attribution." *Journal of Personality and Social Psychology* 46, 1: 44–56.

Herek, Gregory M., and John P. Capitanio. 1996. "'Some of My Best Friends': Intergroup Contact, Concealable Stigma, and Heterosexuals' Attitudes toward Gay Men and Lesbians." *Personality and Social Psychology Bulletin* 22, 4: 412–424.

Herek, Gregory M., and Eric K. Glunt. 1993. "Interpersonal Contact and Heterosexual's Attitudes toward Gay Men: Results from a National Survey." *Journal of Sex Research* 30, 3: 239–244.

Herman, Jody L. 2013. "Gendered Restrooms and Minority Stress: The Public Regulation of Gender and its Impact on Transgender People's Lives." *Journal of Public Management & Social Policy* 19, 1: 65–80.

Herszenhorn, David M. 2013. "On Holding Hands and Fake Marriage: Stories of Being Gay in Russia." *New York Times*, November 6. http://www.nytimes.com/2013/11/07/world/europe/stories-of-being-gay-in-russia.html.

Hetherington, Marc J. 2001. "Resurgent Mass Partisanship: The Role of Elite Polarization." *American Political Science Review* 95, 3: 619–631.

Hewstone, Miles, and Rupert J. Brown. 1986. "Contact Is Not Enough: An Intergroup Perspective on the 'Contact Hypothesis.'" In *Contact and Conflict in Intergroup Encounters*, edited by Hewstone and Brown, 1–44. New York: Basil Blackwell.

Hicks, Josh. 2015. "New LGBT Protections to Take Effect without Gov. Hogan's signature." *Washington Post*, May 25. http://www.washingtonpost.com/local/md-politics/new-lgbt-protections-to-become-law-in-md-without-gov-hogans-signature/2015/05/24/1c11e57a-018a-11e5-833c-a2de05b6b2a4_story.html.

Holland, Jesse J. 2007. "Bill Stalls over Transgender Protections." *USA Today* (AP story), October 2. http://usatoday30.usatoday.com/news/nation/2007-10-02-925595794_x.htm.

Hood, Ralph W., Jr., Peter C. Hill, and Bernard Spilka. 2009. *The Psychology of Religion*, 4th ed. New York: Guilford.

Hopper, Robert. 1998. "What Do We Know about Telephone Conversation?" In *Progress in Communication Sciences: Advances in Telecommunications*, vol. 15, edited by Harmeet Sawhney and George A. Barnett, 29–44. Stamford, CT: Ablex.

Horton, John J., David G. Rand, and Richard J. Zeckhauser. 2011. "The Online Laboratory: Conducting Experiments in a Real Labor Market." *Experimental Economics* 14, 3: 399–425.

Horwitz, Sari. 2014. "Same-Sex Marriages in Utah Legal under Federal Law, Attorney General Holder Says." *Washington Post*, January 10. http://www.washingtonpost.com/world/national-security/holder-same-sex-marriages-in-utah-legal-under-federal-law/2014/01/10/f08f363a-7a19-11e3-af7f-13bf0e9965f6_story.html.

Hovland, Carl I., Irving L. Janis, and Harold H. Kelley. 1953. *Communication and Persuasion: Psychological Studies of Opinion Change*. New Haven, CT: Yale University Press.

Human Rights Campaign. 2014. "New CBS News Poll Shows a Majority of Hispanics/Latinos Support Marriage Equality." *HRC.org*, August 8. http://www.hrc.org/press-releases/entry/new-cbs-news-poll-shows-a-majority-of-hispanics-latinos-support-marriage-eq.

Hutchings, Vincent L., and Nicholas A. Valentino. 2004. "The Centrality of Race in American Politics." *Annual Review of Political Science* 7: 383–408.

Iyengar, Shanto, and Donald R. Kinder. 1987. *News That Matters*. Chicago: University of Chicago Press.

Jackson, Melinda S. 2011. "Priming the Sleeping Giant. The Dynamics of Latino Political Identity and Vote Choice." *Political Psychology* 32, 4: 691–716.

Jackson, John E., and Ken Kollman. 2011. "Connecting Micro- and Macropartisanship." *Political Analysis* 19, 4: 503–518.

Jackson, Linda A., Linda A. Sullivan, and Carol N. Hodge. 1993. "Stereotype Effects on Attributions, Predictions, and Evaluations: No Two Social Judgments Are Quite Alike." *Journal of Personality and Social Psychology* 65, 1: 69–84.

Jacobs, Lawrence R., and Robert Y. Shapiro. 2000. *Politicians Don't Pander*. Chicago: University of Chicago Press.

Jacobson, Gary C. 2000. "Party Polarization in National Politics: The Electoral Connection." In *Polarized Politics: Congress and the President in a Partisan Era*, vol. 5, edited by Jon R. Bond and Richard Fleisher, 17–18. Washington, DC: CQ Press.

Janis, Irving L., and Leon Mann. 1977. *Decision Making*. New York: Free Press.

Jealous, Benjamin, Silas Lee, and Matt A. Barreto. 2012. "NAACP Battleground Poll." November 8. naacp.3cdn.net/193d69817d2aeeffc0_xnm6bc42h.pdf.

Jervis, Robert. 1976. *Perception and Misperception in International Politics*. Princeton, NJ: Princeton University Press.

Johnson, Megan K., Wade C. Rowatt, and Jordan P. LaBouff. 2010. "Priming Religious Concepts Increases Racial Prejudice." *Social Psychological and Personality Science* 1, 2: 119–126.

Johnson, Megan K., Wade C. Rowatt, and Jordan P. LaBouff. 2012. "Religiosity and Prejudice Revisited: Ingroup Favoritism, Outgroup Derogation, or Both?" *Psychology of Religion and Spirituality* 4, 2: 154–168.

Jones, Billy E., and Marjorie J. Hill. 1996. "African American Lesbians, Gay Men, and Bisexuals." In *Textbook of Homosexuality and Mental Health*, edited by Robert P. Cabaj and Terry S. Stein, 549–561. Washington, DC: American Psychiatric Press.

Jones, Edward E. 1990. *Interpersonal Perception*. New York: W. H. Freeman.

Jones, Robert P., Daniel Cox, and Juhen Navarro-Rivera. 2014. "A Shifting Landscape: A Decade of Change in American Attitudes about Same-Sex Marriage and LGBT Issues." http://publicreligion.org/site/wpcontent/uploads/2014/02/2014.LGBT_REPORT.pdf.

Judd, Charles M., and Bernadette Park. 1993. "Definition and Assessment of Accuracy in Social Stereotypes." *Psychological Review* 100, 1: 109–128.

Kam, Cindy D. 2005. "Who Toes the Party Line? Cues, Values, and Individual Differences." *Political Behavior* 27, 2: 163–182.

Kaplan, Thomas. 2011. "Groups Spent $1.8 Million in Same-Sex Marriage Push." *New York Times*, July 18. http://cityroom.blogs.nytimes.com/2011/07/18/groups-spent-1-8-million-in-same-sex-marriage-push/.

Karlan, Dean, and John A. List. 2007. "Does Price Matter in Charitable Giving? Evidence from a Large-Scale Natural Field Experiment." *American Economic Review* 97, 5: 1774–1793.

Katz, Jonathan M. 2015. "North Carolina Allows Officials to Refuse to Perform Gay Marriages." *New York Times*, June 12, A14. http://www.nytimes.com/2015/06/12/us/north-carolina-allows-officials-to-refuse-to-perform-gay-marriages.html.

Keck, Thomas. 2009. "Beyond Backlash: Assessing the Impact of Judicial Decisions on LGBT Rights." *Law and Society Review* 43, 1: 151–186.

Keisling, Mara. 2013. "A Huge Small Step: The Obama Administration Delivers Big." *Huffington Post*, June 14. http://www.huffingtonpost.com/mara-keisling/a-huge-small-step-the-obama-administration-delivers-big_b_3444713.html.

Kelley, Harold H. 1973. "The Processes of Causal Attribution." *American Psychologist* 28, 2: 107–128.

Kiesler, Charles A., Barry Collins, and Norman Miller. 1969. *Attitude Change: A Critical Analysis of Theoretical Approaches*. New York: Wiley.

Kiley, Jocelyn. 2014. "61% of Young Republicans Favor Same-Sex Marriage." *Pew Research*, March 10. http://www.pewresearch.org/fact-tank/2014/03/10/61-of-young-republicans-favor-same-sex-marriage/.

Kinder, Donald R. 2007. "Curmudgeonly Advice." *Journal of Communication* 57, 1: 155–162.

Kinder, Donald R., and Lynn M. Sanders. 1996. *Divided by Color: Racial Politics and Democratic Ideals*. Chicago: University of Chicago Press.

Klar, Samara. 2013. "The Influence of Competing Identity Primes on Political Preferences." *Journal of Politics* 75, 4: 1108–1124.

Klarman, Michael J. 2013. *From the Closet to the Altar: Courts, Backlash, and the Struggle for Same-Sex Marriage*. New York: Oxford University Press.

Koole, Sander L., Michael E. McCullough, Julius Kuhl, and Peter H. M. P. Roelofsma. 2010. "Why Religion's Burdens Are Light: From Religiosity to Implicit Self-Regulation." *Personality and Social Psychology Review* 14, 1: 95–107.

Kopan, Tal. 2014. "10 Things to Know: Arizona SB 1062." *Politico*, February 27. http://www. politico.com/story/2014/02/arizona-sb1062-facts-104031.html.

Kristof, Nicholas. 2014. "Professors, We Need You!" *New York Times*, February 16, SR11. http://www.nytimes.com/2014/02/16/opinion/sunday/kristof-professors-we-need-you. html.

Krosnick, Jon A., and Laura A. Brannon. 1993. "The Impact of the Gulf War on the Ingredients of Presidential Evaluations: Multidimensional Effects of Political Involvement." *American Political Science Review* 87, 4: 963–975.

Krysan, Maria, and Mick P. Couper. 2003. "Race in the Live and the Virtual Interview: Racial Deference, Social Desirability, and Activation Effects in Attitude Surveys." *Social Psychology Quarterly* 66, 4: 364–383.

Kuklinski, James H., and Norman L. Hurley. 1994. "On Hearing and Interpreting Political Messages: A Cautionary Tale of Citizen Cue-Taking." *Journal of Politics* 56, 3: 729–751.

LaCour, Michael J., and Donald P. Green. 2014. "When Contact Changes Minds: An Experiment on Transmission of Support for Gay Equality." *Science* 346, 6215: 1366–1369.

Lane, Emily. "Bobby Jindal Plans to Issue an Executive Order Enforcing Intent of Religious Freedom Bill." *Nola.com*, May 19. http://www.nola.com/politics/index.ssf/2015/05/ bobby_jindal_executive_order_r.html.

Lau, Richard R., and Redlawsk David P. 2001. "Advantages and Disadvantages of Cognitive Heuristics in Political Decision Making." *American Journal of Political Science* 45, 4: 951–971.

Lass, Norman J., Celest A. Almerino, Laurie F. Jordan, and Jayne M. Walsh. 1980. "The Effect of Filtered Speech on Speaker Race and Sex Identifications." *Journal of Phonetics* 8, 1: 101–112.

Lass, Norman J., John E. Tecca, Robert A. Mancuso, and Wanda I. Black. 1979. "The Effect of Phonetic Complexity on Speaker Race and Sex Identifications." *Journal of Phonetics* 7, 2: 105–118.

Lau, Richard R., and David P. Redlawsk. 2006. *How Voters Decide: Information Processing in Election Campaigns*. New York: Cambridge University Press.

Lavariega Monforti, Jessica. 2014. "Identity Revisited: Latino(as) and Panethnicity." In *Latino Politics en Ciencia Política: The Search for Latino Identity and Racial Consciousness*, edited by Tony Affigne, Evelyn Hu-DeHart, and Marion Orr, 51–73. New York: New York University Press.

Lavariega Monforti, Jessica, and Melissa R. Michelson. 2014. "Multiple Paths to Cynicism: Social Networks, Identity, and Linked Fate among Latinos." In *Latino Politics en Ciencia Política: The Search for Latino Identity and Racial Consciousness*, edited by Tony Affigne, Evelyn Hu-DeHart, and Marion Orr, 92–112. New York: New York University Press.

Lavine, Howard, Christopher Johnston, and Marco Steenbergen. 2012. *The Ambivalent Partisan: How Critical Loyalty Promotes Democracy*. New York: Oxford University Press.

Lax, Jeffrey R., and Justin Phillips. 2009. "Gay Rights in the States: Public Opinion and Policy Responsiveness." *American Political Science Review* 103, 3: 367–386.

Layman, Geoffrey C., and Thomas M. Carsey. 2002. "Party Polarization and 'Conflict Extension' in the American Electorate." *American Journal of Political Science* 46, 4: 786–802.

Lazarsfeld, Paul. F., Bernard Berelson, and Hazel Gaudet. 1948. *The People's Choice: How the Voter Makes Up His Mind in a Presidential Campaign*. 2nd ed. New York: Columbia University Press.

Lee, Frances. 2009. *Beyond Ideology: Politics, Principles, and Partisanship in the US Senate*. Chicago: University of Chicago Press.

Leeper, Thomas J. 2012. "Information Choice and Opinion Change Over Time." Paper presented at the Annual Meeting of the Midwest Political Science Association, Chicago.

Lenz, Gabriel S. 2009. "Learning and Opinion Change, Not Priming: Reconsidering the Priming Hypothesis." *American Journal of Political Science* 53, 4: 821–837.

Lerner, Adam B. "Bobby Jindal Issues Religious-Freedom Order." *Politico*, May 19. http://www.politico.com/story/2015/05/bobby-jindal-religious-freedom-executive-order-118115.html.

Letchworth, George A. 1968. "Attitude Change over Time as a Function of Ego Involvement, Communicator Credibility and Number of Exposures to the Communication." Ph.D. dissertation, University of Oklahoma. Dissertation Abstracts International, 29, 2802A.

Levendusky, Matthew. 2009. *The Partisan Sort: How Liberals Became Democrats and Conservatives Became Republicans*. Chicago: University of Chicago Press.

Levine Jeffrey, Edward G. Carmines, and Robert Huckfeldt. 1997. "The Rise of Ideology in the Post-New Deal Party System, 1972–1992." *American Politics Quarterly* 25, 1: 19–34.

Lewis, Gregory B. 2003. "Black-White Differences in Attitudes toward Homosexuality and Gay Rights." *Public Opinion Quarterly* 67, 1: 59–78.

Lewis, Gregory B., and Charles W. Gossett. 2008. "Changing Public Opinion on Same-Sex Marriage: The Case of California." *Politics and Policy* 36, 1: 4–30.

Lewis, Gregory B., and Charles W. Gossett. 2011. "Why Did Californians Pass Proposition 8? Stability and Change in Public Support for Same-Sex Marriage." *California Journal of Politics and Policy* 3, 1: 1–20.

Liptak, Adam. 2013. "Weighing Free Speech in Refusal to Photograph Lesbian Couple's Ceremony." *New York Times*, November 18, A14. http://www.nytimes.com/2013/11/19/us/weighing-free-speech-in-refusal-to-photograph-ceremony.html.

Liptak, Adam. 2014. "Supreme Court Delivers Tacit Win to Gay Marriage." *New York Times*, October 7, A1. http://www.nytimes.com/2014/10/07/us/denying-review-justices-clear-way-for-gay-marriage-in-5-states.html.

Lopez, Mark Hugo. 2013. "Three-Fourths of Hispanics Say Their Community Needs a Leader: Most Latinos Cannot Name One." Pew Research Center, October 22. http://www.pewhispanic.org/2013/10/22/three-fourths-of-hispanics-say-their-community-needs-a-leader/.

Luhtanen, Riia, and Jennifer Crocker, 1992. "A Collective Self-Esteem Scale: Self-Evaluation of One's Social Identity." *Personality and Social Psychology Bulletin* 18, 3: 302–318.

Lupia, Arthur. 1994. "Shortcuts versus Encyclopedias: Information and Voting Behavior in California Insurance Reform Elections." *American Political Science Review* 88, 1: 63–76.

Lupia, Arthur, and Mathew D. McCubbins. 1998. *The Democratic Dilemma: Can Citizens Learn What They Need to Know?* New York: Cambridge University Press.

Lupia, Arthur, Mathew D. McCubbins, and Samuel L. Popkin. 2000. *Elements of Reason: Cognition, Choice, and the Bounds of Rationality*. New York: Cambridge University Press.

Lupu, Noam. 2013. "Party Brands and Partisanship: Theory with Evidence from a Survey Experiment in Argentina." *American Journal of Political Science* 57, 1: 49–64.

Maheswaran, Durairaj, and Shelly Chaiken. 1991. "Promoting Systematic Processing in Low-Motivation Settings: Effect of Incongruent Information on Processing and Judgment." *Journal of Personality and Social Psychology* 61, 1: 13–25.

Mananzala, Rickke, and Dean Spade. 2008. "The Nonprofit Industrial Complex and Trans Resistance." *Sexuality Research and Social Policy* 5, 1: 53–71.

Mansbridge, Jane J. 2003. "Rethinking Representation." *American Political Science Review* 97, 4: 515–528.

Marinucci, Carla. 2014. "Bill to Repeal Transgender-Student Law Falling Short." *SFGate. com*, January 8. http://www.sfgate.com/default/article/Bid-to-repeal-transgender-student-law-falling-5124980.php.

Markoe, Lauren. 2013. "Religious Liberty Double Standards Indicated in New Poll." *Huffington Post*, January 24. http://www.huffingtonpost.com/2013/01/24/religious-liberty-double-standards_n_2537969.html.

Martin, Jenna. 2016. "This Is How Much HB 2 Has Cost Charlotte, per Latest Report." *Charlotte Business Journal*, May 25. http://www.bizjournals.com/charlotte/news/2016/05/25/this-is-how-much-hb-2-has-cost-charlotte-per.html.

Maza, Carlos. 2014. "Debunking the Big Myth about Transgender-Inclusive Bathrooms." *Media Matters*, March 20. http://mediamatters.org/blog/2014/03/20/debunking-the-big-myth-about-transgender- inclus/198530.

McBride, Sarah. 2015. "Infographic: The Discrimination That Remains beyond Marriage." Center for American Progress, June 29. https://www.americanprogress.org/issues/lgbt/news/2015/06/29/116143/infographic-the-discrimination-that-remains-beyond-marriage/.

McCabe, Brian J., and Jennifer A. Heerwig. 2012. "Reframing the Marriage Debate: Wording, Context, and Intensity of Support for Marriage and Civil Unions." *International Journal of Public Opinion Research* 24, 4: 429–449.

McCarty, Nolan, Keith T. Poole, and Howard Rosenthal. 2011. "Political Polarization." http://voteview.com/political_polarization.asp.

McClendon, Gwyneth H. 2014. "Social Esteem and Participation in Contentious Politics: A Field Experiment at an LGBT Pride Rally." *American Journal of Political Science* 58, 2: 279–290.

McConnaughy, Corrine, Ismail K. White, David L. Leal, and Jason P. Casellas. 2010. "A Latino on the Ballot: Explaining Coethnic Voting among Latinos and the Response of White Americans." *Journal of Politics* 72, 4: 1199–1211.

McCullough, Michael E., and Brian L. B. Willoughby. 2009. "Religion, Self-regulation, and Self-control: Associations, Explanations, and Implications." *Psychological Bulletin* 135, 1: 69–93.

McGaughy, Lauren. 2013. "Shreveport Becomes Second City in Louisiana after New Orleans to Pass Non-discrimination Ordinance." *Nola.com*, December 10. http://www.nola.com/politics/index.ssf/2013/12/fairness_ordinance_shreveport_lgbt_gay_la.html.

McGaughy, Lauren. 2014a. "Louisiana Attorney General Hires Special Counsel to Fight Challenges to Gay Marriage Ban." *Nola.com*, February 26. http://www.nola.com/politics/index.ssf/2014/02/gay_marriage_louisiana_special.html.

McGaughy, Lauren. 2014b. "LGBT Housing Non-discrimination Bill Killed by Louisiana Lawmakers." *Nola.com*, March 31. http://www.nola.com/politics/index.ssf/2014/03/lgbt_gay_louisiana_housing_dis.html.

McGuire, William J. 1964. "Inducing Resistance to Persuasion: Some Contemporary Approaches." In *Advances in Experimental Social Psychology*, edited by Leonard Berkowitz, 191–229. New York: Academic Press.

McKay, Ryan, Charles Efferson, Harvey Whitehouse, and Ernst Fehr. 2011. "Wrath of God: Religious Primes and Punishment." *Proceedings of the Royal Society B: Biological Sciences* 278, 1713: 1858–1863.

McVeigh, Rory, and Maria Elena Diaz. 2009. "Voting to Ban Same Sex Marriage: Interests, Values, and Communities." *American Sociological Review* 74, 6: 891–915.

Messner, Michael A. 2002. *Taking the Field: Women, Men, and Sports*. Minneapolis: University of Minnesota Press.

Michelson, Melissa R., Neil Malhotra, Andrew Healy, Donald P. Green, Allison Carnegie, and Ali Adam Valenzuela. 2012. "The Effect of Prepaid Postage on Election Turnout: A Cautionary Tale for Election Administrators." *Election Law Journal* 11, 3: 279–290.

Mill, John Stuart. 1989. *"On Liberty" and Other Writings*. Edited by Stefan Collini. New York: Cambridge University Press.

Miller, Hayley. 2016. "HRC Honors International Day of Transgender Visibility 2016." March 31. http://www.hrc.org/blog/hrc-honors-international-day-of-transgender-visibility-2016.

Miller, Joanne M., and Jon A. Krosnick. 2004. "Threat as a Motivator of Political Activism: A Field Experiment." *Political Psychology* 25, 4: 507–523.

Miller, Melissa. 2011. "Petition of the Day." *SCOTUSblog*, August 1. http://www.scotusblog.com/2011/08/petition-of-the-day-133/.

Miller, Norman. 1965. "Involvement and Dogmatism as Inhibitors of Attitude Change." *Journal of Experimental Social Psychology* 1, 2: 121–132.

Miller, Norman, Marilynn B. Brewer, and Keith Edwards. 1985. "Cooperative Interaction in Desegregated Settings: A Laboratory Analogue." *Journal of Social Issues* 41, 3: 63–79.

Miller, Warren E., and J. Merrill Shanks. 1996. *The New American Voter*. Cambridge, MA: Harvard University Press.

Minkoff, Michelle, Maloy Moore, Sandra Poindexter, and Ben Welsh. N.d. "Proposition 8 Campaign Contributions." *Los Angeles Times*. http://projects.latimes.com/prop8/.

Molloy, Parker Marie. 2014. "Md. Gov. Signs Trans Nondiscrimination Bill into Law." *Advocate*, May 15. http://www.advocate.com/politics/transgender/2014/05/15/md-gov-signs-trans-nondiscrimination-bill-law.

Moore, Mignon. 2010a. "Black and Gay in L.A.: The Relationships Black Lesbians and Gay Men Have to their Racial and Religious Communities." In *Black Los Angeles: American Dreams and Racial Realities*, edited by Darnell Hunt and Ana-Christina Ramon, 188–214. New York: New York University Press.

Moore, Mignon R. 2010b. "Articulating a Politics of (Multiple) Identities: LGBT Sexuality and Inclusion in Black Community Life." *Du Bois Review* 7, 2: 315–334.

Moscowitz, Leigh. 2013. *The Battle over Marriage: Gay Rights Activism through the Media*. Urbana: University of Illinois Press.

Movement Advancement Project. 2016. http://www.lgbtmap.org/equality-maps.

Mucciaroni, Gary. 2011. "The Study of LGBT Politics and Its Contributions to Political Science." *PS: Political Science & Politics* 44, 1: 17–21.

NCAVP. 2015. "Lesbian, Gay, Bisexual, Transgender, Queer, and HIV-Affected Hate Violence in 2014." A Report from the National Coalition of Anti-Violence Programs. http://www.avp.org/storage/documents/Reports/2014_HV_Report-Final.pdf.

Nevarez, Griselda. 2015. "'Familia Es Familia' Fosters Acceptance of LGBT Latino Family Members." *NBCnews.com*, May 22. http://www.nbcnews.com/news/latino/familia-es-familia-urges-acceptance-lgbt-latino-family-members-n361991.

Newport, Frank. 2012a. "The Political Impact of Obama's Same-Sex Marriage Announcement." *Polling Matters*, May 10. http://www.gallup.com/poll/154628/six-say-obama-sex-marriage-view-won-sway-vote.aspx.

Newport, Frank. 2012b. "Seven in 10 Americans Are Very or Moderately Religious." December 4. http://www.gallup.com/poll/159050/seven-americans-moderately-religious.aspx.

Nicholson, Stephen P. 2012. "Polarizing Cues." *American Journal of Political Science* 56, 1: 52–66.

NFL. 2014a. "NFL Statement on Michael Sam." NFLCommunications.com, February 9. http://nflcommunications.com/2014/02/09/nfl-statement-on-michael-sam/.

NFL. 2014b. "NFL says it's following controversial Arizona bill." www.nfl.com, February 25. http://www.nfl.com/news/story/0ap2000000329267/article/nfl-says-its-following-controversial-arizona-bill.

Norton, Aaron T., and Gregory M. Herek. 2013. "Heterosexuals' Attitudes toward Transgender People: Findings from a National Probability Sample of US Adults." *Sex Roles* 68, 11–12: 738–753.

Novkov, Julie. 2008. "The Miscegenation/Same-Sex Marriage Analogy: What Can We Learn from Legal History." *Law & Social Inquiry* 33, 2: 345–386.

Novkov, Julie, and Scott Barclay. 2010. "Lesbians, Gays, Bisexuals, and the Transgendered in Political Science: Report on a Discipline-Wide Survey." *PS: Political Science & Politics* 43, 1: 95–106.

Nownes, Anthony J., and Daniel Lipinski. 2005. "The Population Ecology of Interest Group Death: Gay and Lesbian Rights Interest Groups in the United States, 1945–98." *British Journal of Political Science* 35, 2: 303–319.

NPR. 2012. Obama's Gay Marriage Stance Stirs Black Community. *NPR, All Things Considered*, May 11. www.npr.org/2012/05/11/152520955/obamas-gay-marriage-stance-stirs-black-community.

Obama, Barack. 2013. "Congress Needs to Pass the Employment Non-Discrimination Act. *Huffington Post*, November 3. http://www.huffingtonpost.com/barack-obama/enda-congress_b_4209115.html.

O'Donoghue, Julia. 2013. "LSU Poll Finds Louisiana Opposes Gay and Transgender Discrimination." *Nola.com*, December 18. http://www.nola.com/politics/index.ssf/2013/12/louisiana_lgbt_discrimination.html.

Olson, Laura R., Wendy Cadge, and James T. Harrison. 2006. "Religion and Public Opinion about Same Sex Marriage." *Social Science Quarterly* 87, 2: 340–360.

Oppel, Richard A., Jr. 2013. "Texas and 5 Other States Resist Processing Benefits for Gay Couples." *New York Times*, November 11, A12. http://www.nytimes.com/2013/11/11/us/texas-and-5-other-states-resist-processing-benefits-for-gay-couples.html.

Ortíz, Gabe. 2016. "Being Gay in America Is Still a Radical Act." *Washington Post*, June 13. https://www.washingtonpost.com/posteverything/wp/2016/06/13/being-gay-in-america-is-still-a-radical-act/.

Overman, Steven J., and Kelly Boyer Sagert. 2012. *Icons of Women's Sport: From Tomboys to Title IX and Beyond*, vol. 1. Santa Barbara, CA: Greenwood.

Paciotti, Brian, Peter Richerson, Billy Baum, Mark Lubell, Tim Waring, Richard McElreath, Charles Efferson, and Ed Edsten. 2011. "Are Religious Individuals More Generous, Trusting, and Cooperative? An Experimental Test of the Effect of Religion on Prosociality." In *The Economics of Religion: Anthropological Approaches (Research in Economic Anthropology, Volume 31)*, edited by Lionel Obadia and Donald C. Wood, 267–305. Bingley, UK: Emerald Group Publishing Limited.

Page, Benjamin I., and Robert Y. Shapiro. 1992. *The Rational Public: Fifty Years of Trends in Americans' Policy Preferences*. Chicago: University of Chicago Press.

Petrow, Steven. 2016. "Laverne Cox: The Transgender Person in Your Living Room." *Washington Post*, May 19. https://www.washingtonpost.com/lifestyle/style/laverne-cox-the-transgender-person-in-your-living-room/2016/05/19/522a5206-1dcb-11e6-b6e0-c53b7ef63b45_story.html.

Pettigrew, Thomas F., and Linda R. Tropp. 2006. "A Meta-analytic Test of Intergroup Contact Theory." *Journal of Personality and Social Psychology* 90, 5: 751–783.

Petty, Richard E., and John T. Cacioppo. 1981. "Issue Involvement as a Moderator of the Effects on Attitude of Advertising Content and Context." In *Advances in Consumer Research*, vol. 8, edited by Kent B. Monroe, 20–24. Ann Arbor, MI: Association for Consumer Research.

Petty, Richard E., and John T. Cacioppo. 1984. "The Effects of Involvement on Responses to Argument Quantity and Quality: Central and Peripheral Routes to Persuasion." *Journal of Personality and Social Psychology* 46, 1: 69–81.

Petty, Richard E., and John T. Cacioppo. 1986. "The Elaboration Likelihood Model of Persuasion." In *Communication and Persuasion*, edited by Petty and Cacioppo, 1–24. New York: Springer.

Pew Forum on Religion and Public Life. 2008. *U.S. Religious Landscape Survey.* http://religions.pewforum.org/pdf/report-religious-landscape-study-full.pdf.

Pew Research Center. 2013a. "Growing Support for Gay Marriage: Changed Minds and Changing Demographics." March 20. http://www.people-press.org/files/legacy-pdf/3-20-13%20Gay%20Marriage%20Release.pdf.

Pew Research Center. 2013b. "In Gay Marriage Debate, Both Supporters and Opponents See Legal Recognition as 'Inevitable.'" June 6. http://www.people-press.org/files/legacy-pdf/06-06-13%20LGBT%20General%20Public%20Release.pdf.

Pew Research Center. 2015. "Support for Same-Sex Marriage at Record High, but Key Segments Remain Opposed." June 8. http://www.people-press.org/files/2015/06/6-8-15-Same-sex-marriage-release1.pdf.

Pew Research Center. 2016. "Support Steady for Same-Sex Marriage and Acceptance of Homosexuality." May 12. http://www.pewresearch.org/fact-tank/2016/05/12/support-steady-for-same-sex-marriage-and-acceptance-of-homosexuality/.

Pew Research Center for the People and the Press. 2012. September. iPOLL Databank, Roper Center for Public Opinion Research, University of Connecticut. http://www.ropercenter.uconn.edu/data_access/ipoll/ipoll.html.

Phillips, Amber. 2016. "How Loretta Lynch's Speech Brought Some Transgender Advocates to Tears." *Washington Post*, May 11. https://www.washingtonpost.com/news/the-fix/wp/2016/05/11/loretta-lynchs-speech-just-made-her-a-hero-to-transgender-activists/.

Piacenza, Joanna. 2015. "State of the States on Same-Sex Marriage." Public Religion Research Institute, February 11. http://publicreligion.org/2015/02/state-of-the-states-on-gay-marriage/#.VW8vc-dyq4Z.

Pichon, Isabelle, Giulio Boccato, and Vassilis Saroglou. 2007. "Nonconscious Influences of Religion on Prosociality: A Priming Study." *European Journal of Social Psychology* 37, 5: 1032–1045.

Pierceson, Jason. 2013. *Same-Sex Marriage in the United States: The Road to the Supreme Court.* Lanham, MD: Rowman & Littlefield.

Pinello, Daniel R. 2003. *Gay Rights and American Law.* New York: Cambridge University Press.

Pitkin, Hanna. 1967. *The Concept of Representation.* Berkeley: University of California Press.

Platow, Michael J., Maria Durante, Naeidra Williams, Matthew Garrett, Jarrod Walshe, Steven Cincotta, George Lianos, and Ayla Barutchu. 1999. "The Contribution of Sport Fan Social Identity to the Production of Prosocial Behavior." *Group Dynamics* 3, 2: 161–169.

Porterfield, Elaine. "Washington State Florist Sued Again for Refusal to Service Gay Wedding." *Reuters.com*, April 19. http://www.reuters.com/article/2013/04/19/us-usa-gaymarriage-washington-idUSBRE93I08820130419.

Potok, Mark. 2011. "Anti-gay Hate Crimes: Doing the Math." Southern Poverty Law Center Intelligence Report, February 27. https://www.splcenter.org/fighting-hate/intelligence-report/2011/anti-gay-hate-crimes-doing-math.

Price, Vincent, Lilach Nir, and Joseph N. Cappella. 2005. "Framing Public Discussion of Gay Civil Unions." *Public Opinion Quarterly* 69, 2: 179–212.

Public Policy Polling. 2013. "Clinton Tied or Ahead against GOP Candidates in Louisiana." February 14. http://www.publicpolicypolling.com/pdf/2011/PPP_Release_LA_021413.pdf.

Pullella, Philip. 2015. "LGBT Catholic Group Gets VIP Treatment at Vatican." *Huffington Post* (Reuters story), February 18. http://www.huffingtonpost.com/2015/02/18/gay-catholic-group-gets-v_n_6704738.html.

Putnam, Robert, and David E. Campbell. 2010. *American Grace: How Religion Divides and Unites Us.* New York: Simon & Schuster.

Pyszczynski, Thomas A., and Jeff Greenberg. 1981. "Role of Disconfirmed Expectancies in the Instigation of Attributional Processing." *Journal of Personality and Social Psychology* 40, 1: 31–38.

Rahn, Wendy M. 1993. "The Role of Partisan Stereotyping in Information Processing about Political Candidates." *American Journal of Political Science* 37, 2: 472–496.

Ramakrishnan, Karthick, Taeku Lee, and Miriam Yeung. 2013. "Where Do AAPIs Stand on Critical Issues? Findings from the 2012 National Asian American Survey." Asian American/Pacific Islanders in Philanthropy Webinar, April 29. http://www.naasurvey.com/resources/Home/NAAS12-April29-funder-briefing-web.pdf.

Ramsey, Nick. 2012. "Catholic Priest Defends Marriage Equality." *MSNBC.com*, November 8. http://www.msnbc.com/the-last-word/catholic-priest-defends-marriage-equality.

Randolph-Seng, Brandon, and Michael E. Nielsen. 2007. "Honesty: One Effect of Primed Religious Representations." *International Journal for the Psychology of Religion* 17, 4: 303–315.

Redlawsk, David P., Andrew J. W. Civettini, and Karen M. Emmerson. 2010. "The Affective Tipping Point: Do Motivated Reasoners Ever 'Get It'?" *Political Psychology* 31, 4: 563–593.

Reid-Smith, Tris. 2013. "Olympic Committee Threatens to Punish Athletes Who Fight for Gay Russians." *Gay Star News*, August 12. http://www.gaystarnews.com/article/olympic-committee-threatens-punish-athletes-who-fight-gay-russians120813#sthash.tl8KLu49.FclM4iE3.dpuf.

Religious Action Center. 2013. "Reform Movement Coordinates Letter of Support from Sixty Faith Groups on Behalf of Employment Non-Discrimination Act." July 8. http://www.rac.org/reform-movement-coordinates-letter-support-sixty-faith-groups-behalf-employment-non-discrimination.

Rhine, Ramon J., and Laurence J. Severance. 1970. "Ego-Involvement, Discrepancy, Source Credibility, and Attitude Change." *Journal of Personality and Social Psychology* 16, 2: 175–190.

Richinick, Michelle. 2015. "Pope Francis Suggests Gay Marriage Threatens Traditional Families." *MSNBC.com*, January 16. http://www.msnbc.com/msnbc/pope-francis-suggests-gay-marriage-threatens-traditional-families.

Riggle, Ellen D. B., and Barry L. Tadlock, eds. 1999. *Gays and Lesbians in the Democratic Process: Public Policy, Public Opinion, and Political Representation.* New York: Columbia University Press.

Rimmerman, Craig. 2002. *From Identity to Politics: The Lesbian and Gay Movements in the United States.* Philadelphia: Temple University Press.

Rimmerman, Craig. 2007. *The Lesbian and Gay Movements: Assimilation or Liberation?* Boulder, CO: Westview Press.

Roarty, Alex. 2013. "Poll: End Workplace Discrimination against Gays." *National Journal*, December 10. http://www.nationaljournal.com/congressional-connection/coverage/poll-end-workplace-discrimination-against-gays-20131210.

Robinson, Carin. 2010. "Cross-Cutting Messages and Political Tolerance: An Experiment Using Evangelical Protestants." *Political Behavior* 32, 4: 495–515.

Rohall, David E., Melissa A. Milkie, and Jeffrey W. Lucas 2013. *Social Psychology: Sociological Perspectives*, 3rd ed. New York: Pearson Higher Education.

Rohde, David W. 1991. *Parties and Leaders in the Post-Reform House*. Chicago: University of Chicago Press.

Rosenberg, Gerald. 2008. *The Hollow Hope: Can Courts Bring About Social Change?* 2nd ed. Chicago: University of Chicago Press.

Rossi, Peter H., Mark W. Lipsey, and Howard E. Freeman. 2003. *Evaluation: A Systematic Approach*. Thousand Oaks, CA: Sage.

Rubino, Rich. 2015. "Unlike Father, Rand Paul Is Willing to Alter His Positions to Win." June 10. *Huffington Post*, http://www.huffingtonpost.com/rich-rubino/unlike-father-rand-paul-i_b_7038088.html.

Rutchick, Abraham M. 2010. "Deus ex Machina: The Influence of Polling Place on Voting Behavior." *Political Psychology* 31, 2: 209–225.

Santos, Fernanda. 2013. "New Mexico Becomes 17th State to Allow Gay Marriage." *New York Times*, December 20, A22. http://www.nytimes.com/2013/12/20/us/new-mexico-becomes-17th-state-to-legalize-gay-marriage.html.

Saroglou, Vassilis, Isabelle Pichon, Laurence Trompette, Marijke Verschueren, and Rebecca Dernelle. 2005. "Prosocial Behavior and Religion: New Evidence based on Projective Measures and Peer Ratings." *Journal for the Scientific Study of Religion* 44, 3: 323–348.

Sarup, Gian, Robert W. Suchner, and Gitanjali Gaylord. 1991. "Contrast Effects and Attitude Change: A Test of the Two-Stage Hypothesis of Social Judgment Theory." *Social Psychology Quarterly* 54, 4: 364–372.

Scarberry, Nikki C., Christopher D. Ratcliff, Charles G. Lord, Daniel L. Lanicek, and Donna M. Desforges. 1997. "Effects of Individuating Information on the Generalization Part of Allport's Contact Hypothesis." *Personality and Social Psychology Bulletin* 23, 12: 1291–1299.

Schattschneider, E. E. 1960. *The Semisovereign People*. Hinsdale, IL: Holt, Rinehart and Winston.

Scheve, Kenneth, and David Stasavage. 2006. "Religion and Preferences for Social Insurance." *Quarterly Journal of Political Science* 1, 3: 255–286.

Schildkraut, Deborah J. 2013. "Which Birds of a Feather Flock Together? Assessing Attitudes about Descriptive Representation among Latinos and Asian Americans." *American Politics Research* 41, 4: 699–729.

Schulte, Grant. 2010. "Iowans Dismiss Three Justices." *Des Moines Register*, November 3. http://www.desmoinesregister.com/article/20101103/NEWS09/11030390/Iowans-dismiss-three-justices.

Schulte, Lisa J., and Juan Battle. 2004. "The Relative Importance of Ethnicity and Religion in Predicting Attitudes towards Gays and Lesbians." *Journal of Homosexuality* 47, 2: 127–142.

Segura, Gary M. 2012. "Latino Public Opinion and Realigning the American Electorate." *Daedalus* 141, 4: 98–113.

Seidman, Steven, and Chet Meeks. 2011. "The Politics of Authenticity: Civic Individualism and the Cultural Roots of Gay Normalization." *Cultural Sociology* 5, 4: 519–536.

Shang, Jen, and Rachel Croson. 2009. "Field Experiments in Charitable Contribution: The Impact of Social Influence on the Voluntary Provision of Public Goods." *Economic Journal* 119, 54: 1422–1439.

Shapiro, Ilya. 2014. "9 Reasons Why I Support Both Marriage Equality and Arizona's Religious-Liberty Bill." *Forbes*, March 2. http://www.forbes.com/sites/ilyashapiro/2014/03/02/9-reasons-why-i-support-both-marriage-equality-and-arizonas-religious-liberty-bill/.

Sherif, Carolyn W., Merrilea Kelly, H. Lewis Rodgers Jr., and Bennett Tittler. 1973. "Personal Involvement, Social Judgment, and Action." *Journal of Personality and Social Psychology* 27, 3: 311–328.

Sherif, Carolyn W., Muzafer Sherif, and Roger E. Nebergall. 1965. *Attitude and Attitude Change: The Social Judgment-Involvement Approach.* Philadelphia: Saunders.

Shariff, Azim F., Aiyana K. Willard, Teresa Andersen, and Ara Norenzayan. 2016. "Religious Priming: A Meta-analysis with a Focus on Prosociality." *Personality and Social Psychology Review* 20, 1: 27–48.

Sherkat, Darren E., Melissa Powell-Williams, Gregory Maddox, and Kylan Mattias de Vries. 2011. "Religion, Politics, and Support for Same-Sex Marriage in the United States, 1988–2008." *Social Science Journal* 40, 1: 167–180.

Sherrill, Kenneth. 1996. "The Political Power of Lesbians, Gays, and Bisexuals." *PS: Political Science & Politics* 29, 3: 469–473.

Sherrill, Kenneth. 1999. "The Youth of the Movement." In *Gays and Lesbians in the Democratic Process: Public Policy, Public Opinion, and Political Representation*, edited by Ellen Riggle and Barry Tadlock, 269–295. New York: Columbia University Press.

Shoichet, Catherine E., and Halimah Abdullah. "Arizona Gov. Jan Brewer Vetoes Controversial Anti-gay Bill, SB 1062." *CNN Politics*, February 26. http://www.cnn.com/2014/02/26/politics/arizona-brewer-bill/.

Siddiqui, Sabrina. 2012. "Ohio's Black Voters Support Same-Sex Marriage after Obama's Endorsement, Poll Finds." *Huffington Post*, July 3. http://www.huffingtonpost.com/2012/07/03/ohio-black-voters-same-sex-marriage-obama_n_1646189.html.

Silver, Nate. 2015. "Change Doesn't Usually Come This Fast." *FiveThirtyEight.com*, June 26. http://fivethirtyeight.com/datalab/change-doesnt-usually-come-this-fast/.

Sinclair, Betsy. 2012. *The Social Citizen: Peer Networks and Political Behavior.* Chicago: University of Chicago Press.

Skipworth, Sue Ann, Andrew Garner, and Bryan J. Dettrey. 2010. "Limitations of the Contact Hypothesis: Heterogeneity in the Contact Effect on Attitudes toward Gay Rights." *Politics and Policy* 38, 5: 887–906.

Slothuus, Rune, and Claes H. de Vreees. 2010. "Political Parties, Motivated Reasoning, and Issue Framing Effects." *Journal of Politics* 72, 3: 630–645.

Smith, Miriam. 2005. "Social Movements and Judicial Empowerment: Courts, Public Policy, and Lesbian and Gay Organizing in Canada." *Politics and Society* 33, 2: 327–353.

Smyth, Ron, Greg Jacobs, and Henry Rogers. 2003. "Male Voices and Perceived Sexual Orientation: An Experimental and Theoretical Approach." *Language in Society* 32, 3: 329–350.

Sniderman, Paul M., Richard A. Brody, and Phillip E. Tetlock. 1991. *Reasoning and Choice: Explorations in Political Psychology.* New York: Cambridge University Press.

Solomon, Marc. 2014. *Winning Marriage: The Inside Story of How Same-Sex Couples Took on the Politicians and Pundits—and Won.* Lebanon, NY: ForeEdge.

Soule, Sarah A. 2004. "Going to the chapel? Same-sex bans in the United States." *Social Problems* 51, 4: 453–477.

Spears, Russel, Tom Postmes, Martin Lea, and Anka Wolbert. 2002. "When Are Net Effects Gross Products? The Power of Influence and the Influence of Power in Computer-Mediated Communication." *Journal of Social Issues* 58, 1: 91–107.

Staley, Peter. 2013. "Gay Marriage Is Great, but How about Some Love for the AIDS Fight?" *Washington Post*, June 28. http://www.washingtonpost.com/opinions/gay-marriage-is-great-but-how-about-some-love-for-the-aids-fightlove-will-tear-us-apart/2013/06/28/5b18c50c-ddd0-11e2-948c-d644453cf169_story.html.

Stangor, Charles, and David McMillan. 1992. "Memory for Expectancy-Congruent and Expectancy-Incongruent Information: A Review of the Social and Social Developmental Literatures." *Psychological Bulletin* 111, 1: 42–61.

Stanley, Paul 2012. "Black Pastor Resigns from NAACP over Same-Sex Marriage." *Christian Post*, June 7. http://www.christianpost.com/news/black-pastor-resigns-from-naacp-over-same-sex-marriage-76250/.

Stark, Steven. 1993. "President Powell?" *Atlantic*, October. https://www.theatlantic.com/past/politics/policamp/powell.htm.

Stern, Leonard D., Scott Marrs, Murray G. Millar, and Elizabeth Cole. 1984. "Processing Time and the Recall of Inconsistent and Consistent Behaviors of Individuals and Groups." *Journal of Personality and Social Psychology* 47, 2: 253–262.

Stokes, Joseph P., and John L. Peterson. 1998. "Homophobia, Self-Esteem, and Risk for HIV among Black Men Who Have Sex with Men." *AIDS Education and Prevention* 10, 3: 278–292.

Stonecash, Jeffrey M., Mark D. Brewer, and Mack Mariani. 2003. *Diverging Parties: Social Change, Realignment, and Party Polarization*. Boulder, CO: Westview.

Stoutenborough, James W., Donald P. Haider-Markel, and Mahalley D. Allen. 2006. "Reassessing the Impact of Supreme Court Decisions on Public Opinion: Gay Civil Rights Cases." *Political Research Quarterly* 59, 3: 419–433.

Taber, Charles S., and Milton Lodge. 2006. "Motivated Skepticism in the Evaluation of Political Beliefs." *American Journal of Political Science* 50, 3: 755–769.

Tajfel, Henri. 1970. "Experiments in Intergroup Discrimination." *Scientific American* 223, 5: 96–102.

Tajfel, Henri. 1981. *Human Groups and Social Categories*. New York: Cambridge University Press.

Tajfel, Henri. 1982. "Social Psychology of Intergroup Relations." *Annual Review of Psychology* 33, 1: 1–39.

Tajfel, Henri, and John C. Turner. 1986. "The Social Identity Theory of Intergroup Relations." In *Psychology of Intergroup Relations*, edited by Stephen Worchel and William G. Austin, 7–24. Chicago: Nelson-Hall.

Tate, Katherine. 1993. *From Protest to Politics: The New Black Voters in American Elections*. Cambridge, MA: Harvard University Press.

Taylor, Robert Joseph. 1988. "Structural Determinants of Religious Participation among Black Americans." *Review of Religious Research* 30, 2: 114–125.

Taylor, Robert Joseph, Linda M. Chatters, Rukmalie Jayakody, and Jeffrey S. Levin. 1996. "Black and White Differences in Religious Participation: A Multisample Comparison." *Journal for the Scientific Study of Religion* 35, 4: 403–10.

Terrell, Steve. 2014. "Martinez Won't Seek Amendment to Ban Gay Marriage." *Santa Fe New Mexican*, January 6. http://www.santafenewmexican.com/news/local_news/martinez-won-t-seek-amendment-to-bay-gay-marriage/article_f5b6912c-ae06-5c3f-bd3e-0ae7b9db1989.html.

Terry, Deborah J., and Michael A. Hogg. 1996. "Group Norms and the Attitude-Behavior Relationship: A Role for Group Identification." *Personality and Social Psychology Bulletin* 22, 8: 776–793.

TheGrio. 2011. "The 25 Most Influential Black Leaders of All Time." http://www.blackradio-network.com/images/userfiles/25Influential.pdf.

Theriault, Sean M. 2006. "Party Polarization in the US Congress: Member Replacement and Member Adaptation." *Party Politics* 12, 4: 483–503.

Thrasher, Steven. 2012. "Obama Finally Loses Support of a Black Leader over Gay Marriage, and It's . . . Farrakhan!" *Village Voice*, May 31. http://blogs.villagevoice.com/runnins-cared/2012/05/obama_farrakhan.php.

Touré. 2012. "Will Black Voters Punish Obama for His Support of Gay Rights? The President Might Be on the Right Side of History, but He's on the Wrong side of a Crucial Voting Bloc." *Time*, May 9. http://ideas.time.com/2012/05/09/will-black-voters-punish-obama-for-his-support-of-gay-rights/#ixzz2nkqVBoLZ.

Tropp, Linda R., and Stephen C. Wright. 2001. "Ingroup Identification as the Inclusion of Ingroup in the Self." *Personality and Social Psychology Bulletin* 27, 5: 585–600.

Turner, John C., and Michael A. Hogg. 1987. *Rediscovering the Social Group: A Self-Categorization Theory*. Cambridge, MA: Basil Blackwell.

Ura, Alexa. 2015. "Gay Rights Activists: Fight Is Only Just Getting Started." *Texas Tribune*, June 29. http://www.texastribune.org/2015/06/29/gay-activists-next-fight-discrimination-protection/.

Vacchiano, Ralph. 2014. "Michael Sam Coming Out Will Show NFL Locker Rooms Are Ready for Gay Player." *New York Daily News*, February 10. http://www.nydailynews.com/sports/football/vacchiano-plenty-enlightened-locker-rooms-closet-article-1.1609173#ixzz2uRk71QvN.

Valelly, Richard M. 2012. "LGBT Politics and American Political Development." *Annual Review of Political Science* 15: 313–332.

Valentine, David. 2007. *Imagining Transgender: An Ethnography of a Category*. Durham, NC: Duke University Press.

Valentino, Nicholas A. 1999. "Crime News and the Priming of Racial Attitudes during Evaluations of the President." *Public Opinion Quarterly* 63, 3: 293–320.

Valenzuela, Ali A., and Melissa R. Michelson. 2016. "Turnout, Status, and Identity: Mobilizing Latinos to Vote in Contrasting Contexts." *American Political Science Review* 110, 4: 615–630. DOI: 10.1017/S000305541600040X.

Van Tongeren, Daryl R., Daniel N. McIntosh, Jennifer M. Raad, and Jessica Pae. 2013. "The Existential Function of Intrinsic Religiousness: Moderation of Effects of Priming Religion on Intercultural Tolerance and Afterlife Anxiety." *Journal for the Scientific Study of Religion* 52, 3: 508–523.

Victoria, Donna, and Cornell Belcher. 2009. *LGBT Rights and Advocacy: Messaging to African American Communities*. ARCUS Operating Foundation. www.arcusfoundation.org.

Voci, Alberto. 2006. "Relevance of Social Categories, Depersonalization and Group Processes: Two Field Studies of Self-Categorization Theory." *European Journal of Social Psychology* 36, 1: 73–90.

Wald, Kenneth D. 2000. "The Context of Gay Politics." In *The Politics of Gay Rights*, edited by Craig Rimmerman, Kenneth Wald, and Clyde Wilcox, 1–30. Chicago: University of Chicago Press.

Wallace, Sophia J. 2014. "Examining Latino Support for Descriptive Representation: The Role of Identity and Discrimination." *Social Science Quarterly* 95, 2: 311–327.

Wallsten, Kevin, and Tatishe M. Nteta. 2011. "Elite Messages and Perceptions of Commonality." In *Just Neighbors? Research on African American and Latino Relations in the United States*, edited by Edward Telles, Mark Sawyer, and Gaspar Rivera-Salgado, 125–151. New York: Russell Sage Foundation.

Walster, Elaine, Vera Aronson, and Darcy Abrahams. 1996. "On Increasing Persuasiveness of a Low Prestige Communicator." *Journal of Experimental Social Psychology* 2, 4: 325–342.

Walton, Julie H., and Robert F. Orlikoff. 1994. "Speaker Race Identification from Acoustic Cues in the Vocal Signal." *Journal of Speech and Hearing Research* 37, 4: 738–746.

Wann, Daniel L., and Nyla R. Branscombe. 1993. "Sport Fans: Measuring Degree of Identification with Their Team." *International Journal of Sport Psychology* 24, 1: 1–17.

Wann, Daniel L., and Nyla R. Branscombe. 1995. "Influence of Identification with a Sports Team on Objective Knowledge and Subjective Beliefs." *International Journal of Sport Psychology* 26, 4: 551–567.

Wann, Daniel L., and Thomas J. Dolan. 1994. "Spectators' Evaluations of Rival and Fellow Fans." *Psychological Record* 44, 3: 351–358.

Wann, Daniel L., and Michael P. Schrader. 1996. "An Analysis of the Stability of Sport Team Identification." *Perceptual and Motor Skills* 82, 1: 322.

Washington Post Poll. 2011. July. iPOLL Databank, Roper Center for Public Opinion Research, University of Connecticut. http://www.ropercenter.uconn.edu/data_access/ipoll/ipoll.html.

Weeks, Matthew, and Mark A. Vincent. 2007. "Using Religious Affiliation to Spontaneously Categorize Others." *International Journal for the Psychology of Religion* 17, 4: 317–331.

Weigel, David. 2012. "Maryland: A 36-Point Black Surge of Support for Gay Marriage." *Slate,* May 24. http://www.slate.com/blogs/weigel/2012/05/24/maryland_a_36_point_black_surge_of_support_for_gay_marriage.html.

White, Ismail K. 2007. "When Race Matters and When It Doesn't: Racial Group Differences in Response to Racial Cues." *American Political Science Review* 100, 2: 339–354.

Whitley, Bernard E. 2009. "Religiosity and Attitudes toward Lesbians and Gay Men: A Meta-analysis." *International Journal for the Psychology of Religion* 19, 1: 21–38.

Wicklund, Robert A., and Jack W. Brehm. 1976. *Perspectives on Cognitive Dissonance.* Hillsdale, NJ: Lawrence Erlbaum Associates.

Wilcox, Clyde, and Robin Wolpert. 2000. "Gay Rights in the Public Sphere: Public Opinion on Gay and Lesbian Equality." In *The Politics of Gay Rights,* edited by Craig Rimmerman, Kenneth D. Wald, and Clyde Wilcox, 409–432. Chicago: University of Chicago Press.

Wildermuth, John. 2010. "Prop 8 Spending Found to Have Swayed No Voters." *Sfgate.com,* June 16. http://articles.sfgate.com/2010-06-16/bay-area/21912234_1_same-sex-marriage-campaign-election-day.

Williams, Claire. 2007. "Sexual Orientation Harassment and Discrimination: Legal Protection for Student-Athletes." *Journal of Legal Aspects of Sport* 17, 2: 253–283.

Wilson, Elizabeth J., and Daniel L. Sherrell. 1993. "Source Effects in Communication and Persuasion Research: A Meta-Analysis of Effect Size." *Journal of the Academy of Marketing Science* 21, 2: 101–112.

Worland, Justin. 2015. "Here's Where Same-Sex Marriages Are Still Being Blocked in the U.S." *Time,* June 28. http://time.com/3939202/same-sex-marriage-south/.

Yin, Chien-Chung. 1998. "Equilibria of Collective Action in Different Distributions of Protest Thresholds." *Public Choice* 97, 4: 535–567.

Ysseldyk, Renate, Kimberly Matheson, and Hymie Anisman. 2010. "Religiosity as Identity: Toward an Understanding of Religion from a Social Identity Perspective." *Personality and Social Psychology Review* 14, 1: 60–71.

Zaller, John. 1992. *The Nature and Origins of Mass Opinion.* New York: Cambridge University Press.

General Index

Brian F. Harrison and Melissa R. Michelson, *Listen, We Need to Talk*
Note: References to figures and tables are denoted by '*f*' or '*t*' in italics following the page
number.

Index of Names